How Literature Works

How Literature Works
50 Key Concepts

John Sutherland

Oxford University Press

Oxford University Press

Oxford University Press, Inc., publishes works that further
Oxford University's objective of excellence
in research, scholarship, and education.

Oxford   New York
Auckland   Cape Town   Dar es Salaam   Hong Kong   Karachi
Kuala Lumpur   Madrid   Melbourne   Mexico City   Nairobi
New Delhi   Shanghai   Taipei   Toronto

With offices in
Argentina   Austria   Brazil   Chile   Czech Republic   France   Greece
Guatemala   Hungary   Italy   Japan Poland   Portugal   Singapore
South Korea   Switzerland   Thailand   Turkey   Ukraine   Vietnam

Copyright © 2011 by Quercus Publishing Plc

First published in the U.S. by Oxford University Press, Inc.
198 Madison Avenue, New York, New York 10016
www.oup.com

Oxford is a registered trademark of Oxford University Press

Library of Congress Cataloging-in-Publication Data

Sutherland, John, 1938-
How literature works : 50 key concepts / John Sutherland.
p. cm.
1. Literature—Terminology. 2. Literary form—Terminology. I. Title.
PN44.5.S88   2011

803—dc22   2010045323

ISBN-13: 9780199794195

5 7 9 8 6

Printed in the United States of America
on acid-free paper

Contents

Introduction *3*

SOME BASICS

01 Mimesis *4*
02 Ambiguity *8*
03 Hermeneutics *12*
04 The Classic *16*
05 Intentionalism *20*
06 The Affective Fallacy *24*
07 Narrative / Story *28*
08 Epic *32*
09 Lyric / Prosody *36*
10 Gothic *40*
11 The Translation Paradox *44*

MACHINERY: HOW IT WORKS

12 Culture *48*
13 Milieu *52*
14 Base / Superstructure *56*
15 The Canon *60*
16 Genre *64*
17 Closure *68*
18 Paradigm Shift *72*
19 Ownership *76*
20 Critical Authority *80*
21 Style *84*

LITERATURE'S DEVICES

22 Allegory *88*
23 Irony *92*
24 Imagery *96*
25 Allusion *100*
26 Defamiliarization *104*
27 Bricolage *108*
28 Metafiction *112*
29 Solidity of Specification *116*

NEW IDEAS

30 Structuralism *120*
31 Deconstruction *124*
32 Textuality *128*
33 Double Bind *132*
34 Postmodernism *136*
35 Heteroglossia *140*
36 New Historicism *144*
37 Postcolonialism *148*
38 Semiology *152*
39 Reception Theory *156*
40 Sexual Politics *160*

WORD CRIMES

41 Plagiarism *164*
42 Obscenity *168*
43 Libel *172*
44 Blasphemy *176*
45 Permissiveness *180*
46 Literary Lies *184*
47 Ghost-Writers *188*

LITERARY FUTURES

48 Fanfic *192*
49 The e-Book *196*
50 Literary Inundation *200*

Glossary *204*

Index *206*

How Literature Works

Introduction

Literary criticism suffers from two opposite objections. One is that the enterprise is too easy ("Anyone can read *Pride and Prejudice* intelligently"). The other is that it is mind-numbingly difficult ("What on earth does 'extradiegetic analepsis in *Pride and Prejudice*' mean? And who cares?").

A first point to be made is the inherently dualistic nature of literary criticism. There is no clear dividing line between theory and practice. Many of the ideas about literature and how best to understand it originate with writers themselves. Indeed, according to T. S. Eliot it is only those who create literature who can write usefully about it. All the rest is what D. H. Lawrence calls "critical twiddle-twaddle."

One would not claim (to take a rather fanciful example) that it is only those who make history who can be historians. And not everyone – indeed relatively few who have thought about it – would agree with Eliot, the author of *The Waste Land* (the greatest poem of the twentieth century) and *The Sacred Wood* (one of the greatest volumes of literary criticism of the century). But ultimately those who merely write, or talk, about literature (particularly those who are paid to do so) should be humble in their judgments and prepared to defer to the comments of those who actually make the stuff. What would one not give for Shakespeare's views on his own drama? Would they not be worth more than all the reams of Shakespearian criticism ever written?

No criticism or "theory" can explain a literary work – that is one of the perennial fascinations of great literature. We still do not wholly understand Shakespeare, even after 400 years of thinking about him. But the well-equipped reader will want to have the best toolkit currently available. This book, and the 50 "big ideas" it contains, aims to assemble just such a kit. Clearly at some point every mature reader will decide on the approaches that work best for them. A new historicist and a structuralist, for example (to take two of the "ideas" discussed below) come at texts from wholly different directions, and the conclusions they reach may well not be compatible. But knowing the different techniques gives the reader a wider set of options – more wrenches in the toolkit, so to speak.

There is one idea above all others that should be borne in mind. Namely that literature is ultimately there to give pleasure. Read intelligently, it is one of the very highest pleasures life has to offer.

01 Mimesis

Mimesis can be defined as "holding a mirror up to nature." The Ancient Greek term – pronounced "my-mees-is" – is preferable to the English translation, "imitation," which carries with it a pejorative overtone of "mere copy." Inadequate too is "representation." Mimesis carries more weight than that word. "The concept of Mimesis," writes Stephen Halliwell, in a recent book on the topic, "lies at the core of the entire history of Western attempts to make sense of representational art and its values." It is both fundamental and, at the same time, fiendishly slippery.

The key to the literary door The problem mimesis raises is perennial, fascinating, and, finally, insoluble. Is literature "true," or is it "false"? It is, of course, both. Or neither – some would argue that the question itself is a "category error" (e.g., "What is north of the North Pole?").

The idea of "mimesis" was put into literary-critical circulation by Aristotle, in his fragmentary treatise *The Poetics*. The title does not indicate an exclusive attention to poetry, but to all literary fabrication. Aristotle was fascinated by the mysterious process by which certain black marks on a white surface or sounds in the ear become, for example, an "epic" (*The Odyssey*).

In his extended defense of mimesis as the way in which that trick is performed, Aristotle was quarreling with an even more authoritative philosopher than himself. Notoriously, in his anatomy of the ideal state, *The Republic*, Plato exiled the poets. He admired the aesthetic quality of their "imitations" (they would, he decreed, go into the wilderness outside the city gates "garlanded"), but their creations were intrinsically superficial, subjective and untrue. The critic Mark Edmundson puts it wittily: "Literary criticism in the West begins with the wish that literature disappears."

timeline

*c.*429 BC	*c.*380 BC	*c.*335 BC
Sophocles' *Oedipus Rex* (Aristotle's perfect tragedy)	Plato's *Republic* (the poet is exiled for his "imitations")	Aristotle's *Poetics* defends concept of mimesis as centr to art and literature

For Plato, literature was the mere shadow of reality. Truth was the province of the philosopher-king, not the artist. Worse than that, poetry inspired emotional, not rational, responses. Mimesis created "Beautiful Lies." It led to bad decisions and bad living. Life requires cool heads and clear eyes.

Refuting Plato Aristotle refutes the primary Platonic objection (historical untruth) elegantly – turning the dagger against its wielder. Literary art (epic, tragedy, comedy, lyric), he points out, is unfettered by the accidents and randomness of mere history and can therefore, employing that literary freedom, articulate essential, eternal, or higher truths.

For example: there never was a woman called Anna Karenina who committed adultery, abandoned her family and killed herself at a railroad station. She is fiction. But the proposition with which Tolstoy's novel opens – "Happy families are all alike; every unhappy family is unhappy in its own way" – has the status of what another novelist, in *her* opening sentence, called "a truth universally acknowledged." Fiction, in this line of argument, can be truer than fact. It can, in Graham Greene's phrase, get to "the heart of the matter." Society needs literature's truths.

Aristotle's defense against Plato's second objection – that mimetic art and literature overstimulates the emotions (our eyes moisten at the death of Leonardo DiCaprio in *Titanic*, but we pass by, hard-eyed, the beggar outside the cinema) – is less convincing. Aristotle concedes that art does indeed move us: that is one of its primary reasons for existence. Athenian women, he records, had been known to miscarry and boys to faint when watching tragedy. But the emotion that literature generates, he goes on to argue, is "cathartic."

Mimesis is the primary dramatic phenomenon: projecting oneself outside oneself and then acting as though one had really entered another body, another character.
Friedrich Nietzsche

1581
Sir Philip Sidney's *The Defence of Poesy* offers pro-Aristotelian "apology" for mimesis

1872
Nietzsche's *The Birth of Tragedy* echoes Aristotle's view about mimesis as basis of dramatic art

1946
Publication of Erich Auerbach's authoritative *Mimesis: The Representation of Reality in Western Literature*

"Catharsis," like "mimesis," is a word that does not yield easily to translation. It can imply "purge," or "laxative." Or, more relevantly here, a medicinal *tempering* of the emotions. The lines from Milton's hyper-Aristotelian verse drama, *Samson Agonistes*, are often quoted in this context: "calm of mind, *all passion spent.*" Paradoxically (Aristotle loved paradoxes), art works us up, but leaves us less, not more, emotional, and better able to make rational decisions. Plato, in other words, should welcome literature as something that clears the mind.

The problem of the catharsis theory It's an elegant riposte but it has something of the sleight of hand about it. A recurrent objection against the "cathartic" line of defense is that it necessarily overvalues literature for its "affective" quality: how we respond to it. Taken to its logical extreme, "catharsis" could be thought to imply that the art that moves us most must be the best literature. Which, on the basis of the teardrops it generates, would make some Mills and Boon "weepies" better novels than *Pride and Prejudice*.

Shakespeare versus Aristotle

Shakespeare was as fascinated by the idea of mimesis as all great writers are. In the instruction Hamlet gives the players visiting Elsinore, he tells them to "hold as "twere the mirror up to nature." The idea of the mirror is a favorite with those explaining the relationship of literature to the "real" world ("nature"). Stendhal described the novel as a "mirror in the roadway." But, as any fairground "hall of fun" testifies, mirrors do not always reflect true.

Shakespeare himself has fun with the "realism paradox" in *A Midsummer Night's Dream*, where the more the mechanicals try to depict their play realistically – having a character with a lamp portray the moon, etc. – the less realistic their performance becomes. Elsewhere in the same play, Shakespeare says, "the lunatic, the lover and the poet / Are of imagination all compact." In other words, mimesis is realism plus a bit of moonshine.

> ❝No serious person has the time to be a great writer. The serious person produces propaganda, party pamphlets, not 'works of art.'❞
>
> E. M. Forster – not, one presumes, entirely seriously

Controversy has raged for centuries around Aristotle's theory of mimesis and what it means for literature and society. Plato, as has been said, booted the poet out of the Republic; Aristotle wishes to keep him / her as an honored citizen within the city walls. George Orwell, in his essay "Inside the Whale," argued that exile is, ideally, where the writer should be. Society (particularly totalitarian society) swallows up the domesticated writer, as Leviathan does Jonah. Better Solzhenitsyn, kicked into exile in 1973, than those hacks who stayed as privileged members of the Soviet "Writers' Union."

Strategically, Orwell argued, the place to be is outside the beast, harpoon in hand, not in its belly. James Joyce, with a more modernist outlook, believed the writer should create in a condition of "silence, *exile*, and cunning."

The Marxist writer Bertolt Brecht founded his aesthetic on contradiction of Aristotle's mimesis and literature or drama that is so "magnetically" real that we are sucked in and "carried away." We should sternly resist the lure of mimesis, Brecht insisted. It is the drug of literature. The quarrels go on, and will do as long as there is literature.

the condensed idea
It's not real, but it can be true

O2 Ambiguity

"When I use a word," says Humpty Dumpty, "it means just what I choose it to mean – neither more nor less." The question is, retorts Alice, "whether you CAN make words mean so many different things." Alice, the most sensible of girls, is right, of course. But nowhere do words mean more things more ways than in literature. Put another way, literature is ambiguity raised to the highest degree. The aim, at its noblest, is not to confuse, but to capture the irreducible complexity of things and of language.

The inherent slipperiness of literature Literature is, of its very nature, polyvalent – it can mean different things at the same time. Historically it can also mean different things at different times (think of *Uncle Tom's Cabin* in 1864, during the Civil War, and in 1964, on the implementation of the Civil Rights Act, when the term "Uncle Tom" had become a deadly insult between African Americans). Biographically too, a work of literature can mean different things at different times of one's life. Jack Kerouac's "Beat Bible" *On the Road* is a different novel for me now than it was for the 17-year-old, romantically footloose, writer of this book.

This multi-meaningfulness operates from the level of whole text to the single word. Take the work T. S. Eliot called the "Mona Lisa of Literature," Shakespeare's *Hamlet*. Every age interprets the play's enigmas differently, sometimes wildly so (is Hamlet mad, enquired Oscar Wilde; or merely the critics of *Hamlet*?). The nineteenth century saw the Prince of Denmark as a noble philosopher. Coleridge hazarded, proudly, that he had a "smack of Hamlet" in himself. In the twentieth century, it's not unusual for Hamlet to be seen by feminist critics as a homicidal, sexually predatory brute, spouting stale truisms and obnoxious self-pity.

timeline

1755	1929
Samuel Johnson's *Dictionary* establishes that words can mean different things in different contexts	I. A. Richards's *Practical Criticism* founds new school of criticism, on centrality of literary ambiguit'

Ambiguity and the headless Frenchman

Literature explores, with its unrivaled subtlety, the linguistic ambiguities that we happily live with in our everyday lives. Consider, for example, the statements: "Coke refreshes," "coke ruins lives" and "coke burns." What do you picture in those three statements? English, it has been observed, is unusually rich in ambiguity, and English literature is all the better for it. One reason that French ("lingua franca") is the preferred language of diplomacy is because it is inherently unambiguous, the least prone to *double entendre*. Picture a Frenchman leaning toward an open train window, unaware that a tunnel is coming up. "Look out!" warns the Englishman alongside him. The Frenchman duly looks out and gets his head knocked off. The shouted instruction *"Attention, monsieur!"* would forestall Gallic decapitation.

Has anyone, over the centuries, got *Hamlet* (or Hamlet) right, or has everyone? Can anyone? *Tot homines, quot sententiae*, the Latin proverb says. There are as many opinions as there are people.

Does the view that Hamlet is a cross-dressed woman (an interpretation that has been seriously advanced), or that he is gay, or that he is the victim of an unresolved Oedipus complex have the same legitimacy as T. S. Eliot's sage deliberations about the Mona Lisa of literature?

Verbal ambiguity Moving down the scale, one can discover polyvalence at the micro-level of the simplest of words. Sticking with *Hamlet*, there is an early exchange between Claudius and his new stepson (whose father Claudius has murdered, although Hamlet does not yet know it) in which the King politely enquires why the dark clouds hang over him. Hamlet replies, cuttingly: "Not so, my Lord. I am too much i" the *sun*." It's a homophonic pun: son / sun. Puns ("puncepts," as some modern commentators call them) embody "ambiguity" in its most crystalline form.

1930	**1947**	**1967**
William Empson publishes *Seven Types of Ambiguity*	Cleanth Brooks's *Well Wrought Urn* does for "new criticism" what Empson did for "practical criticism"	Jacques Derrida's *Writing and Difference* argues that "difference" is the essence of literary expression

❝So far from being Shakespeare's masterpiece, *Hamlet* is most certainly an artistic failure.❞

T. S. Eliot

Ambiguity became the buzziest of buzzwords in the 1930s, with William Empson's monograph *Seven Types of Ambiguity* (1930) leading the way. The book was a version of the 22-year-old Empson's PhD thesis (it actually began as a fortnightly undergraduate essay. He was very smart).

Of the multitude (many more than seven) of ambiguities Empson discerns, consider a particularly brilliant example, from Gerard Manley Hopkins's poem, *The Windhover*. The bird (a falcon) closes its wings when it drops down on its prey, falling like a stone. For Hopkins, the bird is a metaphor for Christ, whose arms were extended like wings on the cross, and folded in the tomb:

> "Brute beauty and valour and act, oh, air, pride, plume, here Buckle! AND the fire that breaks from thee then, a billion Times told lovelier, more dangerous, O my chevalier!"

"Buckle," Empson observed, here means two contrary things. One is "girding," pulling oneself together, as one *buckles* a belt, or *buckles* on armor. The other is "bend-to-breaking" – as in a *buckled* or crumpled bicycle wheel. Which is it in *The Windhover*? Both. Why? Because it's poetry.

Psychoanalytic ambiguities There was another exciting doctrine abroad in the 1930s – psychoanalysis. One of the more daring suppositions among ambiguity hunters (who liked to hang their big game up on imaginary walls, like so many trophies) was that there could be Freudian ambiguities ("slips," or what Freud called "parapraxes") in texts of which the authors themselves were unconscious. Consider what Hamlet mutters to himself before going into his climactic tête-à-tête with his mother, in her "closet" (bedchamber):

> "O heart, lose not thy nature, let not ever The soul of Nero enter this firm bosom, Let me be cruel not unnatural."

Nero, of course, is reported to have killed his mother, Agrippina. This is the primary meaning. Other, more scurrilous accounts record an incestuous relationship between the Emperor (when "heated with wine") and his mother. A bedroom scene is imminent. Has Hamlet resolved his Oedipal complex – or is some awful "unnatural" coupling in prospect? It's hard to think that Shakespeare means us to wonder, but does the text unconsciously prompt us in that direction, implying what its author dare not?

Reverence for the irreducible ambiguity of great literature was codified in a teaching technique labeled "practical criticism" in the UK, and "new criticism" in the US. Educationally it was immensely refreshing, sweeping away the previously reigning orthodoxies of philology. Practical criticism placed the "contextless" literary text in clinical isolation, where it could be subjected to the scalpel-like investigations of "close reading."

But what was this endless hunt for meanings – lemon squeezing, the Marxist critic Terry Eagleton calls it – *for*? Young Empson likened the ambiguity virtuoso to a conjuror pulling rabbits out of a hat. Discovering hitherto undiscovered ambiguities proved you were cleverer than other readers.

But ultimately all this close reading by clever readers did, it was felt, go somewhere important. It validated the best texts, creating, as you went, a canon – the curriculum of worthwhile literature. Ambiguity was the criterion. The more pliant literary texts were – the more lemon juice you could squeeze out of them – the better they were. Some forms and ages of literature lent themselves to the close-reading method better than others: notably "the School of Donne" and "moderns" (like Hopkins). As Empson himself observed, some historical periods – notably the Augustans – were by nature disambiguators. Those periods became unfashionable in the decades when practical criticism was riding high – as, just at the moment, it no longer does.

the condensed idea
Literature speaks with a forked tongue

03 Hermeneutics

Hermeneutics is not a word that falls easily from the mouths of most ordinary readers of literature. It translates – inadequately – as "interpretation": the extraction of meaning(s) from words on the page. Hermeneutics adds to that process of extraction a focus on exactly how the meaning is communicated, and how, once communicated, we on our side "make sense" of it.

One plausible origin of the term is relevant – and witty. Hermes was the messenger of the gods, charged with making divine utterance comprehensible to the less than divine human intelligence. But he is also the mythic patron of liars (don't believe a word this winged-heeled fellow says). Is fiction a pretty pack of lies or higher truth?

What does the literary work mean, and how does it mean? Where, hermeneutics enquires, is meaning located? In the concept-framing mind (this is what the philosophical school called phenomenology suggests)? Or is it embedded in the text (a central tenet of such classroom doctrines as practical criticism and fundamentalist religion)? Is it fused into the medium (as Marshall McLuhan argued)? Or is meaning something created consensually, by social groups – like juries coming, exhaustedly, to a majority verdict that none of them wholeheartedly agrees with?

Is there a single meaning, or as many meanings as there are minds to make or receive them? Is meaning, in itself, stable? How does one account for the fact that works such as *Lady Chatterley's Lover* are interpreted as so poisonously obscene at one period of history (1930–1959) that it is a criminal offence to possess them, yet so innocuous at another period (1983) that they can be broadcast in the UK as a BBC "Book at Bedtime" (American radio rather lags behind)?

timeline

c.315 BC	1850s	1900
Aristotle's "On Interpretation," the earliest surviving commentary on hermeneutics	German theologians pioneer "Higher Criticism" of the Bible	Wilhelm Dilthey's philos theological essay "The F Hermeneutics"

Does time make us more, or less knowledgeable?

Consider the following conundrum. If you were given just one return ride on H. G. Wells's Time Machine, and told that you must use it to understand *Hamlet* better, would you:

1. Put the machine into forward gear, and hurtle yourself millennia into the future, when the last Shakespearian critic has spoken her / his last word on the play?
2. Put the machine into reverse gear, and travel back to the first performance, at the Globe Theatre on the London South Bank in 1601 – taking in the bustle, the smells, the Jacobean staging, lighting, and props, the spectacle of Richard Burbage speaking, for the first time, those lines barely dry on the manuscript? But all this before a single word of criticism existed.

Most readers of literature to whom I've put this puzzle would go back rather than forward. But why?

The un-literary origins of hermeneutics Hermeneutics is, by origin, a philosophical rather than a literary-critical term. The topic was of burning interest to learned German commentators on the Bible in the eighteenth and nineteenth centuries. Was the sacred text to be interpreted literally, or figuratively? Were its meanings debatable? Salman Rushdie found, to his cost (that cost being protective incarceration in the novelist's equivalent of Death Row), that the question is even today a life-and-death matter where divinely authored texts are involved.

Hermeneutical paradoxes Hermeneutics throws up many paradoxes, of which the best known is the so-called "hermeneutic circle" – a kind of hamster-in-a-wheel situation. The root of the problem is as follows: I cannot understand any part of *Hamlet*, unless I understand what the whole play is about (e.g., "a man who cannot

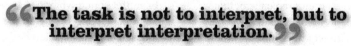

> **The task is not to interpret, but to interpret interpretation.**
>
> Jonathan Culler

1950	**1960**	**1970**
Archibald Macleish's "Ars Poetica" asserts that "A poem should not mean / But be"	Susan Sontag's radical manifesto *Against Interpretation* opposes classic hermeneutic theory	Roland Barthes's analysis of Balzac argues for "the hermeneutic code" as the main stem of literary narrative

make up his mind" – as the voice-over slogan puts it at the beginning of Laurence Olivier's film). But I cannot understand the play as a whole unless I first understand the parts singly (e.g., the centrality of the "to be, or not to be" soliloquy to everything that happens). Ergo, I shall never understand the play, any more than the hamster will escape its treadmill.

There are other paradoxes and puzzles. If a work like Dickens's last novel, *Edwin Drood*, or Nabokov's last novel, *The Original of Laura*, is cut short, halfway (or earlier), by the author's death, can one understand any part of what survives? If a Martian picked up a carburettor, could he (she / it) reconstruct a Ford Fiesta from it?

Another hermeneutic puzzle, which leads to a solution of kinds, is posed by Roland Barthes. If I am reading a crime novel for the second time, and know, this time round, that the butler did it, is the whodunnit better or worse for my improved interpretation of clues that are buried in the text? Clues, that is, which were overlooked on the first reading when I was certain that it was the chambermaid who actually did it.

Sexing up hermeneutics

"In place of a hermeneutics we need an *erotics* of art." So declared Susan Sontag, in her influential 1966 manifesto, *Against Interpretation*. In a decade in which universities, and their disciplines, were being rocked to their foundations by student rebellion, Sontag argued, with eloquent radicalism, that hermeneutics (by which she meant the professionalized *academic* study of literary texts) was not merely obsolete, but as pointless as Swift's scientists laboring to extract sunbeams from cucumbers in *Gulliver's Travels*. What was required, she proclaimed, was a full-bodied, whole-minded engagement with literature. Don't read it, make love to it. Force was added to her injunction by the fact that Sontag was a ravishingly beautiful young woman – epithets not appropriate to the massed and spectacularly unerotic ranks of the tweedy, pipe-smoking, male-dominated Anglo-American professoriate at the time.

"There are meanings within the meanings of H. G. Wells's stories."

V. S. Pritchett

Following up this paradox, Barthes suggests a rule of first and second (and, thereafter, infinitely other) readings. On the first reading we are primarily attentive to what he calls "the hermeneutic code" (i.e., what happens next, with relation to what has gone before). We are gathering data – open-mindedly, unsure of what will be important. In the second reading our response is more situational – we will, for example, pay more attention to what Barthes calls the "symbolic code." His analysis of Balzac's story "Sarrasine" opens with a striking demonstration of the symbolic code. The narrative begins with the narrator sitting on a windowsill, contemplating the natural world of the garden behind him and, at the same time, the artificial world of a sumptuous Parisian ball in front of him. The story that follows is about the sculptor, Sarrasine, who falls in love with an opera singer, La Zambinella. What Sarrasine does not realize – until tragically late – is that "she" is a "he," a castrato. Neither, so cunningly is the tale told, does the reader realize it – on the first reading.

On that first reading the window is neutral scenery. On a second reading the window – the transparent membrane between inside and outside worlds – takes on new significance with what we now know about the sexual ambiguity of the hero/heroine, perched between two sexes.

The attraction of the Barthesian scheme is obvious where canonical literature is involved. We read great works of literature over and over again; or come, the first time, to them having seen TV / film adaptations or with other kinds of plot foreknowledge. Few, nowadays, approach *Pride and Prejudice* – the most widely read classical novel of our age – not knowing, from the opening sentence, that despite all those misunderstandings at the Longbourn ball, Elizabeth will get her Darcy.

the condensed idea
Reading literature and understanding literature are two different things

04 The Classic

**When he addressed the Virgil Society on the subject in
1944 – as European society was consumed in the fires
of world war – T. S. Eliot, while defining "classic" –
evinced some mild concern at current abuse of the
term. "There is a very interesting book," he mused,
"called *A Guide to the Classics*, which tells you how to
pick the Derby winner." This was not what he had in
mind as his subject (the Derby winner the following
year was, ironically, Dante – who was, along with Virgil,
Eliot's example of the incontestably classic writer).**

"Classic" – a debased term? Eliot's question (what is a
classic?) remains tantalizing; and the abuses of the term he joked about
are still everywhere. "Classic comedy" is more likely to mean *Carry On
Up the Khyber* than Aristophanes. Football matches, rock-and-roll, and
tea cakes are all given honorific "classic" status (cigars are also labeled
"Hamlet" – but that, like nags called Dante, is something else).

Overused and abused as the term is, literature still needs it.
Properly applied, the idea of "classic" points toward something that
we hold to be centrally important – although defining that something
is tricky.

Eliot saw classics as fruit of the society in which they happened.
"A classic," he told his Virgilian audience, "can only occur when a
civilization is mature; when a language and a literature are mature. And
it must be the work of a mature mind." He doubtless made this lofty
statement in an auditorium where the blackout blinds were pulled down,
as part of the protective measures against German bombers aiming to
blast the assembled classicists to pieces. Whatever epithet one chose in
1944 for the civilization that had produced Virgil (currently under the
heel of Mussolini), "mature" would not be it.

timeline

1759
Samuel Johnson lays down
principles of neo-classicism
in *Rasselas*

1820s
French critic Sainte-Beuve de
basic distinctions between "
and "romantic" literatures

Frank Kermode's redefinition Frank Kermode addressed himself to the same problem (what is a classic?) in his Eliot lectures (the dead poet being a classic now himself) at the University of Kent in 1973. It was another period of social collapse in Britain. The American withdrawal from Vietnam the year before was accompanied by the OPEC "Oil Shock," which in turn triggered UK inflation rates of 20 percent or more. There were no blinds, but the rolling blackouts produced by the 1973 miners' strike were a painful recent memory. The "winter of discontent" (more electricity cuts) was imminent. We ponder the meaning of the classic most thoughtfully, one may safely assume, when civilization is itself threatened. "Classic" is a category that defines what we regard as culturally important; what, when all else goes under, must be preserved – even, in extreme cases, what we choose to die for.

Both Eliot and Kermode set aside the narrow, but useful, applications of the term: "classical music," or the easy opposition between "classic" and "romantic" writing (what separates Alexander Pope's heroic couplets from William Wordsworth's lyrical ballads).

Refining some of Eliot's ideas, Kermode isolated three key elements in the idea of the classic: imperialism; civilization; antiquity. Classics cross time and transcend national borders. Shakespeare is accepted as a transnational "classic" in Germany, Goethe in England. The huge majority of books do not outlast the period that gave them birth, nor do they migrate to find homes in other languages.

Kermode concurred with Eliot that classics incarnate the highest human standards of mind and morality – they are both civilized and civilizing. And even in a dead language (like the Latin hexameters of the *Aeneid*) they live. Shakespeare speaks to us, although no one today

❝What is a classic? … A delicate question …❞

Charles Augustin Sainte-Beuve

1882

Matthew Arnold outlines his view on the cultural necessity of the classics in *Literature and Science*

1944

T. S. Eliot delivers his lecture "What is a Classic?" to the London Virgil Society

1976

Frank Kermode publishes *The Classic*, based on his "Eliot Lectures" the previous year

Slippery classicisms

Question: What do the following have in common?

The classic work of science fiction: *Fahrenheit 451* (Ray Bradbury)

The classic Western: *Riders of the Purple Sage* (Zane Grey)

The classic romance: *Rebecca* (Daphne Du Maurier)

The classic whodunnit: *The Mysterious Affair at Styles* (Agatha Christie)

The classic thriller: *The Thirty-Nine Steps* (John Buchan)

Answer: The only thing these classics have in common is that they have all outlived their authors, are still read, and constitute the standard by which other works of the same kind are judged.

speaks Elizabethan English, and blank verse is no longer the standard stage medium.

The classic and empire Kermode was sharper in his sociology than Eliot. It was not a civilization but an *empire* – with all the temporal (and, if necessary, brutal) cultural power imperialism implies – that supplied the foundation for the classic. If a language is, as linguists like to joke, a dialect with an army behind it, then classic literature is writing with an *imperium* behind it. This is easily enough tested with reference to the European Union, which currently has some 27 member countries. Which of those countries can be said to have classic literatures, as opposed to some impressive works of literature? The answer would be those which – before the twentieth-century winds of change blew – had great empires (Britain, France, Spain, Italy, Portugal, Germany, Holland, Austria, Belgium). Does Luxembourg have its classics? Or Moldova? Where are their Shakespeares, Racines or Cervantes?

> **Classics? – Old Books which People still Read.**
>
> Frank Kermode

So, if one picks up a Nick Hornby novel in its Penguin Modern Classics livery, what is the assumed connection with Virgil? The implication of its being placed alongside Dickens

> ❝**A classic – something that everybody wants to have read and nobody wants to read.**❞
>
> **Mark Twain**

and Tolstoy is that *High Fidelity* is a book that will last longer than the LP vinyl record to which it is a witty homage, just as *Pickwick Papers* has outlasted the stagecoach or *War and Peace* has outlasted serfdom.

But the criterion of "lastingness" is fiendishly complicated. If Hornby's novel is read, like Tolstoy's, in a hundred years' time (with laborious annotation as to what "record players," "pop charts," and "rock music" were in the 1990s), will it be the same work of literature? Will it, chameleon-like, merely *look* different? Or will it *be* different?

In a brilliant critical move Kermode argues that it is the very pliability of the classic that is its essence. It "accommodates" – makes itself at home – wherever and whenever it finds itself. It is the classic's ability to be both antique, yet modern, its infinite – but never anarchic – plurality that defines it. A work like *King Lear*, Kermode argues, "subsists in change, by being *patient* of interpretation." Every generation will read, or understand, *King Lear* differently insofar as every generation is different from its predecessors. No final version, or interpretation, of the play can be achieved. But every generation will find its own satisfactory interpretation. And the classic is tolerant of each and every different explanation of itself.

the condensed idea
The classic is the gold standard of literature – but all that glistens is not classic

05 Intentionalism

Consider the following statements of literary intent:
1. "Now I will try to write of something else, & it shall be a complete change of subject – ordination" (Jane Austen, to her sister Cassandra, having just finished *Pride and Prejudice*, telling her what the subject of her forthcoming novel, *Mansfield Park*, will be).
2. "[The purpose is] to justify the ways of God to Man" (Milton, in Book One of *Paradise Lost*).
3. "I hope I have taken every available opportunity of showing the want of sanitary improvements in the neglected dwellings of the poor" (Dickens, in his preface to *Martin Chuzzlewit*).

Do authors really know what they are doing? No "Great Books" course would be great without Austen, Milton and Dickens. But if we read *Mansfield Park* for Fanny Price's reflections on slavery, rather than its sage thoughts on the ordination of English clergymen, are we misreading Austen's novel? If we read *Paradise Lost* not for its Christian doctrine but for its poetry, do we misread? If we read *Martin Chuzzlewit* for its unfair (but highly enjoyable) satire on America, rather than its philanthropic (but not entirely visible) anxiety about the lavatories of the poor, have we missed Dickens's point?

The answer to those three questions is a resounding "no." But what does that "no" mean? That we, not the author, "own" the literary work? The embarrassment is often circumvented with some version of "forgive them Lord, for they know not what they do." Creative writers, that is, create things they themselves are not always or entirely aware of. This can be supported by strong evidence. Look, for example, at the title page of Daniel Defoe's *Robinson Crusoe*:

timeline

1719	1820
Alexander Pope's "Essay on Criticism" contends that no writer can achieve more than they consciously intend	Goethe decrees: "In the works of man as in those of nature, it is the intention which is chiefly worth studying"

"The Life and Strange Surprizing Adventures of Robinson Crusoe of York, Mariner: Who lived Eight and Twenty Years, all alone in an un-inhabited Island on the coast of America, near the Mouth of the Great River of Oroonoque; Having been cast on Shore by Shipwreck, where-in all the Men perished but himself. With An Account how he was at last as strangely deliver'd by Pyrates. Written by Himself."

We, in our latter-day wisdom, see *Robinson Crusoe* as a novel – and, more importantly, a primal work that founded the whole subsequent genre of novel writing. Defoe didn't, because he didn't know what a novel was. He wrote one, and made it possible for others to write novels, without ever intending it (his actual intention, biographies inform us, was to make an honest penny. He was 60, hard up, and hit on a brilliant wheeze with his pack-of-lies marooned sailor yarn. The last thing in his mind was founding a genre).

Zappism

The novelist David Lodge created Professor Morris Zapp in his campus novel, *Changing Places*. Zapp is a cigar-chomping, careerist, "stellar" American academic. Lodge had Stanley Fish in mind, and Professor Fish has good-naturedly reveled in the fame of being the "original" of Lodge's satirical creation – sportingly adding that it may be too kind. As Lodge describes him, Prof Zapp believes that "Literature was never about what it appeared to be about ... even the dumbest critic understood that Hamlet wasn't about how the guy could kill his uncle, or the Ancient Mariner about cruelty to animals, but it was surprising how many people thought that Jane Austen's novels were about finding Mr Right." In other words, Literature ain't "about" anything, and the savvy critic ignores whatever the author says it's about.

1946	1967	1977
Wimsatt and Beardsley publish their attack on intentionalism, "The Intentional Fallacy"	E. D. Hirsch Jr. publishes *Validity in Interpretation*, a spirited defense of authorial intention	Roland Barthes' "Death of the Author" denies authorial intention any validity whatsoever

Who is in charge? Like other interesting ideas about literature, "intention" leads us to a thought-provoking impasse. Crudely we can picture it as a never-ending tug of war between the author (who will remind you that "author" = "authority") and the reader(s), who will come back with some variation of "the customer is always right." If modern feminists want to see the heroine of *Jane Eyre* to be the oppressed madwoman in the attic (something, one suspects, that has Charlotte Brontë spinning faster than a Black and Decker drill in her grave at Haworth), so be it. They paid their money, they can think what they like.

Intentionalism sank to its nadir as a critical technique with the rise of new criticism in the US and practical criticism in the UK, in the 1930s. These practices quickly became standard pedagogy in schools, colleges, and universities.

These doctrines fiercely resisted the idea that authors could "dictate" how a work should be read. One detects an underlying political motive in their ferocity. The 1930s was the era of dictators and global totalitarianism – "follow my leader" was the rule, even if it meant total war. "De-authoring" was seen, by the opponents of totalitarianism, as a readerly declaration of independence.

Less politically, the new/practical critics (leaders of the school were Cleanth Brooks and Robert Penn Warren in the US, F. R. Leavis and William Empson in the UK) felt that hunting for intentions was a fatal distraction from the words on the page. When you asked "What does *Keats* mean?" rather than "What does *the poem* mean?" you necessarily raised your eyes from the text of the "Ode on a Grecian Urn," and went burrowing in the secondary material for illumination.

For new critics and practical critics and the generations of readers they instructed (including, as it happened, me), intentionalism was a "fallacy." It had a kind of skull and crossbones pasted on it. It led to dead ends. For these anti-intentionalists, the work of literature should be "orphaned."

> **In every work regard the writer's end, Since none can compass more than they intend.**
>
> Alexander Pope

Stanley Fish's solution But clearly authors' intentions *do* matter. That is a main reason why their names are so prominent on title pages. A way through the impasse is suggested by one of the most subtle modern commentators, Stanley Fish.

> ❝**Intention, a vexed topic that usually brings out the worst in everyone.**❞
> **Stanley Fish**

In his polemical book, *Doing What Comes Naturally*, Fish argues, forcefully, that the solution to the problem lies in "interpretive communities" – i.e., how readers, after careful deliberation, come to a joint conclusion as to how the intention should be understood. An author's statement of intention is not, Fish argues, like a shout of "Fire!" in a theater. No one, wanting to escape imminent, incineration, stops to ask the shouter "What, exactly, do you mean by 'fire?' "

The relationship set up by literature is different. "Intention," Fish plausibly argues, "like everything else is an interpretive fact." We cannot orphan the text from the intention that procreated it. But: "this does not mean that intention anchors interpretation in the sense that it stands outside and guides the process; intention like everything else [in literature] is an interpretive fact; that is, it must be construed."

Unlike "Fire!," or "*Sauve qui peut!*," or "Fire in the hold!," it is quite in order to ask, "What exactly did Milton, at the turn of the seventeenth century, mean by "justify the ways of God"?"

Fish's point is extremely helpful. Intention does not stand outside the textual system, and is susceptible to exactly the same analyses as text itself. Tread carefully and the impasse is passable.

the condensed idea
What a work of literature means is not always what the author means it to mean

06 The Affective Fallacy

Picture the literary act as a long looping arc. At the left-hand starting point is the primal idea, a light bulb suddenly glowing over the author's head. The work then goes through a complex apparatus (literary agent, commissioning publisher, copyeditor, typesetter, printer, binder, wholesaler, retailer) to end with the reader – "consuming" it, with a satisfied burp. From inspiration to expiration. You can pick any point on the arc for your critical examination – but to pick on just one will, almost certainly, lead to distortion and general misunderstanding.

How important are our "feelings?" If judging the work of literature solely by the primal light bulb (i.e., intention) can be called a "fallacy," so too is judging it solely by the burp at the other end of the arc. In fact, one can take it an (indecent) step further. Great tragedy, according to Aristotle, as we have seen, should produce a "catharsis" in the spectator. He only uses the term once, it's untranslatable, and there is dispute about what he meant. But one sense (which survives in our pharmaceutical term "cathartic") is laxative.

This stress on how a work "moves" us (as Ex-Lax moves our bowels) has been called the "affective fallacy" – that is to say, evaluating a work of literature purely, or primarily, on the basis of its emotional impact: how we feel about it. Why this should be proscribed as a "fallacy" can be demonstrated in the following little exchange, which in some form all of us will have heard:

timeline

c.335 BC	1850
Aristotle outlines his theory of "catharsis" in *The Poetics*	Edgar Allan Poe's "Poetic Principle" argues that poet is valuable principally for it effect on the reader

Q. What do you think of Martin Amis's latest novel?

A. I *like* it.

Is the respondent answering, or side-stepping the question? Does it matter, in forming an intelligent critical response, whether a work takes your fancy? We can, surely, say insightful or relevant things about works we heartily dislike. We can like books (many of us do) that our better selves think little of (look at the books we take to the beach every summer).

The "I like it" criterion leads, irritatingly, to a philistine complacency about which E. M. Forster is amusing in *Aspects of the Novel* in which he pictures some stuffed shirt proclaiming "What does a novel do? Why, tells a story of course.... I *like* a story. You can take your art, you can take your music but give me a good story. And I *like* a story to be a story, mind, and my wife's the same." Alas, as Forster sighs, that kind of reader ("I know what I like, dammit") has, traditionally, made up the mass of the fiction-reading market.

But is it really a fallacy? None the less, the likes and dislikes of the common reader (that figure with whom Dr. Johnson "rejoiced" to concur and Virginia Woolf aligned herself) cannot be dismissed as mere philistinism. The commercial facts of literary life will not allow it. Those facts are pressed home on us, every week, with statistical precision, in the form of the best-seller list. The huge bulk of books are bought because readers ("incompetent readers," as Forster sees them) like to read them. What they don't like, they don't buy.

> ❝**Tragedy, then, is an imitation [mimesis] of an action through pity and fear effecting the proper *catharsis* of these emotions.**❞
>
> **Aristotle**

890s	1925	1954	1955
reud introduces "catharsis" s a main component of sychoanalysis	Lev Vygotsky publishes *Art as a Catharsis Theory of Emotions and Fantasies*	Brecht's Berliner Ensemble believes that audiences should be critical, not moved by what they observe on stage	Wimsatt and Beardsley's *Verbal Icon* indicts affective interpretation of literature as a fallacy

Labels say it all

That we should pay some attention to the affective aspect is clear from the "generic" labels attached to styles of entertaining book:

"weepy creepy" (e.g., V. C. Andrews's *Flowers in the Attic*)

"spine-tingler" (e.g., Stephen King's *The Shining*)

"heart-warming romance" (e.g., Colleen McCullough's *The Thorn Birds*)

"tear-jerker" (e.g., Erich Segal's *Love Story*)

"chiller" (e.g., Peter Blatty's *The Exorcist*)

"thriller" (e.g., Frederick Forsyth's *Day of the Jackal*)

"shilling shocker" (e.g., John Buchan's *The Thirty-Nine Steps*)

It's logical to say we do not like this or that ghost story because it did not frighten us, or that we did not like some thriller because it didn't excite us, or that a tear-jerker didn't moisten our eyes. The "effect" is all in all with these popular kinds of book. And is our "educated taste" in higher literature (a term that links literary appreciation with gastronomic) necessarily a bad thing? We don't exactly sniff literature, and roll it appreciatively round the palate like vintage wine – but a cultivated taste for books presumes a somatic (i.e., sensory) response.

How should we respond to the death of Little Nell?

The disfavor for any "affective"-quality literature may be connected with the tight-lipped, emotional control that has, in the modern period, been seen as "good form." Victorians wept buckets at the death of Little Nell. The Irish politician Daniel O'Connell threw the final instalment of the *Old Curiosity Shop* out of the window of the train in which he was traveling, so moved was he. Dockers in New York shouted to the ship bringing the latest copy from England, "Is she dead yet?" This is how Dickens describes the event itself:

> "She died soon after daybreak.... Opening her eyes at last, from a very quiet sleep, she begged that they would kiss her once

again. That done, she turned to the old man with a lovely smile upon her face – such, they said, as they had never seen, and never could forget – and clung with both her arms about his neck. They did not know that she was dead, at first."

I know what I like.
Every Philistine in history

Many of us are more of Oscar Wilde's view that one would need a heart of stone not to laugh. But that, too, perversely, is an "affective response." Laughing, crying, shivering, above all "liking" are things we feel, in the interest of cool rationality, we should control. There is, of course, an interesting historical paradox. The Victorians, when we see photographs of them, invariably have their mouths firmly and grimly clamped shut. Why? Because of Victorian dentistry. Their teeth were so bad. Oscar Wilde was so ashamed of his snaggle-toothed appearance when he smiled or laughed that he placed his hand across his mouth. Weeping was easier. He and his fellow Victorians turned the water works on without shame.

At his public readings, when doing the death of Nancy (in *Oliver Twist*), or Nell, or Paul Dombey, Dickens's pulse rate and blood pressure soared so high that his doctors feared for his life. His life was, in point of fact, shortened by those performances. He was moved – why should we fight it when we read his fiction? Asked what their response to the great deathbed scenes in Dickens or Thackeray (whose death of Colonel Newcome in *The Newcomes* was his prime example) or the death of Thomas Hardy's Jude in *Jude the Obscure*, most contemporary readers would answer "embarrassment." It doesn't necessarily make us better readers.

the condensed idea
Feel free to like or dislike – but don't stop there

07 Narrative / Story

In the foregoing quotation above (see p. 25), from *Aspects of the Novel* (a transcription of his 1927 Clark Lectures at Cambridge), E. M. Forster lays his stress on the term "story." Novelists are storytellers. Eighty years later, giving *his* Clark Lectures, Frank Kermode, mulling over the same topic (specifically with reference to Forster), prefers a different term, "narrative." What is the difference and why has one term replaced the other over the last few decades?

Story and narrative: what's the difference? Story and narrative are not synonyms. Very simply, "story" directs our attention to *what* is told. "Narrative" directs our attention to *how* it is told – to technique, not subject matter.

Novelists themselves have always been fascinated by the technical question of how they should go about their work. There was spirited debate in the eighteenth century as to whether the epistolary method (using letters) of novelists like Richardson, which "wrote to the moment," was more effective than Fielding's "comic epic" technique.

In *Bleak House*, Dickens bisected the line of his story between an omniscient narrator (an "implied" Dickens) and a personage in the novel, Esther, writing autobiographically (anything but omniscient, Miss Summerson does not even recognize her own mother). Dickens, one senses, was trying the techniques out, as a person might go into a shoeshop and try on various footwear before buying two different pairs because he couldn't make his mind up.

timeline

c.335 BC

Aristotle's *Poetics* advocates "unity of action" as essential to narrative

1742

In his preface to *Joseph An…* Henry Fielding defines fictio narrative as the "comic epic in prose'

Historically the novel form became fully self-conscious on this matter with the publication of Henry James's "Art of Fiction" prefaces to the 1908 New York edition of his work. The burden of James's doctrine was simple: "how" was God.

Narrative – the stress on *technique* The Jamesian doctrine can be demonstrated by reference to his best-known work, *The Turn of the Screw*, in which he offers an object lesson on how it should be done. It was designed as a Christmas Eve "gruesome" ghost story, for the Yuletide issue of a best-selling magazine. There is a frame within the frame. The narrator is telling his gruesome tale to a gathering of guests. We listen with them. He opens a document

> "in old, faded ink, and in the most beautiful hand." He hung fire again. "A woman's. She has been dead these twenty years. She sent me the pages in question before she died.... She was my sister's governess," he quietly said. "She was the most agreeable woman I've ever known in her position; she would have been worthy of any whatever. It was long ago, and this episode was long before."

The narrator goes on to read out the governess's narrative. It chronicles her superintendence of two strange children in a sinister country house. Is the house haunted? Are the children possessed? Is the governess the paranoid victim of her own Gothic fantasies?

The story builds to a violent climax – but gradually. It is the inexorable, wholly enigmatic process that grips and terrifies. James's point is that to get your effect (in this case blood-curdling horror), you must twist the story in gradually, like a screw, not hammer it in like a nail.

The art of literature, Henry James tells us, lies in the telling, the *narrating*, not in what is told – the raw materials of fiction are, in

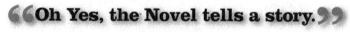

❝Oh Yes, the Novel tells a story.❞
E. M. Forster

1907–1909

nry James outlines his theory
prose narrative in the prefaces
the New York edition of his
vels

1967

In his essay "The Literature of Exhaustion," John Barth argues that traditional narrative resources have been "used up"

1985

Mieke Bal publishes *Narratology: Introduction to the Theory of Narrative*

Narratology: the higher mumbo-jumbo

No branch of literary criticism has attempted to be more scientific than "narratology." It has spawned such awe-inspiring terminology as "narrativity," "narreme," "narratee." Has it disappeared, as anything useful, up its own vocabulary? Frank Kermode (himself the most sophisticated of critics) suggests it has, with this sardonic little riff on how a narratologist might handle the phrase "some months earlier" in a novel: "the narratologist will distinguish analepses as either homodiegetic or heterodiegetic, according to the status, or otherwise, of the story affected by the analeptic intrusion." Any the wiser? I thought not.

themselves, just that: raw. Concentration on narrative has created a critical climate; an orthodoxy and a whole new set of players in the great game of fiction – implied readers, implied authors, unreliable narrators (do we trust everything that Nellie Dean tells Lockwood in *Wuthering Heights*? Do we trust everything Lockwood tells us?).

None the less, with all this welcome sophistication, there remains a strong case to be made for "story." It is possible to "over-narrate." Try to nail something down in a novel, said D. H. Lawrence, and you either kill the novel, or the novel gets up and walks away with the nail.

The death of story-telling? There is another objection. A stress on "narrative" over "story" creates ownership – "liens," as lawyers call them. James, having put so much Jamesian "art" into the work, "owns" *The Turn of the Screw*. No one, by contrast, owns a fairy story like *Cinderella*. The Brothers Grimm or Walt Disney can pick it up and handle it very differently. No one owned the Oedipus legends. Sophocles owned *Oedipus Rex*.

The Marxist critic Walter Benjamin (always more playful than most of his co-ideologues) leapt on the "capitalistic" implications of this distinction between public and private literary ownership. The novel (i.e., the story produced under modern capitalism), Benjamin

"Trust the Tale, not the Teller."
D. H. Lawrence

asserted, represented "the death of story-telling." This startling paradox can be illustrated by the homely example of the "dirty" joke. If, in a school playground, a boy (forgive the sexism) tells a chum a "good joke" – which he would never dare put on paper – and that chum tells another chum and so on, each – in the telling – will change the story in subtle ways.

By the usual Chinese Whispers effect, it may well trickle back, in a week or so, to the original schoolyard teller ("Heard it, ages ago," he ejaculates, contemptuously). But it may well be almost unrecognisable, what with the details it's acquired and lost, in its passage from mouth to ear. Who *owns* that story? Everyone and no one. The narration/narrator arrangement is unfixed. Each teller told it his way.

We can see this played out in newspapers. If there is a big story (the death of Diana), every paper will lead with it – but each will report it differently. Is it the same story in *The Times*, the *New York Times*, or the *News of the World*?

Novelists, typically, take a robust view on the matter. J. D. Salinger's last public act, for example, was to initiate a court to suppress an unauthorized sequel to *The Catcher in the Rye*, called *60 Years Later: Coming Through The Rye*. What made it *his*? The narrating, stupid.

the condensed idea
Don't tell me a story: narrate me a narrative

08 Epic

Epic is a word that is used ubiquitously in modern discourse – as a kind of loose intensifier. See, for example, the following recent (2009) headline from the London *Daily Mail*: *Davina McCall tweets from her snow-bound car as journey home takes epic TEN hours!* A search reveals the word was used 850 times in that one paper in 2009. *Gilgamish, Enuma Elish,* or the *Iliad* were not the day's "epic stories," but matters such as Ms. McCall's unhappily prolonged car journey. The paradox is that we no longer write (and for centuries haven't) the literary form that has supplied this overused epithet. Why don't we have literary epics any more, if the term is so often in our mouths?

Literary epic: definitions Traditionally literary epic has four elements: it is long, heroic, nationalistic and – in its purest form – poetic. Panegyric (extended praise) and lament are main structural ingredients. The first half of *Beowulf* (Britain's earliest surviving epic) is an extended celebration of the hero's prowess in defeating the Grendels, mother and child. The second half laments his death, having incurred fatal wounds in defeating the dragon that terrorizes his kingdom. In epic (see, for example, El Cid and Alfonso VI) there is, typically, friction between hero and monarch – prowess and inherited authority.

Epic exudes confidence about why human beings are on earth. It is, says the critic W. P. Ker, "easy in regard to its subject matter." It knows what it is about and is firm in its moral judgments, particularly where villains are concerned. Leave it to modern writers, like John Gardner, in his 1971 novel, to sympathize with Mrs. Grendel.

timeline

c.790 BC	c.29 BC
Homer's *Odyssey* (putatively) composed	Virgil's *Aeneid* (putatively) composed

It's easy to see why the epic should have wilted in the uncongenial atmosphere of recent times. The modern age does not like epically *long* works – particularly long works of poetry. As Edgar Allan Poe pointed out, the short lyric is the favored form – works that can be "read at a sitting." Thomas Hardy attempted, rashly, at the zenith of his fame, to write an "epic drama," *The Dynasts*. It was intended to be an "Iliad of Europe from 1789 to 1815," with a heroic Napoleon at its center. It is one of the grand failures of twentieth-century literature. For every thousand readers who read Hardy's short lyric poems, there is not one who wades through *The Dynasts*.

Another impediment to modern epic is that modern life lacks "heroes" – at least, in the epic definition of the term. According to Maurice Bowra, epic (he was thinking primarily of Homer) commemorates "the special place for those men who live for action and from the honour which comes from it." Popular fiction (Tom Clancy, Andy McNab) is rich with such figures. But other than in the prostituted *Daily Mail* sense of the term, there are no literary epics about them.

Modern epic: a contradiction in terms? Heroic heroes, and "honor," make today's reading public uneasy. They are happier with anti-heroes, or downright unheroic heroes. Is Emily Brontë's Heathcliff a hero? Is Kingsley Amis's Jim Dixon a hero? Is Dan Brown's Robert Langdon a hero? Yes, in terms of narrative centrality: no, in terms of the old-fashioned "honour" we accord them.

Typically epic belongs to a great age that has passed and at which later ages look back nostalgically – with the sad sense that such greatness is gone for ever. The most venerable epic that has survived to us,

> **Sooner or later there comes a time when the old stories are no longer believed, and then the old poetry loses its hold on an audience which is now instructed by books and newspapers.**
> M. Bowra

*c.*800	1516	1667	1970
Beowulf, the first surviving Anglo-Saxon epic (putatively) composed	Ariosto's *Orlando Furioso* published	Milton's *Paradise Lost* published	John Gardner publishes his novel *Grendel*

The ten all-time greatest poetic epics

The Epic of Gilgamish
(Mesopotamia)

The Odyssey (Ancient Greece)

Mahābhārata (India)

The Aeneid (Rome)

Beowulf (Anglo-Saxon
England)

The Song of Roland (France)

El Cantar de Mio Cid (Spain)

Nibelungenlied (Germany)

Divina Commedia (Italy)

The Lusiads (Portugal)

In film polls taken on the
Internet, Star Wars regularly
tops the lists of greatest epics
in film.

Gilgamish, can be traced back to 2,000 BC. It originated in what is now called Iraq: the cradle of Western civilization.

British literature is founded on an epic, Beowulf, probably composed in the sixth century and transcribed (by an unknown monk) in the tenth. There were attempts to keep the genre alive with Milton's Christian epic, Paradise Lost, and mock-epics such as Pope's The Dunciad (and his immensely popular translations of Homer and Virgil) in the early modern period. Since then, nothing worthy of the name.

The United States is a young country, and its frontier struggles, as civilization spread westward, can be argued to have inspired the last vital manifestation of epic, in the form of the cinema of D. W. Griffith (Birth of a Nation) and the cowboy genre. Demonstrably the epithet "epic" gravitates toward screen heroes such as John Wayne. But not in his non-Western performances.

> **Eschew the monumental. Shun the Epic. All the guys who can paint great big pictures can paint great small ones.**
> **Ernest Hemingway**

> **The art of storytelling is reaching its end because the epic side of truth, wisdom, is dying out.**
>
> Walter Benjamin

Another problem for the modern epic is the nationalistic origin of the genre – more particularly the select league of nations qualified to possess it. Epics are the offspring of "noble and puissant nations," as Milton called them. Could Luxembourg, or the Principality of Monaco, however gifted its authors, host an epic? Could the nationally diffused European Union have one?

When Saul Bellow asked his insolent question, "Where is the Zulu Tolstoy, where is the Papuan Proust?" he was, essentially, making the point that only great civilizations have great literature. And only the greatest of great nations possess epics.

For a variety of reasons, epics are the dinosaurs of literature. They once dominated, by virtue of sheer largeness, but now they are in the museum of literature, not the workshop. When, precisely, did they fade out – and the era of "books and newspapers" (as Bowra calls it) kick in and make them forever impossible? Plausibly in the eighteenth century, with the rise of the novel – sometimes called the "bourgeois epic." Can a novel transcend its bourgeois character and be truly epic? Or is the term, as it might seem, a contradiction (like "jumbo shrimp"). A case can be made for *Tom Jones*, *Middlemarch*, *War and Peace*, and above all – given its allusive title – James Joyce's *Ulysses*. The term fits slightly more easily than Davina McCall's car journey. But at the end of the day, it is an allusion to the real thing, not the thing itself.

the condensed idea
If they are so great, why don't we do them any more?

09 Lyric / Prosody

Of all the short and long poetic forms descended from antiquity (ode, sonnet, epigram, anacreontic, epic, satire, epistle, etc.) the lyric has lasted best. The reason for the triumph of the short lyric, Edgar Allan Poe suggested, was that it represented poetry in its purest form. Like the diamond, lyric poetry is compressed into jewel-like clarity. "I hold that a "long poem" does not exist," Poe declared. "I maintain that the phrase, "a long poem" is simply a flat contradiction in terms." The long poems we revere, he argued, should be seen as necklaces – short lyric moments strung together. It was partly a time and space thing. There was, Poe argued, "a distinct limit ... to all works of literary art – the limit of one sitting." (Woe to the reader who applied Poe's principle to *War and Peace*.)

Must modern poetry keep it short? There was historical justification for Poe's belief in the necessary brevities of art in the modern age. What with railroads (in his day) and all the other transport and communication inventions of the twentieth and twenty-first centuries, life has speeded up dizzyingly. In a crazy-hurry world, who has time to read *Paradise Lost* whole? "Make it New," Ezra Pound commanded fellow poets of the Modernist movement. He could as plausibly have added "and Keep it Short." Life is a nonstop rush hour.

Short as it is, the lyric in English is a highly elastic poetic form. It accommodated the breakaway from rhyme in vers-libre, epitomized in Walt Whitman's flamboyantly unmetrical "Song of Myself."

I celebrate myself, and sing myself,
And what I assume you shall assume,

timeline

*c.*420 BC	*c.*335 BC
Pindar wins eternal fame as leading lyric poet of ancient Greece, and founder of the "Pindaric Ode"	Aristotle lists lyric as one of the forms of poetry in *The Poetics*

For every atom belonging to me as good belongs
to you.

I loafe and invite my soul,
I lean and loafe at my ease observing a spear of
 summer grass.

My tongue, every atom of my blood, form'd from
 this soil, this air,
Born here of parents born here from parents the
 same, and their parents the same,
I, now thirty-seven years old in perfect health begin,
Hoping to cease not till death.

Lyric's relaxed structure also gave free play to the subjective, or
"myself" dimension which has found universal favor over the last
century.

Lyric and the English language More fundamentally, the
lyric has adapted best of all forms to a linguistic truth that gradually
dawned on poets writing in English. Namely that their language is,
phonically, a *stress*, not a *syllabic* system. What does that mean? It's
easily illustrated. Imagine a Frenchman reciting the nursery rhyme
"This is the house that Jack built." He will hit every syllable
equally: "Theese eese zee "ouse zat Jacques beeeelt." Whereas an
English speaker will, following the two strong stress line which is
common in octosyllabic and decasyllabic poetry say something like:
"This is the *house* that *Jack* built."

It was Gerald Manley Hopkins who demonstrated the freedoms
that stress-structured verse (he called it "sprung rhythm")
allowed; as in the grotesquely antisyllabic opening line to "The
Leaden Echo:"

How to kéep – is there ány any, is there none such,
 nowhere known some, bow or brooch or braid or
 brace, láce, latch or catch or key to keep
Back beauty, keep it, beauty, beauty, beauty ... from
 vanishing away?

> **In lyric poetry, truthfulness becomes recognizable as a ring of truth within the medium itself.**
> **Seamus Heaney**

1797	1798	1845	1923
"Ballad year" in Germany – Goethe and Schiller stress the importance of lyric in poetry	Wordsworth and Coleridge publish *Lyrical Ballads,* revolutionizing English poetry	Edgar Allan Poe publishes "The Raven," later hailed as "the most popular lyric poem in the world"	W. B. Yeats is the first lyric poet to win the Nobel Prize for Literature

(Note that Hopkins inserts accents where the stress is to fall –
mimetically that long first line (ending with "keep") is designed to
imitate the ringing of a bell.)

Poetry like Hopkins's offered freedom from all that traditional prosodic
corsetry with offputtingly classical names: hexameters, iambs,
dithyrambs, dactyls, and so on. As it happened, the iambic pentameter
("dee *dum*, dee *dum*, dee *dum*, dee *dum*") remains a popular form (as
does rhyme), but the energies of the English language have always
strained against its foreign strictures, often creating a fascinating
tension between tight and loose. Examples are everywhere, but take
the following, most famous line in English literature: "To be or not to
be, that is the question." If you try and "dee-*dum*" these monosyllabic
words it sounds wrong – like Beethoven played on a music box.

Lyric and the rhythms of modern speech Lyric, with all its
easygoingness, suited the modern world and the modern poet. It
brought poetry and prose into closer conjunction, contradicting
Thomas Gray's rule (expressed in a letter of 1742) that "The language
of the age is never the language of poetry."

Prose and lyric poetry can, however, join up. W. B. Yeats (the most
gifted lyricist of his century) made the point graphically in his edition
of *The Oxford Book of Modern Verse* (1936), when he took a passage of

Poetry, music and the mind's ear

Poetry and music share a number of
technical terms. "Rhythm," notably.
Some of the names given to forms of
poetry indicate a shared origin –
"sonnet," for example, which means
"song." There is, however, a
problem in that in the last five
hundred years at least, one "listens
to music" and one "reads poetry."
Arguably in reading poetry one also
hears it, in the mind's ear, in quite
different ways from what goes on
when one reads, say, a railroad
timetable. The mind "performs"
poetry. That does not always mean
that one can recite it out loud, with the
tunefulness, melody or rhythm it
requires. "I have heard a celebrated
Dante scholar," writes Ezra Pound,
"read the sonnets of the *Vita Nuova*
as if they were not only prose, but
the ignominious prose of a man
devoid emotions: an utter
castration."

prose from Walter Pater, describing Leonardo's *Mona Lisa*, and divided it into 16 lines, as the first "poem" in the anthology. It opens:

> She is older than the rocks among which she sits;
> Like the Vampire,
> She has been dead many times,
> And learned the secrets of the grave;
> And has been a diver in deep seas,
> And keeps their fallen day about her;

Prose or poetry? Both, and a fine lyric *trouvé* as well. The fact remains that poetry – whether short or long – has lost out in the centuries-long battle of literary genres. The novel has won outright. Seventy-five percent of loans from public libraries are fiction: poetry loans are negligible. Poetry rarely, if ever, figures in best-seller lists. Go into any bookstore, and it's a tough job finding any poetry whatsoever. Verse has been exiled to the little magazine, with its little readerships.

Lyric and "song" None the less, in a way that is not immediately apparent, lyric has not merely survived as a living form, but triumphed. The origin of the term is "verse set to musical accompaniment." The lyre is, of course, the instrumental ancestor of the harp, the banjo and

> **The lyric depends on gaps. . . . It is suggestive rather than exhaustive.**
>
> Helen Vendler

the guitar. There is evidence that much Renaissance poetry (like ancient epic) was recited to strumming accompaniment, as was balladry (with the audience dancing as well as listening) and carols (a form of verse in which music is still the other, inseparable, part).

The explosion of popular music in the late twentieth century was, effectively, an explosion of lyric. If one allows that the work of, say, Dylan, Lennon-McCartney, or Morrisey inheres in the words as much as the melodies, there is more poetry being consumed today than at any point in history.

The future of poetry is immense, prophesied Matthew Arnold in the mid-nineteenth century. The airwaves of the twenty-first century bear out his prophecy – although not quite as he had in mind.

the condensed idea
Poetry sings

10 Gothic

It's a term we take for granted without giving it a second thought. If, however, one does give it some thought, "Gothic" is a very odd idea indeed. Go into any high-street bookstore and there will, in all probability, be a shelf helpfully proclaiming its contents: "Horror and Gothic." One conveniently takes down one's preferred Stephen King, James Herbert, Anne Rice or Dean Koontz (or, if sights are higher, Edgar Allan Poe, Emily Brontë or Mary Shelley). What if, instead of "Gothic," it were "Vandalistic," or "Mongol Horde Literature"? The Goths did many things (most of it serious damage). What they singularly did not do was literature. Indeed, it's because of them, and their love of destruction, that we have so little Latin literature surviving to us. Papyrus and vellum burned so merrily.

Why the Goths? The Goths originated in Eastern Europe – well outside civilization. They warred for centuries against the Roman Empire and sacked the Eternal City in AD 410, ushering in half a millennium of the "dark ages." With the destruction of Rome there were no centralized institutions of law, no currency, no commerce beyond primitive barter, no literature, no civilization. Dark indeed. As Richard Davenport-Hines says,

> "The Goths became synonymous with warlike barbarism, "carrying Destruction before them as they advanced, and leaving horrid Desarts every where behind them," as Edmund Burke wrote in 1756. Their love of plunder and revenge ushered in a dark age, and the word "goth" is still associated with dark powers, the lust for domination and inveterate cruelty."

timeline

410	1764	1798
The Goths sack Rome	Horace Walpole publishes *The Castle of Otranto*, generally regarded as the first "Gothic novel" in English	Charles Brockden Brown publishes *Wieland: Or the Transformation*, generally regarded as the first American Gothic novel

The first spine-chiller

Gothic fiction, as a genre, began with Horace Walpole's *The Castle of Otranto* in 1764. It carried the subtitle "A Story, Translated from the original Italian of "Onuphrio Muralto," canon of the Church of St Nicholas at Otranto." All made up, of course – but when did that deter an inventor of Gothic? The narrative opens on the day of the wedding of Conrad, the only son of Manfred, the ruler of Otranto, to Isabella. The ceremony is interrupted by a huge helmet that flies off a nearby statue, killing Conrad. Manfred promptly offers to divorce his wife and marry Isabella, with the cryptic proposal: "In short, Isabella, since I cannot give you my son, I offer you myself." "Heavens!" she retorts, and prudently takes flight through the castle's subterranean vaults. Gothic thrills ensue.

How, then, did "Gothic" become an everyday literary term?

According to Freud, the basic "drives" in the human psyche are destructive and violently appetitive. We are born murderers and rapists. These primal urges are, according to Freudian theory, sublimated into socially acceptable forms: the sadist's primeval knife becomes the surgeon's healing scalpel. A price is paid. At some primeval level we'd rather cut throats than remove appendixes. In his essay "Civilisation and its Discontents," Freud argues that the more civilized we become and the more distant from those primitive drives, the unhappier we must necessarily be.

The attraction of Gothic literature is that it offers a therapeutic escape, safely imaginary, from the controls of order and reason. Hegel observed (thinking of history, not literature), that "The Sleep of Reason Produces Monsters."

817	1818	1847	1946–59	1974
ane Austen ublishes her satire n Gothic fiction, *orthanger Abbey*	*Frankenstein*, by Mary Shelley, published	Emily Brontë's *Wuthering Heights*, generally regarded as the greatest Gothic novel of the nineteenth century	Mervyn Peake's *Gormenghast* trilogy published	Stephen King, the most popular Gothic novelist of modern times, publishes his first novel, *Carrie*

> **Oh! more than Gothic ignorance.**
>
> Squire Western's sister, to her brother, in *Tom Jones*

But as row upon row on the bookstore shelf witness, much as we may respect reason, we also love monsters: at least in books we do. Monsters ravage across the page in our favorite narratives, from Grendel's Mother, through Dracula, to Hannibal Lecter. (As played by Anthony Hopkins, Lecter was voted the most memorable monster in movie history by the American Film Institute in 2003.)

Gothic and the Romantic Movement Romanticism, with its profound doubts about the Enlightenment, found particular creative release in the "sleep of reason." The most popular monster to be created in the nineteenth century, Mary Shelley's Frankensteinian "creature," is, from one angle, a protest against her philosopher father's rationality.

Mary Shelley conceived her story on the Swiss–French border, where Diderot had, 40 years earlier, launched his inflammatory *Encyclopaedia* into prerevolutionary France. How, Shelley's fable queries, did "Reason" (as propagated by the French *philosophes*) degenerate into the "Terror?" It is allegorized in the rational scientist Victor's intended creation of his perfect man, not a second Adam, as his maker hoped, but a monstrous freak:

> "How can I describe my emotions at this catastrophe, or how delineate the wretch whom with such infinite pains and care I had endeavoured to form? His limbs were in proportion, and I had selected his features as beautiful. Beautiful! Great God! His yellow skin scarcely covered the work of muscles and arteries beneath; his hair was of a lustrous black, and flowing; his teeth of a pearly whiteness; but these luxuriances only formed a more horrid contrast with his watery eyes, that seemed almost of the same colour as the dun-white sockets in which they were set, his shrivelled complexion and straight black lips."

A holiday from the constraints of reason? Gothic makes serious points in its sometimes extravagantly unserious way (a best-seller of 2009, one recalls, was *Pride and Prejudice and Zombies* – it sold more that year than Austen's novel). Gothic aims to provoke radically irrational responses and then control them. It allows a little dark age in the mind. It also gives us moral space to consider the place of evil, violence and criminality in our scheme of things. And to indulge complex mixed feelings about them.

> ❝**The principle of the Gothic architecture is infinity made imaginable.**❞
>
> Samuel Taylor Coleridge

Is Hannibal the Cannibal attractive, or repulsive? Both. Take a poll of the most glamorous and sexually attractive hero in British fiction and the bookmakers would give you very short odds on Heathcliff. He has been played by a whole succession of matinée idols, from Laurence Olivier to Ralph Fiennes and Cliff Richard. He is to the classic Victorian novel what James Bond is to the spy novel.

Consider, then, the episode in which – out of wholly malicious motives – Heathcliff seduces Isabella Linton and coerces her into marrying him. Nelly Dean, the housekeeper-narrator at Wuthering Heights, records Heathcliff saying that the first thing he did, on carrying his bride off, "was to hang up her little dog; and when she pleaded for it, the first words I uttered were a wish that I had the hanging of every being belonging to her."

You can do many bad things in English fiction and get away with it. But throttling your wife's harmless little dog is not one of them. It's in character. Later Heathcliff will beat up Isabella unmercifully – the last we see of her she has a black eye. She's lucky he doesn't do worse. He murders the owner of Wuthering Heights who stands in his way.

How can we align his psychopathic brutality and his Byronic allure? The conventions of Gothic fiction – of which Emily Brontë is a leading practitioner – pull off this trick. And in so doing they indicate how literature can reflect the perverse peculiarities of the human personality. You won't find it in Hegel.

the condensed idea
Terrify us, please!

11 The Translatior Paradox

Translation motivates itself by a belief in "essentialism." There is, the translator believes, something at the core of the thing to be translated that can be parceled up and sent across the language barrier without too much loss of quality. "Equivalency" (another favorite term among translators) is the goal. But can true equivalency ever be achieved?

The critic Walter Benjamin, who pondered deeply on the subject, thought not. "All translation," he wrote, "is only a *somewhat provisional* way of coming to terms with the foreignness of languages." With simple informational materials (scientific or technical data, for example), equivalence between languages can be easily achieved (although the directions on self-assembled articles made abroad often contradict this: IKEA, it is jested, has provoked more divorces than adultery).

Can the translation ever rival the original? Literature, with its complex stylistic textures and reliance on nuance, poses problems for the translator. Some authorities (like Benjamin, cited above) maintain that the more literary the text, the less successful any translation must be. Roy Harris, writing in the *TLS* (1987), recycles a favorite demonstration of literary untranslatability: "It is difficult to decide whether translators are heroes or fools. They must surely know that the Afrikaans for "Hamlet, I am thy father's ghost" sounds something like 'Omlet, ek is de papa's spook.'" Little equivalency here.

timeline

*c.*130	*c.*1380
The Greek translation of the Bible, the Septuagint – or "work of seventy translators" – completed	Chaucer translates Boethi *On the Consolations of Philosophy* as *Boece*

Similarly mirth-provoking are the many attempts to translate the title (and, of course, the following text) of one of the most famous and ubiquitously translated novels of the last 50 years. In Danish, *The Catcher in the Rye* comes out as *Forbandede Ungdom* – which back-translates as "Damned Youth." In Swedish, it's *Raddaren i noden*, which back-translates as "Saviour in a Crisis." In Polish, it's *Buszujacy w Zbuzu* – "Romper in the Grain."

> **Poetry is what is lost in the translation.**
> **Robert Frost**

Translation and *The Catcher in the Rye* In literature, the cargo to be translated is not merely semantic. If your culture does not have, in its well-known poetry store, the Burns vernacular poem about catching and rye, do you have the faintest hope of translating Salinger's title into anything other than gobbledygook?

One of the jokes in Salinger's book, of course, is that Holden Caulfield himself does not understand what Burns is going on about – the young preppie being deficient in the vocabulary of vernacular Lowland Scots. He would benefit from a translation into the slang of 1950s America.

O Jenny's a' weet, poor body,
Jenny's seldom dry:
She draigl't a' her petticoatie,
Comin thro' the rye!

1.
Comin thro' the rye, poor body,
Comin thro' the rye,
She draigl't a' her petticoatie,
Comin thro' the rye!

2.
Gin a body meet a body
Comin thro' the rye,
Gin a body kiss a body,
Need a body cry?

3.
Gin a body meet a body
Comin thro' the glen,
Gin a body kiss a body,
Need the warld ken?

4.
Gin a body meet a body
Comin thro' the grain,
Gin a body kiss a body,
The thing's a body's ain.

749	1796	1859	1999
amuel Johnson "imitates" ie 10th Satire of Juvenal as The Vanity of Human Vishes"	Alexander Pope translates *The Odyssey* into neo-classical couplets	Edward Fitzgerald's translation of "Rubaiyat of Omar Khayyam" goes on to be the most popular verse translation of the century	Seamus Heaney publishes his translation of *Beowulf* to huge acclaim

Translation and the Bible

All translations of the first line of the Bible, chronicling the Creation, originate with the Greek:

'Εν ἀρχῇ ἐποίησεν ὁ θεὸς τὸν οὐρανὸν καὶ τὴν γῆνν ὁ θεὸς τὸντὴν

This, however, is how the more famous translations handle that sentence:

In principio creavit Deus caelum et terram (Latin Vulgate)

In the bigynnyng God made of nouyt heuene and erthe (Wyclif's Bible)

In the beginning God created the heaven and the earth (King James's Version)

In the beginning of creation, when God made heaven and earth (New English Bible, 1970)

There is, in these few words, infinite capacity for disagreement (over make/create, for example). And each, of course, is the translation of a translation – perhaps itself secondary – from the original Greek.

In the novel, Holden assumes the "catcher" is there to save the girl. In the poem (and knowing the incorrigibly libidinous Rabbie Burns), it is quite likely that fornication is in prospect. (Mark Chapman, the *Catcher*-infatuated murderer of John Lennon, could also have benefited from a translation. His crazed understanding of the poem was as off-beam as Holden's.)

Literary translation: a peculiar problem The translator of literature is faced with a double bind. He/she must be "faithful." That goes without saying. But a good translation can sometimes only be found by abandoning fidelity altogether and searching for something that will make the same point in the destination language/culture. "*Traduttore, traditore*" – "translator, traitor," as the Italian proverb puts it.

English poses particular problems for the foreign translator because it is so overloaded with loan words and synonyms. There are ten times as many individual words, it has been estimated, in Shakespeare as in Racine. How, then, to translate a line such as Macbeth's "rather will it the multitudinous seas incarnadine?" France (thanks to its academy) does not tolerate neologisms like Shakespeare's "incarnadine." "*Rougir*" (all that French offers, "redden") is very lame.

Translation is not merely required across national frontiers, but across time as well. Few contemporary readers can take on the foundation text of British literature, *Beowulf*, in its original Anglo-Saxon. Chaucer likewise. Time, in this way, makes Martians of us all – alienating us from "our" national literatures.

The greatest writer in the language, Shakespeare, arguably needs updating, particularly for readers coming to him for the first time. Continuing the former example, consider the following original and modernized versions of Macbeth's lament about the blood sticking to his fingers:

> Will all great Neptune's ocean wash this blood
> Clean from my hand? No, this my hand will rather
> The multitudinous seas incarnadine,
> Making the green one red."

> "Will all great Neptune's ocean wash this blood
> Clean from my hand? No, my hand will rather
> Redden the many seas,
> Making the green one red.
> (www.enotes.com/macbeth-text/act-ii-scene-ii)

It makes the lines explicable, but limpness like "redden the many seas" raises the question, can a translation be better than the original (as, it is said, some film adaptations are better than the book of the film), or must it always be worse? Is there always loss? Instinctively one answers yes. Umberto Eco puts a precise percentage on the kinds of loss: "The job of translation is a trial and error process, very similar to what happens in an Oriental bazaar when you are buying a carpet. The merchant asks 100, you offer 10 and after an hour of bargaining you agree on 50."

None the less, globalization is a fact of contemporary literary life. As Vladimir Nabokov (a novelist who wrote in three languages, sometimes translating them) puts it, "The clumsiest of literal translation is a thousand times more useful than the prettiest of paraphrase." It's a pity so many are so clumsy.

the condensed idea
It's impossible – but what option do we have?

12 Culture

"If we take culture seriously, we see that a people does not need merely enough to eat but a proper and particular cuisine.... Culture may even be described simply as that which makes life worth living." So wrote T. S. Eliot in his treatise *Notes Towards a Definition of Culture*, in 1948. Eliot was consciously answering a question that his fellow Harvard graduate, the philosopher William James, had posed in a lecture 50 years earlier, entitled, "What makes Life worth Living?" Culture, Eliot proposed, can fill the empty socket where religion used to be. And literature is a main constituent in a nation's culture.

Mass civilization, minority culture? The idea of culture as *the* vital element in national identity was urged by Matthew Arnold, in his 1860s polemic, *Culture and Anarchy*. There had been, in the run-up to the second Reform Bill of 1867, working-class agitation. Some railings had been destroyed in Hyde Park – not exactly the storming of the Bastille, but a whiff of riot and revolution ("anarchy") was in the air.

Ideas about culture are invariably permeated by prejudice about class. Traditionally – and certainly for Matthew Arnold – culture is the property of society's "civilized" class. This is not, necessarily, the toffs (whom Arnold cheerfully called "Barbarians," preferring as they did horses to Goethe). Barbarians could, being moneyed, serve as useful patrons. So could wealthy members of the commercially enriched middle classes ("Philistines"). The "culture carriers" (*Kulturträger*), as Germans call them (Arnold was a fervent Germanist), will have benefited from class privilege, but float freely in an ambience of "sweetness and light" *in*, but not necessarily *of* the upper and wealthier reaches of society. The lower middle classes and workers (the

timeline

1867–8
Matthew Arnold opens what will become a long-running "culture debate" with *Culture and Anarchy*

1948
T. S. Eliot's provocative *Notes Towards a Defin of Culture* is published

"Populace") were, in Arnold's view of things, irredeemably cultureless, as much a lost cause as the beasts of the field.

Do only great civilizations possess culture?

Running through Arnold's argument is an ineffable elitism. You cannot have what the Germans call *Hochkultur* unless you have the trappings of humane education, civilized manners, good taste, and a broad cultivation that takes in travel, music, philosophy and an appreciation of cathedrals and oil paintings. Culture is a whole-mix thing. It is like an orchestra in which literature is a soloist, but one that could not perform without an ensemble of different instruments around it.

James Baldwin, the African American novelist, described high culture eloquently, 100 years later, in his essay "Stranger in the

> **When I hear the word 'culture' I reach for my revolver.**
>
> Commonly ascribed to Herman Goering, but in fact originating with the dramatist Hanns Johst

Test your CL

The University of Virginia Literature Professor, E. D. Hirsch Jr., published *Cultural Literacy: What Every American Needs To Know* in 1987. It became a runaway best-seller, triggering a hot-tempered debate. Hirsch offered a list of 500 things (from *Arabian Nights* to Zola) that every culturally literate person needed to know. In subsequent publications he expanded the list to 5,000. Measure your CL with the following (answers on p.208):

1. LRB NYRB. What do the initials stand for, and which came first?
2. In which novel was "One-Nation Conservatism" invented?
3. Where did Henry Fielding die? Why does it matter?
4. In which work of literature does the theoretical-physics term "quark" originate?
5. Who wrote a poem to the West Wind?
6. Which novel has won the Booker Prize three times?
7. How old was Keats when he died, and what poem did he leave unfinished?
8. Is Moby Dick male or female?
9. Who, or what, is "beloved" in Toni Morrison's 1987 novel?
10. What is an "Alexandrine?"

950s	1987	1987
:hard Hoggart's *Uses of Literacy* d Raymond Williams's Culture and ciety trigger the "Culture Wars"	Allan Bloom makes the argument for cultural conservatism in *The Closing of the American Mind*	E. D. Hirsch Jr.'s *Cultural Literacy* becomes a bestseller

Village." He contrasts his "heritage" with that of the lowest Swiss peasant, ruefully noting "The most illiterate among them is related, in a way I am not, to Dante, Shakespeare, Michelangelo, Aeschylus, Da Vinci, Rembrandt, and Racine; …. Out of their hymns and dances came Beethoven and Bach. Go back a few centuries and they are in full glory – but I am in Africa, watching the conquerors arrive."

> **"Culture is too important to be left to the Cultural Historians."**
>
> Stefan Collini

Note that Baldwin does not say that the "illiterate" *create* the works of Dante, Shakespeare or Racine. But they are organically "related" to them. What establishes that relationship? Rootedness. Culture, as in biology, is a living thing. Deracination – uprooting – kills it, as surely as cutting kills flowers.

The twentieth-century advocate of elite art was the American immigrant turned Englishman T. S. Eliot. The basis of Eliot's idea of culture is "homogeneity." The necessary glue is supplied, primarily, by the Christian, royalist and Conservative traditions that Eliot had embraced on becoming English. Culture's bedrock was faith, and Eliot, notoriously, believed – as a corollary of this fideism:

> "The population should be homogeneous; where two or more cultures exist in the same place they are likely either to be fiercely self-conscious or both to become adulterate. What is still more important is unity of religious background; and reasons of race and religion combine to make any large number of free-thinking Jews undesirable."

That last comment of Eliot's (uttered after World War Two) has given huge offence.

"Working-class culture:" a contradiction in terms?

Even as he wrote, in 1948, voices were being raised against Eliotesque elitism. While accepting that literature/art was the product of class groupings, there were cogent defenses of the intrinsic worth of working-class and "popular" culture, and folk art.

Spearheading the working-class cultural heroes was D. H. Lawrence – a miner's son who had never attended a proper university. Who was the archetypal Lawrentian hero? A gamekeeper who wins an aristocrat's wife – Lady Chatterley – with such lover's lines as: "Tha's got the nicest arse of anybody."

" The commercialization of culture culminates in absurdity. "
Theodore Adorno

In the 1960s, works such as Lionel Trilling's *After Culture* and Richard Hoggart's *The Uses of Literacy* fueled a lively Anglo-American debate on the subject.

Powerful voices from the left were demanding respect for culture that was neither elitist, provincial, metropolitan nor monocultural and which had been too long suppressed or marginalized.

The debate formed into a school. "Cultural Studies" was grafted on to Humanities educational curricula and became a subject in its own right ("courses on Mickey Mouse and Danielle Steel" sneered the sceptical ranks of cultural traditionalists). While literature remained a principal interest, the focus was broadened – often to the point of total diffusion. Canon-busting ("counter-culture") became a competitive academic sport.

The danger was that Cultural Studies, freed from canonical boundaries, became a study of everything and anything. One professor, at Princeton, a star in the new academic firmament, devoted himself to study of the TV weather channel.

Broadening of the cultural aperture in this way, argued Allan Bloom, led, paradoxically, to what he called "The Closing of the American Mind:" "What is advertised as a great opening is a great closing. No longer is there a hope that there are great wise men in other places and times who can reveal the truth about life – except for the few remaining young people who look for a quick fix from a guru."

In the last decades of the twentieth century, with an arch-conservative in the White House, revolvers blazed as traditionalists fought back in the so-called "Culture Wars." It was tweed jackets versus low-rider jeans at dawn.

the condensed idea
Culture is to society what honey is to the bee-hive

13 Milieu

Literature, proclaimed the French sociologist Hippolyte Taine, did not come out of the air. It was conditioned by three earthy elements: *race, milieu, moment*. The first and last slip into English without needing translation – although "race" is nowadays a hotter potato than it was for a Frenchman of the 1890s. English, however, has no exact equivalent term for *milieu*. It means, loosely, "socio-literary context." But something more than that. Putting a meaning on that "something more" is tricky.

What does the word mean? "Milieu" is one of those simple-sounding ideas that quickly lead the unwary into a thicket of complexity. What, for example, would be the milieu(x) from which a work like *The Great Gatsby* emerged? Obviously "the Jazz Age" – a term invented by Scott Fitzgerald himself – suggests itself as a prime candidate. So does "the Roaring Twenties." This was the decade in which Fitzgerald's career (himself in his twenties) took off meteorically, fueled by "the Great Experiment," Prohibition. The Volstead Amendment introduced what Fitzgerald called "the most expensive orgy in history," only terminated by "Black Thursday," in October 1929, when Wall Street collapsed. That "orgy" is definitely a milieu.

Then there is Gertrude Stein's comment about "the Lost Generation" – those writers who, in the postwar ideological malaise, drifted away from mainstream America and its values, many taking up residence in Paris.

Fitzgerald, along with his Parisian *confrère* Hemingway, was one of Stein's doomed crew. Hemingway and Fitzgerald (as well as Thomas Wolfe and Ring Lardner) shared the most famous editor of the twentieth century, Maxwell Perkins. It was a distinguished literary

timeline

1714	1863
The Scriblerians – the first literary "club" in England –is formed, with Pope, Goldsmith and Swift as members	Hippolyte Taine proclaims his *race milieu moment* triad as the constitutive forces of literature

stable. A milieu, one might think. Fitzgerald, unlike Hemingway or Wolfe, was a cradle Catholic, and a Southerner – the son of a Civil War veteran. A milieu? He was named in honor of a distant relative, Francis Scott Key, who wrote the American national anthem, *The Star-Spangled Banner*. He was a Princetonian (it was at university that he formed his friendship with Edmund Wilson). One could go on.

Like Tennyson's Ulysses, Fitzgerald could say, "I am a part of all that I have met" – and was, since *Gatsby* is an early work, still in the process of meeting. Extracting a neat milieu from all these circumstances is as hard as bottling fog. It would require a shelf-full of monographs – books that are, in point of fact, still being written.

Milieu versus coterie Milieu aligns itself with an analogous Gallicism for which there is no exact English equivalent, but which is easier to work with – *coterie*. It means, literally, "mutually creative company." Examples of literary coteries might be the Bloomsbury Group, the Black Mountain Poets, or the Beats. Writers in such coteries do not operate as a collective with a joint identity (sometimes, indeed, they do not even know each other socially). But they share a network of beliefs, concepts, and practices.

One can, for example, trace any number of filaments connecting the so-called "Bloomsberries." Lytton Strachey's Oedipal anti-Victorianism (expressed in the group's bible, *Eminent Victorians*) connects with Roger Fry's aesthetic post-Impressionism, and Virginia Woolf's "stream of consciousness" narrative techniques. G. E. Moore's philosophical liberalism permeates the fiction of E. M. Forster. Rarely, if ever, did this

> **"A fashionable milieu is one in which everybody's opinion is made up of the opinion of all the others. Has everybody a different opinion? Then it is a literary milieu."**
>
> **Marcel Proust**

1900–1910	1955	1960s
The "Bloomsbury Group" is formed around the authors Virginia Woolf, E. M. Forster, and Lytton Strachey	The "Beat Generation" bohemian writers coalesce in San Francisco around Kerouac, Burroughs and Ginsberg	The Liverpool Poets popularize spoken verse and poetry "events" in the home city of the Beatles

Milieu – does it still mean anything, in English or French?

The further back you go in literary history, the easier it is to make use of Taine's idea. You wouldn't be fully equipped to appreciate Augustan satire unless you knew about the convivial Kit Kat Club, of which Alexander Pope and Jonathan Swift were stars. So too the "Lakers," as they were called – the Romantic poets and writers (Coleridge, Southey, De Quincey) who clustered round Wordsworth in the Lake District. In the modern period, it is much less easy to sketch in any meaningful milieu round an author. What, for example, is the milieu of Salman Rushdie? Born in Bombay, brought up in Karachi, educated at Rugby School and Cambridge University, earning his reputation as a British-based writer writing for an English-speaking readership, now resident mainly in America. Mobility (physical and social) and globalization has rendered the idea of a stable milieu invalid. It makes more sense to see the modern author against a flickering series of milieux, none lasting more than a moment.

coterie muster for afternoon tea in Gordon Square, London WC1. But they had something vital in common.

The danger of a triad like Taine's is that it suggests that literary genius is put through a kind of socio-historical mangle to be produced, in its finished form, at the other end. But used sensitively, it roots literature in the soil from which it grows. A work such as James Shapiro's prize-winning study of Shakespeare, *1599*, stresses the significance of "moment." Could Fitzgerald have written *The Great Gatsby* in 1935, rather than 1925, in the midst of the Great Depression? – probably not: or at least not in the same way.

One of the most useful things a critic can do is to evoke the moment and milieu of a work of literature. Take, for example, this from Stanley Wells's *Shakespeare and Co.*, vividly evoking the South Bank theater world just before the first night of *Hamlet*:

> "Early one morning in 1600 or 1601, boys ran around London sticking up bills announcing that if you went to the Globe playhouse on the south bank of the River Thames that afternoon

> **❝The best job that was ever offered to me was to become a landlord in a brothel. In my opinion it's the perfect milieu for an artist to work in.❞**
>
> **William Faulkner**

you could see a new play called *Hamlet*. They pasted the bills on the doors of taverns and houses, and on pissing posts provided for the convenience of those who walked the streets. The lads pulled down out-of-date bills announcing earlier performances and chucked them away."

The race problem "Race" is something else. Paul de Man (in his wartime years as a neo-Nazi hack) published an article in Belgium's leading newspaper, *Le Soir*, entitled "The Jews in Contemporary Literature," in which he asserted:

"Their cerebralness, their capacity to assimilate doctrines while maintaining a cold detachment from them, would seem to be very precious qualities for the work of lucid analysis that the novel requires. But in spite of that, Jewish writers have always remained in the second rank ... and so ... are not among the most important figures, and especially not among those who have had some decisive influence on literary genres."

One can see the political point of this in a Nazi-occupation milieu. It rationalizes, and confirms, state-sanctioned anti-Semitism. Does it have any literary-critical value in assessing, say, the poetry of Heinrich Heine? No.

However vivid, however brilliantly or sensitively evoked literary milieux and moments are, they cannot "explain" a work of great literature ("race" certainly can't). What they can do is to stage, or background, the work so that we understand it better.

the condensed idea
Not where the author, but the author's work comes from.

14 Base / Superstructure

The base/superstructure model is Marxist in origin, although it has been adopted as an article of faith by European socialism and liberals generally. George Orwell, in *The Road to Wigan Pier*, his monograph about the British coal industry in the 1930s, puts the base idea trenchantly:

> "It is only because miners sweat their guts out that superior persons can remain superior. You and I and the editor of the *Times Lit. Supp.*, and the Nancy poets and the Archbishop of Canterbury and Comrade X, author of *Marxism for Infants* – all of us *really* owe the comparative decency of our lives to poor drudges underground, blackened to the eyes, with their throats full of coal dust, driving their shovels forward with arms and belly muscles of steel."

Marxist origins Base/superstructure is a temporal as well as spatial thing. Superstructural activity – writing literature, for example – is necessarily *secondary* in the historical – or even the day-to-day – sequence. Bertolt Brecht's earthy injunction, *"Erst fressen!"* ("Grub comes first!") puts it bluntly. The echoing "Culture second!" needs no saying. Marx himself put the primary/secondary aspect more wordily in *A Contribution to the Critique of Political Economy*. It is a much-quoted passage:

> "In the social production of their existence, men inevitably enter into definite relations, which are independent of their will, namely [the] relations of production appropriate to a given stage in the

timeline

1859	1883
Karl Marx introduces the concept of base / superstructure in *A Contribution to the Critique of Political Economy*	After Marx's death Friedrich Eagles refine the concept

development of their material forces of production. The totality of these relations of production constitutes the economic structure of society, the *real foundation*, on which arises a legal and political *superstructure*, and to which correspond definite forms of consciousness."

Brecht is pithier and Orwell more eloquent. But the key terms in Marx's phraseology are "real foundation" and "superstructure." Literature is the product of what Marx elsewhere terms "surplus value" – disposable leisure time, money, and a full belly. The refined, Proustian belch after the Brechtian grub. Moreover, as Marx observes, what is going on down below will affect what is happening on top. It is not a simple cause and effect. Street violence can, for example, generate counter-revolutionary, or escapist literature. But, Marx insists, you cannot disconnect literature – or any other superstructural activity – from its host society.

Is it useful? Yes There are attractive aspects to the base/superstructure idea. It neatly explains, for example, the hierarchy of cultural forms and media in terms of economic and industrial progress and the wealth they generate. Dance, street theater, oral poetry require little in the way of finance. They thrive, even in prehistory. A film like *Avatar*, which broke box office records in 2010, required $300m in upfront finance and a technology (itself immensely expensive) that only became available in the twenty-first century. The commercial theater that made Shakespeare possible was itself made possible by the explosive economic energies, commerce, and industrial wealth among the middle classes released by London's urbanization in the seventeenth century.

The novel, the only major literary form whose birth we can confidently date, is congenital with early capitalism in the eighteenth century. The primal text, *Robinson Crusoe*, is plausibly an allegory of

> **❝Wellington said that an army moves on its belly. So does a London theatre. Before a man acts he must eat. Before he performs plays he must pay rent.❞**
> **George Bernard Shaw**

1920	**1937**	**1940s–1950s**
Antonio Gramsci refines the idea of base / superstructure further, bringing the two into closer connection	Orwell refines the idea in his study of British coal-mining, *The Road to Wigan Pier*	Brecht promulgates the importance of the socio-economic "base" in his plays and theater

"homo economicus" – how an individual, with nothing but his inborn talent, makes himself a landowner and rich. Defoe's novel would not have been possible until circuits of manufacture (printing) and supply (bookshops, libraries) and money to buy books (*Robinson Crusoe* cost the goodly sum of a guinea) were available to a literate reading public. Why did we not have *Hamlet* or *Robinson Crusoe* (let alone *Avatar*) in the fifteenth century? Because the "base" wasn't there to make them possible – any more than men could fly to the moon in 1869.

Is it too easy? The danger of base/superstructure is that it quickly becomes reductionist – it's too easy an explanation. Clear-cut division between the two vertical sectors (cake/icing on the cake) is nowadays generally regarded as "vulgar" Marxism. New Marxists have complicated the model (on which Marx himself devoted relatively little analysis) vastly and unvulgarly.

A major source of complication is the relationship between producers of material value in the base ("hand-workers," as Victorians called them) and producers of immaterial "consciousness" ("brain-workers") in the superstructure. Put bluntly, if you were Orwell's coal-miner, what would you feel about the idle classes above ground with time to read *The Road to Wigan Pier*?

Follow the money

One useful way of looking at base/superstructure in terms of literary careers is to look at what money does to them creatively. Dickens and George Eliot, for example, were the two best-paid novelists of their time. Both of them received record (for the time) payments of £10,000 for a single novel (*Romola* and *Our Mutual Friend*). What is notable, however, is that as their late-life remuneration increased to these unprecedented heights, the intervals between their works increased from one to as much as four years. This did not mean they were writing more slowly, but more artfully, and they could, for example, introduce foreign settings since they could afford to travel in style. Nor, of course, should it be assumed that the more carefully composed work was better (*Romola* is considered Eliot's least readable, if most deeply researched, novel). But it always pays to pay attention to what a writer was paid. It is a basic fact.

The same problem was given a vivid illustration in H. G. Wells's 1895 novel, *The Time Machine*. In that story, the traveller uses his wonderful new machine to go to the year 802,701. There he discovers that humankind has devolved into two contrary species: the effete Eloi, who spend their lives in a kind of Garden of Eden, doing nothing but play; and the cannibalistic Morlocks, slaving in a subterranean factory world, emerging only at night, to eat Eloi. The Eloi are, of course, versions of the *fin de siècle* decadents, notably Oscar Wilde and his followers. The Morlocks are what the contemporary novelist George Gissing called "Workers in the Dawn" – the laboring masses.

> **"Literature is not just the passive reflection of the economic base."**
> Terry Eagleton

Is the relationship of base person and superstructure person necessarily antagonistic? Must those relegated by historical destiny to the base be either submissive worker bees or cannibals? What of those societies, and cultures that have no "economic base?" Periclean Athens could boast a Sophocles and an Aristotle, not simply because of their native genius, but because there were five slaves (and women, who, as Aristotle said, were the same thing) for every free man. Where is the slave's or woman's *Oedipus Rex*?

The easy deduction that "consciousness" is the exclusive preserve of the superstructure is, on closer inspection, untenable; similarly that "production" is the exclusive property of the base. There is creativity at all levels of society. The superstructure also "produces" – ideology and political thought, for example. That immaterial product affects, and transforms, what is happening throughout the whole body of society, top to bottom. In other words, superstructure can materially influence base, as well as vice versa.

It's stimulating. But at the end of the day the base/superstructure model is useful principally insofar as thinking about it leads us to discarding it as anything other than a metaphorical stepping stone to more interesting (super-superstructural?) things. Used this way, the idea serves a very useful purpose.

the condensed idea
The foundations of literature are not literary

15 The Canon

"Canon" became a current term some centuries ago in Christian theological discourse. Etymologically it can be traced back to the ancient Greek for "measuring rod." The "canon of scripture" are those texts regarded as authentically biblical (the discards are "apocryphal"). Over time, "canonical" came to indicate those texts all devout Catholics should read. Those they should not read were listed in the *Index Librorum Prohibitorum*. "Canon" and "censorship" are always close cousins, dependent as they are on authority. What are the literary applications of the canonical idea? Are they useful?

What is a literary canon? Around 30 years ago, the term "canon" was imported to cover that nucleus of literature that was worthy of study at university, or of immortality in "classic" reprint libraries (e.g., Penguin Classics), or that would be prescribed on "Great Books 101" foundation courses, or found in the anthologies of literature marketed for educational institutions. Before the 1960s, the term would have meant nothing to well-read people, as regards the literature they read, or were expected to read if they wanted the respect of their peers.

The literary canon has since become the most exclusive of clubs. Entrance is a fiercely contested matter, leading to "canon wars." The canon's central membership (Shakespeare, Virginia Woolf, for example) is fixed for long periods, but not immutable. Even Shakespeare cannot be certain of always holding his place. At the fringes, it is as fluid and fuzzy as this week's best-seller lists. Are H. G. Wells, Theodore Dreiser, or Rebecca West in there? Sometimes yes, sometimes no.

timeline

AD90

Hebrew biblical canon established

1779–1781

Samuel Johnson's *Lives of the Most Eminent Poets* nominate 52 writers who constitute the canon of English verse

> **Is it possible to envisage a future British or American culture in which *King Lear* would not be an important work of art, worthy of membership in the canon?**
>
> Jeremy Hawthorn

Educationally, the canon exists primarily to winnow out from the chaff what Arnold calls "the best that has been thought and said in the world:" literature's richest harvest. There is, however, a secondary, hardly less important function. One "consumes" literature, but unlike other consumables (yesterday's hamburger, for example), it does not disappear once consumed, digested and excreted. Literature accretes.

In Chaucer's *Canterbury Tales*, it is a matter of wonderment that the Clerk (the term meant something akin to our word "scholar") had half a dozen books on his study bookshelf. That comprised most of what was available in the fifteenth century. With the Google Library Project's arrival in the second decade of the twenty-first century, the modern clerk will have access to 15 million volumes in the palm of his hand.

There was no need for a "literary canon" until the arrival of printing had enlarged the store of available literature from a hillock to a mountain. The canon tends to be fixed in size; the apocrypha – or noncanon – grows inexorably. *Vita brevis, ars longa*, says the classical proverb: "Life is short, art is long." The problem is, it gets longer all the time.

Early literary canon-making When Samuel Johnson, at the behest of the London booksellers, compiled his *Lives of the Most Eminent Poets*, in the mid eighteenth century, the epithet, and the limited number (52 – one for every week of the year), represented a canonical procedure. It was, however, at the end of nineteenth century, with the emergence of a truly "mass" literary culture, that canonization got going in force. It took the form of classic reprint libraries (some, like Everyman and World's Classics, still survive) that

1796	**1861**	**1906**	**1962**
The "apocrypha" (non-canonical books of the Bible) are dropped from the King James text	Palgrave's *Golden Treasury of English Songs and Lyrics* is published. It dominates school curricula for decades	Everyman's Library begins to establish an informal canon of "great works"	First *Norton Anthology of English Literature* published

effectively reduced what every "well-read" citizen should read to a manageable hundred or so texts. For the student and pupil, anthologies such as Palgrave's "Golden Treasuries" of verse established themselves. At the same period in the 1890s, the best-seller list appeared. It too thinned out the "must-reads" of the moment into a manageable quantum. Reduction was the driving force.

The canon and education One of the attractions of the study of classics in schools and universities has always been the small size and fixity of the corpus. Virtually the whole of classical Latin and Greek canonical literature can be contained on one CD disc. And, of course, it never grows. So too with Anglo-Saxon poetry, which until a few decades ago was the foundation element in English studies.

Modern literature is a much less compactable thing. There are currently around 150,000 titles published every year in the two major English-speaking markets. Some 10 percent of those are classified as "literature," swelling the two million or so literary titles already stored in the British Library and the Library of Congress (and, imminently, on Google). A modern-day clerk would need to live to the age of Methuselah to read even a fraction of them.

The state-ordained curriculum.

British government, via its education ministries, has taken on itself the responsibility for establishing what is the canon of British literature – as prescribed for the school examinations that are the gateway to university study. Texts appropriate for study at Key Stage 4 include some works by the following authors: Douglas Adams, Richard Adams, Fleur Adcock, Isabel Allende, Simon Armitage, Alan Ayckbourn, J. G. Ballard, Pat Barker, Alan Bennett, Alan Bleasdale, Bill Bryson, Angela Carter, Bruce Chatwin, Brian Clark, Gillian Clarke, Robert Cormier, Jennifer Donnelly, Keith Douglas, Roddy Doyle, Carol Ann Duffy, U. A. Fanthorpe, John Fowles, Brian Friel, Mark Haddon, Willis Hall, David Hare, Tony Harrison, Susan Hill, S. E. Hinton, Jackie Kay, Harper Lee, Laurie Lee, Andrea Levy, Joan Lingard, Penelope Lively, Liz Lochhead, Mal Peet, Peter Porter, Philip Pullman, Willy Russell, Jo Shapcott and Zadie Smith.

Other "appropriate" writers "from different cultures and traditions" are also listed. Films are suggested as a useful way of getting into Jane Austen.

> **To enter the canon, or more properly, to be entered into the canon is to gain certain obvious privileges. The gatekeepers of the fortress of high culture include influential critics, museum directors and their boards of trustees, and far more lowly scholars and teachers.**
>
> George P. Landow ("lowly" scholar)

Universities, schools and the authorities that set up such things as the "National Curriculum" have become adept at thinning down the canon to anorexic proportions. A Great Books one-semester course will typically, in the US higher education system, allow some 90 to 100 hours" reading. At three minutes a page for prose, and ten minutes for verse, that gives you time – as the calculator glumly estimates – to read *Moby-Dick* and *Hamlet*. So you prescribe a chapter here, a chapter there, a short poem or an anthology (like the best-selling Norton range) that offers manageable excerpts.

It's nonsense, of course. A Victorian fiction course, at the best universities in the Anglo-American world, will prescribe *Hard Times*, *Silas Marner*, *Tess of the D'Urbervilles* and *Jane Eyre* and call it "Victorian Fiction." In fact these half-dozen or so texts give no more idea of what the 70,000 or so works in the field represent than six pebbles will tell you what Chesil Beach looks like. But what option does pedagogy have?

The educational canon is one among many. There are "alternative canons," "queer literature canons," "feminist canons," "science fiction canons" – as many canons as there are specialist interest or affiliation groups There are national variations. *War and Peace* may be canonical for Russians; is it as canonical for – say – the French, who may, prejudicially, have a very different idea of Napoleon from Tolstoy?

the condensed idea
The best that has been
thought and written. Read it!

16 Genre

Genre means different things, according to where you are positioned in the book world. For the retailer of books, it is a shelving and location issue. Topography matters in shops. The massive range of choice – many thousands of very different wares – in even the smallest bookstore creates confusion. Hence, with fiction – always a best-selling line – there will be: "classics," "gay and erotic," "romance," "SF and horror," "teen," and "crime" sections. De facto, from the commercial standpoint, these represent genres. Demand creates them. In times gone by, "Westerns" might have been supplied, for a certain kind of male customer. That genre has largely disappeared. But other genres – the graphic novel, for example – spring up to fill the vacancies.

Genre and book commerce For the bookseller, genre is a pragmatic question of what to put where. It throws up occasional problems. Does, for example, Margaret Atwood's *The Handmaid's Tale* (which won a Hugo and a Nebula – the two top SF prizes) go into the science fiction section, alongside Asimov? Or the modern classics section, alongside Achebe?

For the genre author, the term means something different. It's a kind of club, with a distinct set of rules, conventions, styles and fashions. In 1928, S. S. Van Dine drew up twenty rules for the crime writer, of which the first (and most inviolable) is: "The reader must have equal opportunity with the detective for solving the mystery. All clues must be plainly stated and described."

Within the rules, there is a degree of freedom. But there is a core of shared tools and subject matter. You can pick up ideas, gimmicks, styles from fellow club members.

timeline

c.335 BC	1820s	1868
Aristotle lists different kinds of literature in *The Poetics*	The "Tale of Terror" is popularized by *Blackwood's Magazine* in England and later by Poe in America	Wilkie Collins publishes *The Moonstone*, regarded as the first "true" detective novel in English

Stephen King is honored, but not respected

On 15 September 2003, the National Book Foundation announced that Stephen King, the most famous genre author of his time, would be the recipient of a "lifetime award." In his acceptance speech at the public ceremony on 19 November 2003, King recalled how he and his wife Tabitha "lived in a trailer and she made a writing space for me in the tiny laundry room with a desk and her Olivetti portable between the washer and dryer.... When I gave up on *Carrie*, it was Tabby who rescued the first few pages of single spaced manuscript from the wastebasket, told me it was good, said I ought to go on." The main thrust of King's November speech was ungrateful *Carrie*-style payback. They hadn't emptied a bucket of pig's blood over his head, but the literary establishment was guilty of "tokenism" – treating him, a mere genre writer, like a house Negro with their lifetime award. It was an awkward occasion.

If some innovative genre writer, like Robert Traver, comes up with the idea of the legal thriller (*Anatomy of a Murder*, 1958), it will be picked up and recycled profitably (most profitably by John Grisham). A breakthrough MacGuffin (as Alfred Hitchcock called the plot gimmick that grips the film audience) may also be developed, creatively.

Genre and the imitative author Me-tooism is sanctioned, and even encouraged. Mills and Boon, for example, have established sub-genres around the doctor-nurse scenario, the Georgette Heyer-style Regency romance, or the "governess tale."

The major imprints publish rule books, or templates, for would-be authors. Readers want the cosily familiar rather than the strange.

Often writers of genre hang out together socially: as did the Detective Writers Club in the 1930s. They set up associations with prizes for outstandingly proficient fellow writers in their genre, such as the Edgar

1902
Owen Wister publishes *The Virginian,* the model for innumerable other "Westerns"

1926
Hugo Gernsback launches *Amazing Stories*, which establishes the science fiction genre in its modern form

1984
William Gibson popularizes "cyberpunk" SF, with his novel *Neuromancer*

(named after the "inventor" of the detective story, Edgar Allan Poe) or the Hugo (named after the "inventor" of the term "science fiction," Hugo Gernsback). There is no prize called the Marcel (Proust) or the Franz (Kafka).

These genre prizes will typically be announced and awarded at large conventions, such as Worldcon (World Science Fiction Convention), with thousands of "fans" in attendance. At Worldcon they like to dress, *Galaxy Quest*-style, as their favorite SF characters.

It is a feature of genre that it mobilizes large numbers of dedicated readers, who form affiliation sub-groups of their own (nowadays by website, and web-based "fanzines"). Readers tend to be voracious consumers of their preferred fictional fare. Surveys suggest that devotees of science fiction and crime read up to a dozen titles a month. Genre writers tend, in response, to be prolific. Barbara Cartland had a life score of some 600 titles, aided by a team of amanuenses, turning out her pink and fluffy romances with the efficiency of a Japanese widget factory.

Is genre a fiction-only thing? It's convenient to think of genres (science fiction, romance, PI detective fiction, etc.) as empty boxes, waiting to be filled. But some precision is required. The novel is not, by most definitions, a "genre" but a "form." It is a larger box that contains genres, Russian doll-style.

Does "poetry" contain genres? Does drama? Aristotle talks of comedy and tragedy as dramatic styles. Are epic, lyric, satire, elegy *genres*? Arguably they are, but the term does not sit easily. Fiction is where the word seems most at home. There are, currently, five popular fictional genres in full production: romance (including historical romance), science fiction and fantasy, horror, thriller and crime.

Most practitioners stay within their box. Some, like Stephen King (who has written in all five genres – including a version of the

> **We have a name in the studio, and we call it the "MacGuffin." It is the mechanical element that usually crops up in any story. In crook stories it is almost always the necklace and in spy stories it is most always the papers.**
>
> **Alfred Hitchcock**

Western, with his "Gunslinger" saga) move around. But so brand-loyal are fans that genre writers prudently do not vary their stock in trade too much. It is plausible to see "pornography" as a genre – although it has migrated largely to visual and graphic forms.

There are, roughly speaking, two grand theories of how the imaginative energies of creative fiction disseminate themselves. One is a version of "trickle-down." A "master" like Henry James rewrites the rules for fiction, and disciples learn from him. An alternative view (favored by the Russian formalists) is that the energies explode from below, volcanically.

The second of these theories is the more plausible. Genre, that is, is the magma in which literature finds its primal existence. Analogues for Salman Rushdie's magic realism in *Midnight's Children* (the inter-clairvoyance, for example, of the children born at the moment of India's independence in 1947) are usefully looked for not in Henry James's *What Maisie Knew*, but in John Wyndham's *Village of the Damned* (published, originally, as *The Midwich Cuckoos*).

One of the more interesting literary frontiers is that where hard-boiled genre melts into "high" literature. A. S. Byatt's *Possession: A Romance*, for example, which blends critical theory, Victorian scholarship and traditional female romance. Another striking example is Paul Auster, whose *City of Glass* is offered as a "metaphysical detective story." Its narrative "hook" is a midnight phone call: "It was a wrong number that started it, the telephone ringing three times in the dead of night, and the voice on the other end asking for someone he was not."

The not-someone is "Paul Auster, of the Paul Auster Detective Agency." The recipient of the call is Daniel Quinn, who writes detective fiction (under the pseudonym William Wilson) but who, none the less, pretends, for reasons he himself cannot explain, to be Paul Auster and takes on the case. Genres bend. None the less, there was enough of the old-fashioned page-turner for *City of Glass* to be nominated for an Edgar. Jacques Derrida has given this melting of boundaries a typically Derridean term: degenerescence.

the condensed idea
Tell me a story – just like the last story

17 Closure

Until well into the 1950s, movies would routinely finish with "The End" blazoned in large letters across the screen. They don't end that way any longer – partly because so many film narratives are, nowadays, "open-ended." The Yellow Brick Road led Dorothy and her crew to stunning revelation in Oz's Emerald City. Cormac McCarthy's road goes nowhere. Nothing is revealed, other than more damn road. The most interesting ideas in literature often start with what look like banal questions, such as "Why do we want our narratives to have endings?" Or, to refine the question, why – knowing we want them – do we deny ourselves the gratification of always having them? Why do our literary roads presume destinations, reached or not reached?

Why are ends/endings so important to us? One answer to that question – why do we crave ends? – might be that, as humans, we are physically wired to want them. The Chomskyan linguists argue that we have a "language gene;" do we also have a "closure gene" – a physical predisposition to those two words, "The End?"

Oddly – given the ubiquity of narrative endings in literature – the subject has received little attention.

The critic Frank Kermode, who *has* given it attention, also starts with a homely question. Why, he asks, when the alarm clock by our bed goes "tick tick," does the brain insist on hearing "tick tock?" The reason, he suggests, is our addiction to beginnings and (even more addictively) endings: "Tick is a humble genesis, tock a feeble apocalypse."

timeline

1611	1848
King James Bible makes widely available the "end of days" St. John's Gospel	In *The Communist Manifesto*, Karl Marx predicts the postrevolutionary "withering away of the state"

Big stories: big endings

Our very biggest stories ("supra-literary fictions," as Kermode calls them) are those that regulate Western society: e.g., the Bible, *Das Kapital*, *The Origin of Species*. All can be see to conform, roughly, to a triadic structure: genesis (the beginning), tribulation and apocalypse (the middle game), last judgment (the end); primitive society, revolution, utopia; primal soup, evolutionary diversity, biosystem. These grand fictions demonstrably shape our smaller perceptions. What is Decadence? The ripe (rotten) fruit of *fin de siècle*. The new millennium (*2001* – as in Arthur Clarke's millenarian saga) associates itself, chronologically, with rebirth (Clarke's "starchild"). Even centuries and millennia, it would seem, have their tick and their tock.

Why do we perceive the world in terms of beginnings and endings? The acoustic conundrum led to Kermode's book-long investigation (*The Sense of an Ending*) and his conclusion that human beings reflexively interpret the world around them teleologically – in terms, that is, of beginnings and endings.

The great mass of fiction can be broken down into the three components (1) exposition; (2) complication; (3) resolution. The shape of a typical George Eliot novel, to take a specific example, is similarly: (1) idealism and illusion (Dorothea Brooke wants to be a modern St Theresa); (2) breakdown and disillusionment (Dorothea marries and discovers Edward Casaubon is not the great man she fondly imagined); (3) reconstruction (Dorothea builds a new life out of the wreckage of her old life). But in that novel's last chapter, it was Eliot who insisted that "every ending is a new beginning."

1890s	1967	1992
The *fin de siècle* literary movement becomes a powerful element in European and American literature	Frank Kermode publishes *The Sense of an Ending*	Francis Fukuyama publishes *The End of History and the Last Man*

Endings and the "big stories" Prophecy, myth and propaganda, as Kermode notes, stick very closely to "grand" narratives. Popular and children's literature – with their "once upon a time" and "happy ever after" – also remain close to the providential scheme. "Major literature" varies the formula and, often, plays with it: sceptically and complicatingly. But the formula is always there, whether adhered to or contradicted.

Victorian fiction was addicted to strong affirmative endings. Like old movies, it too appended the redundant information "The End" to the last page of the volume. Typically three "sacramental" moments were drawn on to bring down the curtain: birth, marriage and death. The last pages of Victorian fiction echo with peals of bells, babies" cries and funeral dirges. There are interesting differences, though, particularly among the major authors in the field. Everyone who has read the novel remembers the opening line of *Jane Eyre*: "There was not a possibility of taking a walk that day." Many readers, however, struggle to remember the last words (a common error is to recall the famous "Reader: I married him"). In fact *Jane Eyre* ends: "Amen; even so come, Lord Jesus!" (echoing, as it happens, the last words of the Bible).

Brontë was born in a parsonage, the daughter of a clergyman, married a clergyman, and probably assented to the Anglican creed most Sundays of her life. Her novels all fit, in their conclusions, to a providential view of life. God's ordained end.

Dickens, Brontë's contemporary, was – if his endings are to be credited – less certain. Famously he was uncertain how to end *Great Expectations*. In one coda, the hero, Pip, is reunited with the love of his life and they walk off to what we assume is contented marriage. In an alternative version, the lovers are separated only to meet, years later, in the crowd of Piccadilly Circus. They exchange a few words and go their separate ways.

Why should these few words tacked on to the last page of an 800-page novel matter so much? Because the world views the alternate endings represent infect the whole, like yeast in dough. One ending affirms

❝It ain't over till the fat lady sings.❞
The fat lady, although many who use the term are unaware of it, is Brünnhilde, in the grand climax of *Wagner's Ring Cycle*

providence. In the other, life has no grand meanings or narratives. Dickens finally hedged his bets with a faint hint, inserted into the providential ending, that Pip and Estella might not, after all, stay together.

Playing with the idea The modern author who has most subtly played games with fictional endings is the critic and novelist Umberto Eco. *The Name of the Rose* is a narrative constantly promising, then denying, the closures of conventional fiction. It's like a Sherlock Holmes story in which all the clues are turned up, but the crime they point toward is never solved.

The Name of the Rose can, in this respect (if not in literary quality) be compared with another best-seller, *The Da Vinci Code*. In Dan Brown's novel, the clues so expertly interpreted by the Harvard symbologist Robert Langdon all combine to make a logical conclusion. There was, the ending discloses, a Mrs. Jesus Christ.

In terms of mental disorder, Eco's narrative is like psychosis – everything is clear but nothing makes sense. Brown's narrative is like paranoia, where everything fits into a hidden, but gradually revealed scheme. For the paranoid mind, nothing is accidental. If a stranger looks at you in the street, it is because they are the CIA, plugged into your brain. Paranoia, like prophecy, is rigid. There is nothing unmeaningful, nothing inconclusive – however enigmatic it may superficially appear. The idea is played with, brilliantly, by Thomas Pynchon, in *Gravity's Rainbow*. Why do V2 rockets fall wherever the hero, Slothrop, has an erection? There must be a reason. Paranoia supplies it. He's wired.

Literature, as Kermode puts it, cannot make sense of our lives – and the end points, or destinations that we like to think we are making for. What it can do is "attempt the lesser feat of making sense of the ways we try to make sense of our lives." Explain, that is, why our ears insist on hearing tick-tock not tick-tick.

the condensed idea
Literature loves the finishing touch

18 Paradigm Shif

The term "paradigm shift" is nowadays something of a cliché (it's a favorite among sports journalists, describing some team shake-up). A fairly recent addition to critical vocabulary it was introduced into popular discourse by the historian of science Thomas M. Kuhn, in his 1962 study *The Structure of Scientific Revolutions*. Kuhn began with a simple, vexing observation: Why do scientists quarrel so much among themselves? His "paradigm shift" thesis has been hugely influential and genuinely illuminating. *The Structure of Scientific Revolutions* routinely figures in round-ups of the most important books of the twentieth century.

Shifts in science Kuhn's approach is "meta-topical." He looks at the history of science, in all its many departments, to observe how the discipline moves forward – which demonstrably it does. Very simply, Kuhn perceives three phases, or stages, in science's progress. What he calls "paradigm" is central to each of them. Literally the word means "pattern." Kuhn, however, prefers the overtones of the German word "*Gestalt*," which carries the supplementary sense of "meaningful pattern." One of his illustrative ideas is of the picture that one's eyes initially see as a duck, then, after a second or two, the image, or *Gestalt*, recomposes itself as a rabbit.

For scientists, a paradigm is a field (e.g., Einstein's General Theory of Relativity) within a larger field (theoretical physics) within a still larger field (science). In all these fields certain constituents are held together by common variables.

timeline

1390s	1750s
Chaucer breaks away from other dialects to establish "English" as the language of literature	The Augustans break with "barbarous" earlier literature to "polish" English literature along neo-classical lines

The first of Kuhn's stages is "pre-paradigmatic." It's a kind of bubbling intellectual primal soup. All theories contest among themselves without any becoming orthodoxy or consensual. Then one theory establishes itself as dominant, firms up, and develops a community of co-theorists and instructors around itself. It becomes, as Kuhn puts it, "normal." The energies of the community are devoted to confirmation and – more aggressively – the defense of its core belief. Careers and eminence are invested in the preservation of the ruling "normal" paradigm. Disagreement is routinely seen as heresy.

> **We can't solve problems by using the same kind of thinking we used when we created them.**
>
> **Albert Einstein**

This, "normality" as Kuhn calls it, is the second stage. The third stage is "revolutionary." So well defended is the normal that its fortifications can only be overcome by assault. If successful (not all revolutions are or deserve to be), there occurs a "paradigm shift," equivalent to a scene change in theater. A new normality will now emerge, conforming to the new paradigm. For example: until the middle of the twentieth century there was a "normal" view among cosmologists that the universe was in steady state (the most famous proponent was Fred Hoyle). Then came the "Big Bang" theory, and – after much quarreling – a new paradigm. It is a tenet in Kuhn's model that all paradigms are provisional.

Can we transfer the idea to literature? Interestingly Kuhn had been a student of humanities before moving to the history of science. Can one transfer his idea of the "paradigm shift" to literature? On the face of it, yes, one can. The idea explains a lot and paints a plausible big picture. Literature too moves through historical time, redefining its dominant styles or "schools" conflictually by something akin to a series of "normalities" and "revolutions."

The Augustan era's mission to civilize the "barbarous" canon of English literature – by translation, if necessary – into more polished forms of expression was, one might think, just such a revolution. So too was Coleridge and Wordsworth's proclaimed aim to banish the

1790s	1890s	1962
The "revolutionary" romantic movement establishes itself against worn-out neo-classicism	"Modernism" discards "worn out" romanticism	Thomas S. Kuhn publishes *The Structure of Scientific Revolutions*

Literary criticism: history or science?

Is the study of literature (and the informed reading of it) "historical" or "scientific?" Both sides of the argument have their advocates. No scientist sees the history of science as anything other than interesting – they would no more use their predecessors'' work than a modern astronomer would use Galileo's feeble (but history-making) telescope for present-day history-making research. Literary courses, by contrast, at school and university, are overwhelmingly backward-looking. It was not until well into the twentieth century that the Oxford curriculum admitted any literature after 1830 (and even that was labeled "modern"). Attempts to "scientify" the discussion of literature were dismissed as what D. H. Lawrence calls "twiddle-twaddle." With the recent "theory" revolution, "twiddle-twaddle" has become an orthodoxy. The conflicts between the different theoretical schools – formalists, neo-Marxists, poststructuralists, new historicists – conform eerily to what Kuhn describes in *The Structure of Scientific Revolutions*.

"gaudy and inane phraseology" and stylistic mannerisms of those over-polished Augustans, with their manifesto volume *Lyrical Ballads*. "Surgery for the Novel: Or a Bomb!" proclaimed D. H. Lawrence, one of the storm-troopers of modernism. Exit genteel Edwardianism, stuffy Victorianism and all that post-Romantic old hat. A paradigm shift is coming.

As Kuhn pictures it, "normality" does not roll over and die quietly. It fights back, savagely. Its life is at stake. Alfred Noyes (a leading Edwardian poet of the old school) greeted James Joyce's newly published *Ulysses*, in 1922, with the following blast, published under the headline "Literary Bolshevism" in the *Sunday Chronicle*:

> "I have picked out *Ulysses* because it brings to a head all the different questions that have been perplexing literary criticism for some time past. There is no answer possible in this case. It is simply the foulest book that has ever found its way into print.... The writing of the book is bad simply as writing, and much of it is obscure through sheer disorder of the syntax. But – there is no foulness conceivable to the mind of madman or ape that has not been poured into its imbecile pages."

Ulysses would, said Noyes, warming to his theme, "make a Hottentot sick." None the less, "modernism" carried through its revolution, only to be attacked, in its turn, by the apostles of postmodernism.

> **❝I must create a system, or be enslaved by another man's.❞**
>
> **William Blake**

One of the attractions of Kuhn's model – whether applied to science or humanities – is that it conceives knowledge as the outcome of perpetual battle. Conflict creates light, as well as heat. But in science, the idea of progress is valid in ways that it can never be in literature. The best science is the newest. No university course teaches Copernican, heliocentric cosmology as an equal but alternative theory to, say, Stephen Hawking's cosmology.

Does literature "advance" over time? There is good evidence that, however joltingly, science advances. Does literature advance in a similar way? Is the Shakespeare–Tom Stoppard relationship the same as the Copernicus–Hawking relationship? Literature changes over historical time; but can its forever remade newness be called "progress?" In the absence of tests of verifiability and falsifiability (science's method), the question does not admit of an easy answer.

New literature does not blot out old. Noyes, for example, is still riding high. His poem "The Highwayman" is on the National Curriculum as part of the British literary heritage that all children should know. This does not mean that Joycean modernism "failed" – in the sense, say, that some revolutions fail. What it means is that we cannot easily define what progress is in literature – if anything.

There is revolution, yes, certainly, and paradigm-shifting in plenty. But where those events are taking literature is never entirely clear. There are those who perceive decline and degeneration. It makes more sense to see literature as a constant quest to adjust to a changing present.

the condensed idea
It's a battlefield

19 Ownership

If you go into a car showroom and plunk down the however many dollars/pounds/euros posted on the windshield in the forecourt, sign various documents and drive off, there is no question. The vehicle is yours. You own it. But, in a sense, you don't. The point can be demonstrated by a mind game. Supposing you replicate, exactly, the car you've just bought (say a Prius Hybrid), down to the last nut, bolt and chrome trim. You then mass-produce it under a different marque: "Notprius," say. What would then happen is the mother of all lawsuits. Every new car is swaddled in thousands of invisible patent liens.

Multiple owners – but which of them is dominant?

Ownership of literature, if one follows the whole arc, is much more complex than the above example about the new car. Say a writer – Anthony Trollope – writes a novel. The "Chronicler of Barsetshire" (who preferred "outright sale," on the grounds that it made things simpler) duly sells his manuscript novel to a publisher. The publisher, who now "owns" the work, down to the last Trollopian comma, prints and binds thousands of copies and sells them on to bookshops. They, having paid the wholesale price, "own" the Trollopian stock. Customers then buy them, paying the retail price. They, at the end of the line, now "own" their book. In 1931, 50 years after Trollope's death, the book enters "the public domain." No one now owns the copyright.

At every stage of this complicated selling-on process, the book in question is identified as "Trollope's novel." How can this be? How can an author sell something, and still, in a sense, own it?

timeline

1616	1710	1894
Ben Jonson publishes his collected works, the first author to lay claim to his own writing in this way	The Queen Anne copyright act establishes the nature of literary property	The US belatedly signs to international copyrig protection

The candy store conundrum

When department retailers such as Woolworth's "five and ten cent" (in the UK "threepenny and sixpenny") stores came on the scene in the 1930s, a popular moral brain-teaser was: "What would happen if all the lights went out?" Would the customers, that is, stuff their pockets with all the free sweets they could grab? The Internet has created just such a lightless literary candy store. It's the Wild West, the Barbary Coast, Liberty Hall. Copyright has no writ there. Technology typically outraces the law in this way.

Automobiles were thundering homicidally along the roads before universal driving licensing was brought in. Literary ownership on the web is still very patchy. But one possible glimpse of the future is the Creative Commons initiative, founded in San Francisco as a nonprofit organization in 2001. Under the "copyleft" slogan, CC allows participating creators to indicate which rights they wish to retain, and which they agree to put in the public domain. Wikipedia is a main participant.

The explanation is to be found in the elegant legal formulation of literary copyright – a statute as finely framed itself as any work of literature. Copyright presumes authorship – a primal owner. There was, of course, literature before there were authors to own it.

No one can attach an authorial label to *Gilgamish*, the Old Testament, or *Beowulf*. It is doubtful that Homer was an author in the modern sense – he may have had the same status as Toyota: a convenient brand name for a many-handed composition. Similarly, folk literature such as the ballad, or popular legend (the Robin Hood stories) is "unowned."

1928
The Berne Convention introduces the notion of authors possessing inalienable "moral rights" to their work

1990
The World Wide Web radically reduces the effectiveness and policing of traditional copyright regulation

1996
The European Union extends copyright for 50 years after an author's death

Should we abolish literary ownership/authorship?

Roland Barthes (a main article of whose literary faith was "the death of the author" – by critical assassination if necessary) liked to cite the orchestral team behind medieval texts – the dictator, the scribe, the illuminator, the commentator (margins were left for his contributions), the copyist. Where is the "author" in this ensemble? The modern analogy would be with film – before, that is, French new criticism came in with the idea of the "auteur" director, a concept that has never taken much hold among the general cinema-going public.

There was, self-evidently, authorship in ancient Greece and Rome. It established itself in Britain with the arrival of printing. Arguably the first author in the modern sense, in Britain, was Ben Jonson, who superintended the production, under his own name, of his collected works. They were not, however, "protected" in the same way that – say – Jonson's other personal property was.

Copyright and ownership The great 1710 law of copyright was urged into existence by London booksellers who wanted to protect (primarily) their expensive editions of Shakespeare. It was, principally, a trade protection (the "right to copy"). Authors' rights were a secondary consideration. The law itself, however, presumed a primal creator – a "Shakespeare" at the start of it all. This was legally necessary for the complex subsequent transfers of, and limitations on, property rights.

Crucially the thing that was protected was the *immaterial form of words*. The immateriality required a leap of imagination. It supposed a kind of spectral, Platonic idea of the literary work, which, whatever material forms it might take, remained inviolate. A corollary (inherent in the prefix "copy") was that it was only the form of actual words, not its "design," or "architecture," that was protected.

> **Intellectual property is an important legal and cultural issue. Society as a whole has complex issues to face here: private ownership vs open source, and so on.**
>
> Tim Berners-Lee, inventor of the World Wide Web

There is, in literature, "no copyright in ideas." Thus if someone like Ward Moore invents the "alternative universe" scenario in science fiction (with *Ring in the Jubilee*), Philip K. Dick is free to borrow and develop it (in *The Man in the High Castle*).

This is one of the primal freedoms of literature – one that makes the me-tooism of "genre" possible.

The down side is clear enough. Paraphrase – saying the same thing in different words – slips the copyright noose. If, for example, one were to take famous opening of *The Catcher in the Rye* ("If you really want to hear about it," etc.) and paraphrase ("Should you be intensely curious," etc.) and go on right the way through the narrative in that paraphrasing way to the novel's last, resonant words about not telling anyone anything ("keep your thoughts to yourself") one would not have come up with a literary masterpiece, but would one be legally in the clear? Technically, yes, I suspect one might be. But the law has never been entirely precise on the matter, and is becoming even less so. Following the European model, in the 1980s, Anglo-American law incorporated the idea of an author's "moral right" to the "expressive heart" of what they write. It was under the provisions of this modification that J. D. Salinger was able to prevent the biographer Ian Hamilton paraphrasing the contents of his private correspondence (thus killing Hamilton's proposed biography).

The current law of copyright – on which all our understanding of literary ownership is based – is 300 years old, and at least (with the arrival of the Internet) 30 years out of date. Changes are coming. But, as Hamlet says, the law never hurries. It took Anglo-American law 30 years to come up with an efficient driving licence system – and arguably – America (at least) has still to frame an adequate law for fire-arms.

> **We can say nothing but what hath been said. . . . Our poets steal from Homer.**
> **Robert Burton**

the condensed idea
Literature is harder to keep hold of than a piece of wet soap

20 Critical Authority

The Booker Prize was set up in 1969 to identify and reward the "best novel of the year." It is now plausibly regarded (not least by itself) as the premier literary prize of its kind in the world. Its judgments are universally taken as sound, unbiased and authoritative. Papal, almost. It takes its place alongside other "certification of highest quality" prizes: the Costa (formerly the Whitbread), the Pulitzer, the Goncourt, the Orange, the T. S. Eliot Prize for Poetry, the Queen's Gold Medal for Poetry, the Man Booker International Prize, the Nobel Prize (the last three are for literary careers more than individual works). How obediently does the reading public accept the decisions these authoritative prizes make on its behalf?

Are prizes reliable judges of literary worth? The following novelists won the Booker Prize (since 2002 the Man Booker Prize) in the first decade of the twenty-first century: J. M. Coetzee, Anne Enright, Yann Martel, DBC Pierre, John Banville, Margaret Atwood. Top short-listed novelist over the years, by yards, has been Ian McEwan, whose *Amsterdam* won in 1998. Hardly a contest goes by without protest that McEwan has not won, whenever he has a new work out.

On 8 December 2009, the *Guardian* newspaper ran one of its "Comment is Free" threads, inviting bloggers to nominate the worst book of the decade. It was a red flag of a question, and the journalists who framed it manifestly expected respondents to dump on the likes of Paulo Coelho/Katie Price/Dean Koontz/Jackie Collins and their (supposedly) depraved ilk.

timeline

1559

The *Index Librorum Prohibitorum* (the books forbidden for the faithful to read) is introduced by the Catholic Church

1670s

Thomas Rymer's criticisms of Shakespeare make him the first authoritative literary critic in England

If this was indeed their expectation, the CiF team were utterly confounded. The manifestly bad books of the decade they had in mind were totally ignored. What, almost unanimously, the 892 respondents chose to target were "the most over-rated Booker winners."

> **[The] reader constitutes the authority for the meaning of the text.**
>
> Catherine Belsey

Outright rebellion No punches were pulled. Over 200 respondents went for Ian McEwan (there was scarcely a voice raised in his defense). Others mauled included most of the Booker laureates and many of the runners-up of the decade. All these books had won golden notices from reviewers in the most authoritative opinion-forming journals around – not least the *Guardian*'s own distinguished stable of literary commentators.

Vox populi Guardianisti, it was clear, did not want its opinion formed, thank you very much. Typically rebellious was the following, from mastershake (all the respondents wrote through noms de web):

"I think that *On Chesil Beach* and *Saturday* are the two worst books I've read this decade. Unmitigated, smug, self-satisfied rubbish from beginning to end. No redeeming features at all. Yet they still got near-universally good reviews in the broadsheets. What is it going to take for literary journos to wake up to the McEwan myth?"

At least mastershake was relatively restrained in his deprecation. The same could not be said of Stuart Evers's verdict: "In a shit-soaked field of its own is *Saturday* by Ian McEwan." This critical terminology of the bathroom was echoed by *Waldhorn*: "What fun to share the knowledge that one is not alone in thinking that *Saturday* is the most self-indulgent piece of literary masturbation to be produced in this or any other decade." And by johnnyt64: "Oh, how I long to take my copy [of *Saturday*] down from a bookshelf and quote from it to back up my opinion but I long ago shat on it, threw it into my garden and set it alight. It was the only cathartic act that seemed appropriate." "A mind numbing piece of crapola," taxpayertogo concluded.

1750s	1868	1920	1994
Samuel Johnson establishes himself as the model of the authoritative English literary critic	Matthew Arnold publishes his *Essays in Criticism*, advocating the central importance of the literary critic	S. Eliot publishes *The Sacred Wood,* which sets the tone for subsequent literary criticism	Harold Bloom publishes *The Western Canon: The Books and School of the Ages*

Who is the Mr. Big in literary criticism today?

One of the ways scholars, critics, and pundits measure their stature is by how often their work is cited by their peers. Scores are precisely recorded in the massive *Arts and Humanities Citation Index*. It's a fascinating databank. The rise of French theorists in the early 1980s, for example, is precisely registered, with Michel Foucault and Roland Barthes being among the top cited authorities in all the arts and humanities fields, with many hundreds of hits each. The following are scores from the latest *AHCI*:

Terry Eagleton: 415
Frank Kermode: 208
Elaine Showalter: 154
Jacques Derrida: 164
Michel Foucault: 72
Roland Barthes: 64
Germaine Greer: 24

Modesty should forbid, but won't: John Sutherland has a very respectable 218.

The Life of Pi, said AR27, was of a quality "an 8 year old would be embarrassed to submit as homework." Another critic confided, "I never actually finished that novel because I found it so smug, twee, and boring – wow – this must truly be the worst book ever published." Other "worst ever" candidates were proposed: "I hated *The Gathering* by Anne Enright ... dull dull dull ..." "Margaret Atwood's *Oryx and Crake* must be a contender for most over-rated ..." "I didn't like Ishiguro's *Never Let Me Go*, pretty shit, actually ..." "I hate *The Line of Beauty* – reading it felt like being very badly constipated ..." "Banville's *The Sea* – "literary onanism ..." I'm inclined to agree – it's a cold pudding of lugubrious prose ..." "*Vernon God Little* definitely the silliest Booker winner ... a truly shite book ..." "The ghastly modern Oirish school of Banville, Toibin, Enwright [*sic*] et al. ...Oh, and Coetzee's *Disgrace*: inexplicable characters, jaw-droppingly bad dialogue."

It went on. What was noticeable, as well as the chorus of derogation, was angry class resentments. Katsushika joined the McEwanphobic chorus, but what particularly got under his/her skin was class: "Ian McEwan's *Saturday* was unmitigated shite. Especially the first thirty pages that I actually read. I started pissing myself with laughter when he started describing the main character's *bluesman* son. And I was somewhat unsurprised that our middle-class hero has an unpleasant encounter with an oik later on.'

❝Like thatching or clog dancing, literary criticism seems to be something of a dying art.❞

Terry Eagleton

Anger or revolution? Another rage was that against the perceived conspiracies of the London literary world: "There's something truly horrible," wrote Absoluteboon, "about the way the literati slaver and foam over McEwan." That Enright and Banville won, wrote OZKT29B, was "proof that the Booker don't mean shit."

"I rejoice to concur with the common reader," said Dr Johnson – alias "the Great Cham" (or rule-giver). What he meant was that he rejoiced when the common reader concurred with him. Since the death of T. S. Eliot, there has been no authoritative literary legislator, of undisputed Johnsonian status, in Britain or America.

Critical sans-culottism of the kind the twenty-first century is witnessing tends to coincide with liberating new technologies. Printing, self-evidently, was one. The new literary initiatives (notably the Romantic movement) triggered by the French Revolution can be linked to the portable printing press (no more complicated than an ironing board, and easily hidden), which, in the run-up to 1789, permitted "under the cloak" publications (subversive pamphlets, pornography, libels of all kinds).

The student uprisings and general intellectual-ideological turmoil of the 1960s coincided with the paperback revolution and underground newspapers. And today we have the Internet, which has made everyone, potentially, their own *TLS* or *NYRB*.

Where this revolt will go, only time will tell. Will it blow itself out, or change the landscape? One thing is certain, Great Chams are, for the moment anyway, alongside the diplodocus in the company of extinct species.

the condensed idea
I'll make my own mind up, thank you very much

21 Style

"The most durable thing in writing is style, and style is the most valuable investment a writer can make with his time. It pays off slowly, your agent will sneer at it, your publisher will misunderstand it, and it will take people you have never heard of to convince them by slow degrees that the writer who puts his individual mark on the way he writes will always pay off." So wrote Raymond Chandler, arguably the most stylish writer ever to have written a crime novel. Few artists succeed in creating their own style – as another great instrumentalist, the trumpeter Miles Davis, once put it, "it takes a long time to play like yourself." Most never get there.

Everyone has one, and they are all different In January 1996, a novel called *Primary Colors* swept, overnight, to the top of the American best-seller charts and stayed there for the best part of a year. It was a political fiction (the "primary" in the title was a pun, referring to the bruising selection process an American president has to go through).

One of the features of the novel that titillated the public taste was that the author was billed as "Anonymous." Even senior publishers at Random House, it was said, did not know his/her identity.

Primary Colors was a *roman-à-clef*. But no one who had turned on a TV set in the 1990s needed any key as to who the main characters were intended to represent. The hero, Jack Stanton, was "the most enigmatic American alive" – William Jefferson Clinton – and the narrative was an inside story of Clinton's 1992 election campaign, no holds barred.

timeline

1590s	1667
"Senecan" versus "Ciceronian" style wars dispute which prose style is more appropriate	John Milton invents a Latinate English diction for his Christian epic, *Paradise Lost*

The author was identified by a stylistician, Professor Don Foster, as Joe Klein (a journalist with a substantial corpus of published work). Foster, a specialist in Shakespeare (also employed on occasion by the FBI), had applied his stylometric techniques to the text of *Primary Colors* and found a fit with Klein's prose. Every one of us, linguists like Foster assume, has our own particular style – our idiolect – something as uniquely "us" as our fingerprints or DNA.

Foster was also employed, in his forensic capacity, in the FBI hunt for the Unabomber, who accompanied his outrages with long rambling manifestos to the newspapers. Ultimately the idea about idiolect depends on a theory of what language is – a theory elegantly propounded by the Swiss scholar Ferdinand de Saussure.

Style: the linguist's explanation Language, Saussure theorized, could be seen as something binary. There was *langue*, which represented the vast notional pool. No one had ever, or could ever, map all the possible permutations of grammar, syntax and lexical items that make up *langue*. What *could* be anatomized was *parole* – speech acts, or individual uses of language. It was Joe Klein's *parole* that Foster, aided by his computer analysis, used to identify the correct authorial "hand."

"Idiolect" is preferable to "style" (a term that goes back to a person's individual use of the stylus, or pen: signatures on our bank checks still witness to the uniqueness of a person's penmanship). A preferable term is "color." Each of us colors, or stains, what we write with ourselves. We are what we write and what we write is us.

Anyone with an ear for literature will be able to pick up the individual colors of a famous writer. When in 1798 he read the words (later incorporated into the *Prelude*) "uncertain heaven received/Into the

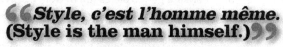

> **Style, c'est l'homme même.
> (Style is the man himself.)**
> Sainte Beuve

1798	1924	1950s
Wordsworth rejects the Augustan phraseology in favor of the style of "man speaking to man"	The linguist Jesperson defines "free indirected" or "represented" speech	Samuel Beckett popularizes "minimalist" literary style

bosom of the steady lake," Coleridge wrote: "I should have recognised [them] anywhere; and had I met these lines, running wild in the deserts of Arabia, I should have instantly screamed out 'Wordsworth!' "

He would have recognized them because they were so intrinsically Wordsworthian. When she read the elaborately anonymous *Waverley*, Maria Edgeworth clapped the volume shut with the ejaculation "*Aut Scotus, aut Diabolus*" – "Either Scott wrote it or the devil did."

The style of others: free indirect discourse Writers' styles change over the course of their careers, though not usually as to be wholly out of character. But there are situations in which a skilled author does not want his or her "stain" on what they are creating. Drama is one such situation in which authors have to find *paroles* that may be alien to themselves. Mimicry is required. None the less, experts like Foster argue that even characters as opposed in every way as – say – Othello and Iago have enough trace elements of Shakespeare in them to be identified as his work.

Styles within styles

Consider the following statement, by Raymond Chandler (again):

> "The best writing in English today is done by Americans, but not in any purist tradition. They have roughed the language around as Shakespeare did and done it the violence of melodrama and the press box. They have knocked over tombs and sneered at the dead. Which is as it should be. There are too many dead men and there is too much talk about them."

What Chandler implies here is that there are national styles (English/American), there are period styles (there were no press boxes in Shakespeare's England) and, by implication, there are genre styles (Chandler, for example, confessed to deriving much of the Chandlerian style from his fellow "hard-boiled" crime writer, Dashiell Hammett). One of the most difficult problems for the cultivated literary ear is to distinguish these larger, collective styles from the individual literary voice.

Idiolect presumes we can never escape from ourselves. We are locked inside our own style. And yet writers constantly attempt to break out into the minds, lives and speech patterns of others. Novelists have developed a particular technique for it – "free indirect style" (FIS) or "discourse."

> **Style is the mind skating circles around itself as it moves forward.**
>
> **Robert Frost**

FIS allows the narrative to slip inside the thought processes – not necessarily wholly verbalized – of a character. Handled well, it gives the reader a vivid sense of "being" that other character. Virginia Woolf was a virtuoso performer on the FIS instrument. Take the following passage from *Mrs. Dalloway* (the heroine, Clarissa, is walking from Westminster to Bond Street in London, on a fine June morning). Whose voice does the reader "hear?"

> "For having lived in Westminster – how many years now? over twenty, – one feels even in the midst of the traffic, or waking at night, Clarissa was positive, a particular hush, or solemnity; an indescribable pause; a suspense (but that might be her heart, affected, they said, by influenza) before Big Ben strikes. There! Out it boomed. First a warning, musical; then the hour, irrevocable. The leaden circles dissolved in the air. Such fools we are, she thought, crossing Victoria Street."

The last remark about "crossing Victoria Street" is clearly authorial. The rest is Clarissa Dalloway. But would a middle-aged Conservative politician's wife come up with that metaphor about leaden circles dissolving in the air? There is a tang of Woolf among the Dalloway here. The beauty of free indirect discourse is just that – it is free.

the condensed idea
Everyone may have one, but a good style is very hard to come by

22 Allegory

Literature's cleverest trick is to say one thing by means of saying something entirely different. Allegory belongs alongside simile ("my love is like a red, red rose") and metaphor ("O Rose, thou art sick") but is not, like them, a one-off device or ornament. It is more properly seen as a system, extended over length – sometimes the whole of the work (as in, for example, the successive books of Spenser's *The Faerie Queene* – the first of which allegorizes "holiness," the second "temperance," and so on). A narrative (like Bunyan's *Pilgrim's Progress*) can be an allegory. It can't be, in its totality, a metaphor. How, then, does allegory do its trickery and why is literature so fond of this device?

Plato uses allegory to clinch his point One of the earliest, and most vivid, allegories is that of "the cave," in Plato's *Republic*. Socrates is talking to Glaucon, instructing him on the nature of knowledge, and the limits set on it by the human condition. "Let me show in a *figure*," he says, "how far our nature is enlightened or unenlightened:"

"Behold! human beings living in a underground den, which has a mouth open towards the light and reaching all along the den; here they have been from their childhood, and have their legs and necks chained so that they cannot move, and can only see before them, being prevented by the chains from turning round their heads. Above and behind them a fire is blazing at a distance, and between the fire and the prisoners there is a raised way; and you will see, if you look, a low wall built along the way, like the screen which marionette players have in front of them, over which they show the puppets."

timeline

c.610 BC

Aesop's *Fables* allegorize the human condition in terms of animal narratives

c.360 BC

Plato uses his "cave' allegory in *The Republic* to illustrate the limitations of human perception

can a writer be allegorical despite himself?

Edgar Allan Poe was a sworn foe to allegory, something he associated – disapprovingly – with his contemporary, Nathaniel Hawthorne. According to Poe: "if allegory ever establishes a fact, it is by dint of *overturning a fiction*.... Under the best circumstances, it must always interfere with that *unity of effect* which, to the artist, is worth all the allegory in the world." Allegory undermined realism, the basis of modern fiction. But can a work like Poe's *The Masque of the Red Death* be read *un*allegorically? It opens, sonorously: "The *Red Death* had long devastated the country. No pestilence had ever been so fatal, or so hideous....There were sharp pains, and sudden dizziness, and then profuse bleeding at the pores, with dissolution." Prince Prospero (an allusion to *The Tempest*) ordains an end-of-the-world fancy dress party. The narrative is conducted through seven (mystical number) chambers, the whole *Totentanz* taking place under a gigantic, ticking ebony clock. Allegorical? Surely yes, Edgar.

This is not a fable about unfortunate potholers but an allegory of the sadly handicapped way (as Plato saw it) that we benighted humans will always know the real world.

But why doesn't Socrates just say it straight out? Why draw on a "figure" to get the message across? Many reasons suggest themselves. Not least, of course, his allegory beautifies. It can also be said to crystallize. And it makes what he is saying memorable. Once read or heard, no one ever forgets that Platonic image.

Modern thoughts about allegory Serious dispute over the merits of allegory began with interpretation of the Bible in the nineteenth century, as its literal holy writ wilted in the face of science, rationalism and Enlightenment scepticism. Could a man survive for three days inside the intestines of a whale, as we are told Jonah did,

1590	1678	1863	1979
Spenser's *The Faerie Queene* allegorizes the cardinal virtues in a poem of epic length	Bunyan's *Pilgrim's Progress* allegorizes human life in terms of a pilgrimage toward the Celestial City	Charles Kingsley publishes *The Water-Babies: a Fairy Tale for a Land-Baby*	Paul de Man publishes *Allegories of Reading*

only to be spat up, good as new, on land? No. It's an allegory, of course, for the enslavement of the Israelites in the bowels of Egypt.

Schopenhauer in *The Horrors and Absurdities of Religion* is eloquently satirical on the subject of allegory.

His essay takes the form of a dialogue – or quarrel – between Philalethes (who demands the truth, the whole truth, and nothing but the truth) and Demopheles, who argues that "you've got to see that the needs of ordinary people have to be met in a way they can understand." They have no greater need than religion, and allegory is the only way they can take it in:

> "Religion is truth allegorically and mythically expressed, and so rendered attainable and digestible by mankind in general. Mankind couldn't possibly take it pure and unmixed, just as we can't breathe pure oxygen; we require an addition of four times its bulk in nitrogen. In plain language, the profound meaning, the high aim of life, can only be unfolded and presented to the masses symbolically, because they are incapable of grasping it in its true signification."

"Philosophy," he sagely observes, "is not for everyone." Neither, of course, is economics. The financial catastrophe that ravaged the Western world in 2009 was conveyed "allegorically and mythically" in terms the everyday victim could understand – such as "credit crunch," "toxic loan," "double dip recession."

> **The greatest thing by far is to be a master of metaphor. It is the one thing that cannot be learned from others; it is also a sign of genius, since a good metaphor implies an eye for resemblance.**
>
> Aristotle

Written and pictorial allegory was at its most sophisticated in the medieval and Renaissance periods. It persists in modern literature as enriched texture rather than an obtrusive device. Allegory, at all periods, requires sophisticated readers capable of holding two very different kinds of truth simultaneously in their minds. Is Dorothea Brooke's the story of one remarkable (fictional) woman, or the story of a nineteenth-century (factual) Everywoman? We must maintain both hypotheses in a kind of tension when we read *Middlemarch*.

Not to perceive allegorical meanings is to blunder into comical literalism, as did the

Country Life reviewer of Kenneth Grahame's delightful anthropomorphic allegory, *Wind in the Willows*, who complained that the depiction of Ratty (the amiable rodent who loved "messing about in boats") was zoologically inaccurate. True enough, but foolish.

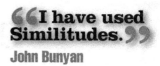

"I have used Similitudes."

John Bunyan

The allegorical twist in the tail H. G. Wells's *The War of the Worlds*, a work thrown off by a young man in the 1890s, is among the most read of early science fiction romances. One reads it as a rattling invasion yarn about bloodsucking aliens – inspired by the recent "discovery" of canals on Mars. But just once, in passing, Wells brushes his authorial finger across a button that transforms the whole work:

> "And before we judge of [the Martians] too harshly we must remember what ruthless and utter destruction our own species has wrought, not only upon animals, such as the vanished bison and the dodo, but upon its inferior races. The Tasmanians, in spite of their human likeness, were entirely swept out of existence in a war of extermination waged by European immigrants, in the space of fifty years. Are we such apostles of mercy as to complain if the Martians warred in the same spirit?"

The novel, the reader apprehends, allegorizes European colonialism and its genocides. Sticking to the mid-1890s, is *Dr. Jekyll and Mr. Hyde* a Gothic tale of demonic possession, or an allegory about the unconscious self that, in Vienna, Freud was beginning to make sense of? Is Oscar Wilde's *Dorian Gray*, with his real self in the attic, a fantasy, or an allegory of the subterfuges forced on the "love that dare not speak its name" in the 1890s?

Schopenhauer fondly believed that man would grow out of its allegorical primitivism "as out of his childhood clothes." He was wrong. Ambiguity points us to words meaning more than one thing. Allegory enlarges that double meaning to whole texts. If you want naked, unvarnished, single truth, as does Philalethes, don't go to literature. If you want many truths, compressed into their full complexity, literature is exactly the place to go.

the condensed idea
Allegory keeps readers on their toes

23 Irony

At its simplest, irony is saying one thing and meaning another. To that extent, the device aligns itself with allegory and metaphor and all the other indirectness of literature. But unlike allegory (see p. 88), irony's primary aim is not to make complex things simpler. Just the opposite. The etymological origin of the word – the Greek *eironeia* – translates as "deception," "hypocrisy" or "lie." In literature, irony makes simple things more slippery – but by doing so, truer to life. If the blunt definition of literary realism (*vraisemblance*) is "lies like truth," irony would have us believe that "lies *are* truth." Live with it.

The favorite device of the angry author Irony is typically accompanied by the four 's's: sarcasm, satire, subversion and scepticism. It often depends on tone of voice. Depending on how it's stressed "that's *terrific*" – for example – can mean it really is terrific ("Well done"), or it's awful ("God, what an idiot you are").

Irony lurks everywhere in modern literature. When Evelyn Waugh calls his novel *Decline and Fall*, he does not mean that the 1930s London of the Bright Young Things (itself an ironic label) resembles imperial Rome. Just the opposite. What Waugh has in mind is something more along the lines of Nick Flynn's über-ironic title, *Another Bullshit Night in Suck City*.

When Orwell names "the last man in Europe" (as he called the hero of *Nineteen Eighty-Four*) "Winston Smith," he makes an ironic conjunction between the greatest war leader of the twentieth century

timeline

1729
Swift publishes (anonymously) his "Modest Proposal," generally regarded as the most brilliantly ironic short text in English Literature

1813
Jane Austen's ironic skills a novelist reach their heig in *Pride and Prejudice*

and a nobody. Reading modern literature, it is wise to keep one's nostrils always on the twitch for the sharp tang of such irony.

It goes beyond a local effect sniffed here and there to a generally, and incorrigibly, disillusioned view of life. Hardy entitled one of his books *Life's Little Ironies*. All his volumes could be so titled – with the proviso that the irony is not always so little. Take the following, from his *Satires of Circumstance*:

> In the Cemetery
> "You see those mothers squabbling there?"
> Remarks the man of the cemetery.
> One says in tears, "Tis mine lies here!"
> Another, "Nay, mine, you Pharisee!"
> Another, "How dare you move my flowers
> And put your own on this grave of ours!"
> But all their children were laid therein
> At different times, like sprats in a tin.
> And then the main drain had to cross,
> And we moved the lot some nights ago,
>
> And packed them away in the general foss
> With hundreds more. But their folks don't know,
> And as well cry over a new-laid drain
> As anything else, to ease your pain!

As a world view, irony undercuts idealism, optimism, faith with razor sharpness. Nothing stands up after irony's cruel, hamstringing slash. When a future king of England stalks on stage to tell the audience:

> "Now is the winter of our discontent
> Made glorious summer by this sun of York"

he does not mean something along the lines of F. D. Roosevelt's (wholly unironic) campaign song "Happy Days are Here Again" but "don't you believe it:" some very unhappy days are in prospect. It was Laurence Olivier's brilliant perception, in his 1955 film, that Gloucester is less an evil monster than a master ironist – and to give him a knowing leer with that "winter of our discontent" utterance.

1894	1974	1990s
Thomas Hardy publishes the collection of tales, *Life's Little Ironies*	Wayne C. Booth publishes his authoritative study of the device, *The Rhetoric of Irony*	"Postironic" becomes a popular term in literary discussion, with the same general effect as "postmodern"

Irony lurks everywhere There was, in the late twentieth century, a veritable rage for ironic reinterpretation of canonical works of literature. Nothing now meant what it seemed to mean. Eurekas went up all over the "deep reading" world (as the critic Wayne C. Booth called it) when yet another conventional reading was overthrown by the discovery of some hitherto undetected irony. *Othello* suffered terribly from the "ironizing" tendency. For centuries Shakespeare's hero had been played as "the noble Moor." But then the irony-hunters began looking at his last, great speech, in which he declares himself one "who loved not wisely but too well."

Is this true? Did he not murder an entirely innocent, meek wife – whose last words are an attempt to exculpate her murderer – out of motives of injured pride and rank stupidity? We should put more credence on Emilia's furious utterance that he is "ignorant as dirt." Othello dies having learned nothing, apologizing for nothing, praising himself outrageously. Noble? Surely you are being ironic?

Why is it so attractive? Irony releases a lot of interpretative power. Authors can mean something quite other from what, on the

A masterpiece of irony

In any poll of classically ironic works of literature, *The Monkey's Paw*, by W. W. Jacobs (spoofed, memorably, in an episode of *The Simpsons*), would score high. A relic from the Orient – a monkey's paw – grants the possessor three wishes. A suburban family, the Whites, come by the magic paw. The father asks it for £200 to clear the family mortgage. The next day, the Whites's only son is killed in an industrial accident at work. The firm gives Mr. White £200 compensation. He then wishes his son back from the dead – he returns a decomposing corpse, battering at the door of the house they now own. With his last wish, the father must wish his son dead again. The knocking on the door stops, the wind howls, a lamp flickers, forlornly, in the street outside.

face of it, they seem to mean. They can play games with the simple reader. For decades, Scobie, the hero of Graham Greene's *The Heart of the Matter*, was seen as an honorable man, caught in an impossible dilemma. Committing suicide was, ethically, the right thing for Scobie (nicknamed "Aristides the Just") to do; but as a Catholic, it was the worst possible thing for him to do. Readers' hearts ached for the man. Then, in a preface to a late edition of the work, Greene announced that Scobie was an utter prig. All those readers had got him wrong – they had missed Greene's irony. Silly them.

Wayne C. Booth, mentioned above, makes – in his authoritative book on the subject – a useful distinction between what he calls "stable irony" and "unstable irony." The distinction can be illustrated in the work that is probably the most virtuosic exercise in irony in English literature, *Gulliver's Travels*.

In the first of the four books, the hero's trip to Lilliput, the satire is generally seen as directed against Queen Anne's court, and the little yes-men she surrounded herself with. The ironies are controlled and shot off like well-aimed poison-tipped arrows. But in the fourth book (Gulliver among the equine Hounhyhyms), an out-of-control Swift seems to be raging against the whole world. It's ironic – but what point is being made? Gulliver, if not Swift, seems to be a candidate for the strait jacket. Do we despise the whole human race as much as Swift's extravagantly misanthropic hero? No.

Irony, when used or perceived, has the odd effect of making you feel very smart. You see what others are too dull to see – the doubleness of it all. Clever me.

> **Clap an extinguisher upon your irony if you are unhappily blessed with a vein of it.**
> Charles Lamb

the condensed idea
The camera may never lie.
Literature does. and cleverly

24 Imagery

The idea of imagery brings in the vexed question of what one *reads*, and what one *sees* while reading, with the aid of what Wordsworth memorably called "the mind's eye." It's tricky, since clearly what one sees, with the two actual eyes in one's head, is small black marks on a white surface. One will have to wait for the development of neuro-criticism, employing some advanced magnetic field imaging equipment, to know what the exact nature of the two kinds of apprehension is. What one knows so far, and rather fuzzily, suggests that two different areas of the brain are involved.

What does it mean to "see" literature? Over-visualization, some critics argue, is a vice because (that familiar objection) it distracts close attention from the words on the page to something not on the page. But in some areas of literature, imagery – pictures in the head – can be argued to have a primary role and, indeed, to be vital to full appreciation.

Imagism, as a poetic school in the early twentieth century, spun off from French symbolism and an interest in the ideogrammatic and pictographic systems of China and Japan. The instantaneity of these nonphonic, nonsequential calligraphies circumvented, in a small way, the "hermeneutic circle" problem (see p. 13) – that you couldn't understand the parts unless you understood the whole, but you didn't understand the whole until you'd taken in the parts. Ezra Pound – a fervent Orientalist – famously shrank a long poem about the French Metro into one image, something consumed in a single "eye bite:"

> The apparition of these faces in the crowd;
> Petals on a wet, black bough.

He instructed his friend T. S. Eliot to do much the same kind of drastic shrinkage in the fourth section of *The Waste Land*, reducing a long

timeline

18 BC	1780–1800
In his *Ars Poetica*, Horace advocates *ut pictora poesis* – as in pictures, so in poetry	William Blake prints his poetry, embellished with his own pictorial imagery

narrative to the vivid imagery of Phlebas the Phoenician, gradually decomposing as he bobs in the waves.

What does imagery do that other devices can't? The image crystallizes. It makes the linear spatial, and can, when used by a great writer, enrich rather than impoverish meaning. Imagery-hunting was found particularly illuminating by mid-twentieth-century interpreters of Shakespeare. It was noted that in the text of *Hamlet*, for example, there are a string of references to hidden infection – hinting at venereal disease. There is, as Hamlet puts it, "something rotten in the court of Denmark." This idea of syphilitic decay at the core – confirmed by a score or so of similar images, in various mouths – operates like a Wagnerian leitmotif in the play. One sees it, in the mind's eye.

Meaningful image clusters were highlighted in other plays ("nature imagery" in *King Lear*, "blood imagery" in *Macbeth*, even imagery

> **Is this a dagger I see before me?**
> Shakespeare, *Macbeth*

Are images necessarily visual?

Terms such as "the mind's eye" (itself a visual image) suggest that imagery is, essentially, a thing of the eye. But, contradiction in terms that it may be, one can also "smell" an image (through the "mind's nose"), as in Lady Macbeth's hallucinatory: "Here's the smell of the blood still: all the perfumes of Arabia will not sweeten this little hand. Oh, oh, oh!" And one can apprehend an image (through the "mind's fingers"), as when Angus says of Macbeth himself, "Now does he feel/His secret murders sticking on his hands" (like tacky, congealing blood). Or one can taste an image (through the "mind's tongue"), as in Keats's

> O for a beaker full of the warm South!
> Full of the true, the blushful Hippocrene,
> With beaded bubbles winking at the brim,
> And purple-stainèd mouth.

Are images necessarily visual? In optometry, yes; in literature, no.

1820s	1900s	1926	1951
Jonathan Keats argues that the poet should embellish poetry with as much imagery as it can carry	Keats The Imagist group establishes itself as a leading poetic style in England	I. A. Richards, in *Practical Criticism*, attacks "over-visualization" as a vice in the reading of poetry	I. Wolfgang Clemen publishes his groundbreaking monograph *The Development of Shakespeare's Imagery*

imagery in *Antony and Cleopatra*). It's significant that Shakespeare (like Wagner) is taken in through the ear, not the eye, when we go to the theater. Drama, unlike the novel read at bedtime, is an audio-visual experience.

Historically, Shakespeare's use of imagery (he would not have recognized the word, in the sense we are using it, but he certainly knew what he was doing) can be traced back to the "emblem books" that he would have known from childhood. "Time," for example, is typically depicted in Renaissance emblems as a beautiful woman, in rapid motion, with a fringe on her brow, but bald at the back at her head. What does the image mean? That time has to be taken "by the forelock." As the most famous emblematist, Francis Quarles, put it, in an explanatory caption: "Make use of time if thou lovest eternity; yesterday cannot be recalled; tomorrow cannot be assured; only today is thine, which if thou procrastinate, thou losest; and which lost is lost forever. One today is worth two tomorrows."

Shakespeare alludes to the emblem, with an image, in Ulysses' comment to Achilles in *Troilus and Cressida*:

Time hath, my lord, a wallet at his back
Wherein he keeps alms for oblivion.

"Act now," the wily Ulysses counsels, "or it will be too late." He hammers the instruction home with the image of the wallet.

The explanatory image Imagery used in this way is "ecphrastic" – it makes things *real*. But like the verb "realize," it carries with it a sense of creating a deeper understanding. One thinks of it primarily as a poetic device, but prose writers use imagery as well. A famous example is the description of the fog – a London "pea-souper" (itself a proverbial image) – that opens *Bleak House*. Meteorologically, fog was a common metropolitan weather condition, but as an image, it depicts the obfuscating, poisonous miasma spewed out by British law.

> **Every thing possible to be believed is an image of truth.**
>
> William Blake

"The raw afternoon is rawest, and the dense fog is densest, and the muddy streets are muddiest near that leaden-headed old obstruction, appropriate ornament for the threshold of a leaden-headed old corporation, Temple Bar. And hard by Temple Bar, in Lincoln's Inn Hall, at the very heart of the fog, sits the Lord High Chancellor in his High Court of Chancery."

Nowhere in his extensive private notes on his novels does Dickens use the word "image" – although he does instruct himself, on occasion, to "strike the keynote." It took critics and readers the best part of a century to find a way of describing what Dickens was doing with his fog description. One is reminded of Freud's modest comment, "Everywhere I go I find that a poet has been there before me." Freud himself was fascinated by images. In his first major monograph, *On the Interpretation of Dreams*, imagery (usually translated as "symbolization") figures prominently.

For Freud, dreams are an image-laden language in which the purpose of the image is not to make something very clear (as do the seventeenth-century emblem books) but to keep secret ("latent") what is too dangerous to make clear ("manifest"). Explicit sexual meaning is, specifically, masked, or cunningly disguised, by imagery, thus:

> "All elongated objects, sticks, tree-trunks, umbrellas (on account of the opening, which might be likened to an erection), all sharp and elongated weapons, knives, daggers, and pikes, represent the male member. A frequent, but not very intelligible symbol for the same is a nail-file (a reference to rubbing and scraping?). Small boxes, chests, cupboards, and ovens correspond to the female organ; also cavities, ships, and all kinds of vessels."

The notion of the secretive image is perennially fascinating. Dan Brown uses it in the most popular novel of the twenty-first century, *The Da Vinci Code*. The story opens with the world-famous professor of religious symbology, Robert Langdon, being challenged with an image (involving a corpse, a Leonardo painting and a cabbalistic inscription) that only a professor of religious symbology at Harvard University has a chance of interpreting – and perhaps not even him.

the condensed idea
A picture is worth a thousand words – but usually doesn't require as many

25 Allusion

One of the most the most famous, and original, novels of modern times: *The Catcher in the Rye*, begins with a first sentence protestation that the reader need expect no "David Copperfield kind of crap." But original as Salinger's novel is, it consciously drags another novel in its train (albeit "kind of crappily"). Works of literature, we should realize, are not islands, entire of themselves. They connect with other works – invisibly and visibly. The most visible, controlled and *knowing* form of connection (other than outright plagiarism) is allusion.

How is it different from other kinds of literary reference? It may look like what theorists like to call "intertexuality" (see p. 129), but allusion quacks rather differently. It is not a genetic thing – like shared DNA – but a device, a tool, effectively, with which the author can do interesting things and create interesting effects.

In the above example from *The Catcher in the Rye*, Holden is drawing up his contract with the reader; what he will do, and what he will not do. The terms of that contract would have been very different had the key sentence read, simply: "all that kind of crap." It would, essentially, have stated the same thing. But the Dickensian allusion – "David Copperfield kind of crap" – brings another work of literature into play. It enlarges the perspective, and complicates it. And makes it, despite Holden's disavowal, intensely literary.

The allusion presumes, of course, a reader who is well read: or at least, well read up to American high school standard. It would not work as

timeline

c.1380

Chaucer opens his *Canterbury Tales* with a florid allusion to Petrarch

c.1610

Shakespeare, in the character of Caliban in *The Tempest*, alludes to Montaigne's essays on the cannibal well were Holden to say "all that Proustian kind of crap:" even though *À la Recherche du Temps Perdu* is as much an introspective recollection of adolescent crises as is *David Copperfield*.

Varieties Allusion can be intra- or extra-literary; it can refer to things inside books, or outside them. Dickens, for example, in the second paragraph of *Great Expectations*, has his hero, Pip, recall going down to look at the gravestones of "five little brothers of mine – who gave up trying to get a living, exceedingly early in that universal struggle." Serialized as it was in early 1860, at a period when the world was buzzing with excitement about "evolution," every wide-awake reader would have picked up the allusion to the third chapter ("Struggle for Existence") of Darwin's *Origin of Species* (published in November 1859), which he opens by saying: "Nothing is easier than to admit in words the truth of the universal struggle for life." Those allusive words will flavor the whole of Pip's life story.

Allusion can be used to suggest overall meanings to be encountered in a work. Titles – typically allusive-heavy elements – do this with great force and economy. Take, for example, the work routinely described as "the most read novel to have come out of Africa," Chinua Achebe's *Things Fall Apart* (1958).

The narrative is set in the 1890s, just at the point when Western missionaries arrive on their "civilizing" (i.e., colonizing) mission to eastern Nigeria. The novel follows the doomed career of a village leader, Okonkwo. He is not strong enough to resist the force of Western colonialism. Okonkwo is proudly heathen: his gods are Idemili, Ogwugwu, Ababala. But the title points elsewhere, to W. B. Yeats's chiliastic poem "The Second Coming:"

> Turning and turning in the widening gyre
> The falcon cannot hear the falconer;
> Things fall apart; the centre cannot hold;
> Mere anarchy is loosed upon the world.

The allusion in Yeats's own title is to the Book of Revelation, which forecasts the second coming of Christ after the apocalypse. What is the

1922	1955	2000
T. S. Eliot opens his epochal modernist poem *The Waste Land* with a barrage of allusion	Philip Larkin's "I remember I remember" alludes to Thomas Hood's poem, with the same title, written a century before	The Coen brothers' movie, *O Brother Where Art Thou?*, is based on a witty allusion to *The Odyssey*

How well read are you?

Titles – that part of the work of literature that calls out most loudly to the reader – are often heavily allusive. What are the allusions in the following titles? (Answers on p.208.)

1 *Portrait of the Artist as a Young Dog* (Dylan Thomas)

2. *The Remembrance of Things Past* (C. K. Scott Moncrieff's translation of Proust's *À la recherche du temps perdu*)

3. *For Whom the Bell Tolls* (Ernest Hemingway)

4. *Lucky Jim* (Kingsley Amis)

5. *Far from the Madding Crowd* (Thomas Hardy)

6. *Tender is the Night* (Scott Fitzgerald)

7. *Of Human Bondage* (Somerset Maugham)

8. *The Grapes of Wrath* (John Steinbeck)

9. *A Passage to India* (E. M. Forster)

10. *Arcadia* (Tom Stoppard)

effect of that double allusion (Yeats/Revelation) on the novel? That something terrible will happen (the destruction of Okonkwo, unsurprisingly), with the promise – in the distant future – of salvation (i.e., independence for the as yet unborn state of Nigeria).

Yeats is also alluded to in the title of Cormac McCarthy's novel, *No Country for Old Men* (the novel behind the 2007 Oscar-winning film). The allusion, rather less clear cut, is to the poem "Sailing to Byzantium," with its opening lines:

> That is no country for old men. The young
> In one another's arms, birds in the trees
> – Those dying generations – at their song

The old, the poem argues, must withdraw into the eternity of art, symbolized by Byzantium (Constantinople). They can no longer live the sensory life of the young. The allusion points toward the central character, Ed Tom Bell, a frontier lawman out of his time in the lawless fallen world of the Mexican–American border.

McCarthy – who loves allusion – is more direct in his 2006 novel, *The Road*. In this apocalyptic scenario, the allusion, ironically, is to Frank Baum's *The Wizard of Oz*, and the "Yellow Brick Road." McCarthy's unnamed hero follows it less happily than Dorothy.

Eliot: master allusionist Allusion works best with a well-read reading public – one which can pick up the echoes. But will even the best read of readers get them all? Take the overtly allusive first five words of the most famous poem of the twentieth century, *The Waste Land* about April being "the cruellest month." The primary allusion is to the opening words of Chaucer's *Canterbury Tales*, "Whan that Aprill with his shoures soote/the droghte of March hath perced to the roote." But Chaucer was alluding, in his turn, to the opening words of Petrarch's Sonnet 42, "The spring returns, the spring wind softly blowing/Sprinkles the grass with gleam and glitter of showers." Petrarch himself was alluding to a whole genre of "spring and rebirth" poems called, in French, *reverdie*. It means, literally, "regreening."

Eliot uses allusion as a framework. Before one even gets to the allusive first five words, there are (in the title, epigraph and dedication) allusions to the anthropologist James Frazer, Petronius and Dante – and so it goes on for the whole five sections of the poem. It's not a mere peacock display of learning. Eliot is asserting, allusively, the traditions within which a modern poet must work.

How disabled is one's reading if one doesn't pick up the Chaucer allusion? Or the Caulfield/Copperfield allusion in *The Catcher in the Rye*? Can we handle Joyce's *Ulysses* if we don't know Homer – at least in translation? Few aspects of literature justify wide and deep reading more persuasively than allusion.

the condensed idea
The reader who reads most gets most

26 Defamiliarizatio

"The purpose of art is to impart the sensation of things as they are perceived and not as they are known. The technique of art is to make objects 'unfamiliar.'"
So wrote Viktor Shklovsky, inventor of the term "defamiliarization." In Russian, there is a less cumbersome word, *ostranenie*, which translates as "making strange." In essence, the idea is itself familiar to every reader. You turn a page – then something distracts you (the doorbell perhaps) – you come back to the book, and you cannot remember, for the life of you, what was on the page you have just turned over. At its best, literature "strikes;" what you read is unforgettable, however loud the doorbell. Defamiliarization is essential to that unforgettability, both fundamental and, at the same time, fiendishly slippery.

Is there an easier way of saying it? The task of literature, Shklovsky said, was to "make the stone stony." One of his favorite examples was that of Tolstoy's short story "Kholstomer." It's an everyday
tale – but rendered vivid by coming from the mouth of a horse.

Poets knew all this long before the critics came up with the word for it. Poets have always been alive to the need to defamiliarize (Aristotle observed as a necessary element in poetry its "strangeness"). Coleridge justified the pseudo-ballad diction of *The Ancient Mariner* as a conscious attempt to tear away the "film of familiarity" that means "we have eyes, yet see not, ears that hear not, and hearts that neither feel nor understand." He did this, in large part, by a *faux* antiquity of diction – something that constantly teeters on the edge of the absurd:

timeline

*c.*332 BC	1817
Aristotle's *Poetics* notes that part of poetry's power is its ability to make familiar things strange	In *Biographia Literaria*, Sar Taylor Coleridge argues th "strangeness" is a central effect in Romantic poetry

It is an ancient Mariner,
And he stoppeth one of three.
"By thy long beard and glittering eye,
Now wherefore stopp'st thou me?"
He holds him with his skinny hand,
"There was a ship," quoth he.
"Hold off! unhand me, grey-beard loon!"
Eftsoons his hand dropt he.

Brecht's "alienation effect" Bertolt Brecht developed the
idea of "defamiliarization" as something central to his theater. The
term he devised was *verfremdung effekt*, which translates commonly as
"the alienation effect" ("distanciation" is a preferable term, avoiding as
it does confusion with Karl Marx's quite different idea of social
alienation). Brecht hated what he called the "magnetic" effect of
popular film and drama. One should not, he believed, be "carried
away" – transported *into* the work. One should keep one's distance.
There must be no "suspension of disbelief" and the illusion that one
was witnessing something "real." One of the ways of "distanciating"
the audience was by "laying bare the device" – making the sets look
like sets, having the actors make clear they were acting.

Brecht went a stage further. Why, he asked, should audiences in
theaters behave as if they were in church? Why should they not be
more like spectators at a football or boxing match? The point of all
this, for Brecht, was to render the audience "critical." He called some
of his plays *Lehrstücke* – teaching pieces. A typical alienation device is

> **Art exists to help us recover the sensation of life; it exists to make us feel things, to make the stone stony. The end of art is to give a sensation of the object as seen, not as recognized.**
> Victor Shklovsky

1917	1940s	1972
Russian critic Viktor Shklovsky argues that "making strange," or "defamiliarization," is the essence of literature	Bertolt Brecht establishes his theater and dramatic works on the principle of "alienation"	John Berger's TV series *Ways of Seeing* introduces a mass audience to the idea of defamiliarization

that in his most famous play, *Mother Courage*. A small merchant who makes her living peddling snacks to the troops (on both sides) in the Thirty Years War she survives. It would be easy to sentimentalize her. But Brecht intends us to see her as a capitalist. He does so by an alienation device – have her furtively cheat the undertaker who is burying her beloved daughter out of a few coppers.

Defamiliarization and alienation techniques became hot topics in the 1920s and 1930s for plausible historical reasons. There was a fear of psychic automation, of the kind allegorized in Fritz Lang's *Metropolis*, at a time when whole populations were reduced to "automata" by totalitarian tyranny. A main element of the Nazi doctrine was *Gleichschaltung* – making everyone the same, making every experience the same, questioning nothing. Brecht was virulently anti-Fascist (and more prudently, in his later career, anti-Stalinist).

Brecht's theory of how plays should be staged has been immensely influential. Historically one can see it redrawing the rules of Shakespeare production, after the first performances of Brecht's

Defamiliarizing lines

The following are among the most joltingly defamiliarizing opening lines in fiction.

One morning, when Gregor Samsa woke from troubled dreams, he found himself transformed in his bed into a horrible vermin. (Franz Kafka's *Metamorphosis* – Gregor, we learn, has become a man-sized bedbug.)

It was a bright, cold day in April and the clocks were striking thirteen. (George Orwell's *Nineteen Eighty-Four*. The novelist Anthony Burgess claimed to have read an Italian translation in which thirteen was corrected to "*uno*" on the grounds, presumably, that the benighted English novelist couldn't even tell the time correctly).

My name was Salmon, like the fish; first name, Susie. I was fourteen when I was murdered on December 6, 1973. (Alice Sebold's *The Lovely Bones*. Susie, we discover, is writing her novel in heaven.)

> **In order to produce A-Effects the actor has to discard whatever means he has learned of persuading the audience to identify itself with the characters which he plays. Aiming not to put his audience into a trance, he must not go into a trance himself.**
>
> **Bertolt Brecht**

Berliner Ensemble in London in the 1950s, and their enthusiastic welcome by the most influential critic of the day, Kenneth Tynan.

The opposite view: Stanislavski Brechtianism ran counter to another, quite contrary and more dominant, theory of dramatic performance. For Brecht, "identifying" with characters (whether it is the actor, the audience or even the playwright who does the identifying) is plain wrong. It leads to an "uncritical" response in the audience. A quite opposite view was advocated by Constantin Stanislavski. For this Russian theorist, the actor (and behind the actor, the dramatist) had, above all, to "get inside" a character – *become* Hamlet, not merely "play" Hamlet. This "method" technique, as it became known in America (where it had a powerful influence on actors such as Marlon Brando) involved a kind of marriage between the performer and the character he/she plays. "Bring yourself to the point of taking *hold* of a role," wrote Stanislavski, "as if it were *your own life*. Speak for your character in *your own person*. When you sense this real kinship to your part, your newly created being will become soul of your soul, flesh of your flesh."

The key to understanding, for Stanislavski, was emotion – intense sympathy. Emotional empathy or cerebral defamiliarization? Stanislavski or Brecht? Twenty-first-century theater is still in two minds on the question.

the condensed idea
Literature kicks

27 Bricolage

Bricolage is an idea put into general circulation by the anthropologist Claude Lévi-Strauss, in his work on myth and *pensée sauvage* (loosely, "the primitive mind"). The term has that *mot juste* quality of other Gallicisms for which English has no exact equivalent, such as *mise en scène, dénouement*. The nearest French–English dictionaries can get is *"bricoler* = to putter." Putterer (*bricoleur*) or putterage (*bricolage*) do not fall happily from the lips. The meaning as more fully defined is "work that is put together from whatever materials come to hand." DIY, one might say. A classic example is the eighteen Watts Towers, in South-Central Los Angeles – handsome structures that were constructed out of street garbage. Much literature can claim to be put together on the same DIY architectural principle.

Anthropological origins of the term For the anthropologist, like Lévi-Strauss, "myth" (*pensée sauvage* – the wisdom of primitive societies) is a prime example of bricolage. Myth explains events in terms of the necessarily limited range of knowledge the myth-maker already has. When people are angry, they shout and throw things about. When Zeus is angry, he thunders and hurls lightning bolts. This is *météorologie sauvage*. Weather myths. The mythology is as valid for the societies that originate it as is climate-change theory for modern Western societies.

There is, however, a difference. Myth presumes knowledge. Science (Ben Franklin and lightning, for example) presumes ignorance and investigates the yet-to-be-known. Scientists see themselves as going into a dark tunnel, and illuminating it as they go. Authors of poems,

timeline

1621

Robert Burton publishes his encyclopaedic miscellany
An Anatomy of Melancholy

1921–1954

Watts Towers constructed in Los Angeles

plays and fiction rarely see themselves doing that; and if they do, it's usually bad poetry, drama and novels that result.

Literary applications The idea of bricolage can be usefully applied to literature. Lévi-Strauss himself took an example from English fiction – Wemmick's house, on the Walworth Road, in *Great Expectations*. Like the builders of Watts Towers, Wemmick has constructed a *faux* British castle out of local building materials, and whatever junk he can scavenge. This is how Pip describes Château Wemmick:

> "Wemmick's house was a little wooden cottage in the midst of plots of garden, and the top of it was cut out and painted like a battery mounted with guns.
>
> "My own doing," said Wemmick. "Looks pretty; don't it?"
>
> I highly commended it. I think it was the smallest house I ever saw; with the queerest gothic windows (by far the greater part of them sham), and a gothic door, almost too small to get in at.
>
> "That's a real flagstaff, you see," said Wemmick, "and on Sundays I run up a real flag. Then look here. After I have crossed this bridge, I hoist it up – so – and cut off the communication."
>
> The bridge was a plank, and it crossed a chasm about four feet wide and two deep. But it was very pleasant to see the pride with which he hoisted it up and made it fast; smiling as he did so, with a relish and not merely mechanically."

Wemmick's "aged p" (his father) informs an inwardly chortling Pip: "This spot and these beautiful works upon it ought to be kept by the Nation, after my son's time, for the people."

> ❝ **Bricolage builds ideological castles out of the debris of what was once a social discourse.** ❞
>
> Claude Lévi-Strauss

1950s–1960s	1962	1980s
William S. Burroughs experiments with his "cut-up" (fish-bowling) technique, a version of bricolage	Claude Lévi Strauss publishes *La Pensée Sauvage*	"Punk" fiction bases itself on its understanding of bricolage

Bricolage and science fiction One can spread the idea of literary bricolage beyond such examples. Consider SF and dinosaurs. When Arthur Conan Doyle wrote *The Lost World*, in 1912, there were parts of the globe still unexplored. It was plausible (at least for readers of fiction; not perhaps for geographers) to suppose recesses of the planet, the Amazon principally, where dinosaurs and other prehistoric beasts might still roam.

Doyle's Professor Challenger novel has been a best-seller for almost a hundred years – regularly revived (or shamelessly ripped off) for film and TV adaptations. But if one flashes forward to a more recent dinosaurian adventure tale, *Jurassic Park*, the explanation has to be different. There was, at the end of the twentieth century, no spot on earth – however remote – where dinosaurs might plausibly roam.

Michael Crichton reached for the more recent discoveries of Crick and Watson about recombinant DNA. Also to hand was the separate fact that prehistoric blood-sucking mosquitoes had been preserved in amber. This created a believable scenario – genetic re-creation: a park that was half Disneyland, half Eden.

Bona fide scientists (probably Crichton himself, who had a degree from Harvard in medical science) regard *Jurassic Park* to be as fanciful

Three French terms (untranslatable, but useful)

Bricolage is not collage, a French word that sounds like it. Collage is derived from the French "to glue" (*coller*), and indicates work in which essentially disconnected elements are stuck together, without any inherent architecture or form (something bricolage aims at). Collage is, primarily, a technique used in pictorial art, although literary examples (Ezra Pound's *Cantos*, Robert Burton's *The Anatomy of Melancholy*) could be so called. Montage (from the French *monter*, to "mount" – as one mounts stamps in an album) describes disparate elements arranged serially, but without connectives, or joining syntax. The introduction of montage into film (where it is a central technique) is usually attributed to the Soviet director Sergei Eisenstein. The shock opening of Dickens's *Bleak House* is an early example of literary montage ("London. Michaelmas term lately over, and the Lord Chancellor sitting in Lincoln's Inn Hall. Implacable November weather.")

as Professor Challenger's expedition into the Cretaceous period lying on the banks of the twentieth-century Amazon. But both authors can be seen as bricoleurs – framing their narratives out of materials to hand, "fragments," as T. S. Eliot says, "shored against my ruins."

Long-lasting works of literature typically adapt to new circumstances in this bricolage way. When H. G. Wells published *The War of the Worlds* in 1895, recent observation of "canals" on Mars made the idea of invasion (by space vehicles fired from cannon) plausible. They land in the Home Counties, of course, because Britain is the global superpower at that date.

In 1939, Orson Welles made a famous radio programme in which he simulated *The War of the Worlds* as a fast-breaking news story. Large chunks of the Eastern Seaboard were panic-stricken, taking the programme as the real thing. What Welles was drawing on was not a pool of anxiety about Martian invasion, but the same kind of thing that was happening in China and Europe. And that would, within months, happen at Pearl Harbor, to be conveyed to the American population by radio-casts that were not fake.

The 1953 George Pal film of *The War of the Worlds* had the Martians (who are never clearly seen) take the planet over with flying saucers – the UFOs that were generating paranoia among sections of the American population in the Eisenhower era. In 1953, it was just feasible to fantasize life on Mars. After the Red Planet had been explored by orbiting telescopes and ground exploration vehicles, the notion of a super-intelligent race there was astronomical nonsense. In the 2005 Tom Cruise–starring film, the aliens come from – who knows where?

In every successive version of *The War of the Worlds*, one sees the framers of the narrative reaching out for the best materials available at the time. This is the essential principle of bricolage. A definitive version of *The War of the Worlds* awaits the final discoveries and conclusions of cosmology. It will be a long wait, with much further bricolage before we get there.

the condensed idea
You have to work with what you've got

28 Metafiction

Metafiction is narrative that knowingly surrenders, and rejoices in, its consciousness of being derivative. As its corpus grows, literature becomes ever more aware of itself. Originality is aimed at – but proves increasingly elusive. There is no wrecking ball in literature, no demolition. The stuff accretes, inexorably, and at an ever faster rate. In Dickens's day, there were under 1,000 new fiction titles produced every year. In the twenty-first century, it's a poor year that doesn't generate 10,000, and 10,000 new echoes in the literary echo chamber.

Is all fiction metafiction? The term "metafiction" is of recent origin – no more than four decades old. But with hindsight, one can detect metafictional elements in the earliest works of literature. *Don Quixote*, for example, is an "antiromance." The melancholy knight, with his cardboard armor and comic misapprehensions of chivalry, is Cervantes" playful metafictional joust with heroic works such as *The Song of the Cid*, and innumerable medieval romances of knight errantry.

Literary parody (e.g., Henry Fielding's *Shamela*, a hilarious take-off of Samuel Richardson's *Pamela*) is one standardized form of metafiction. Homage fiction (e.g., Michael Cunningham's *The Hours* – a tribute to Virginia Woolf's *Mrs. Dalloway*) is another, as is mock epic (e.g., Alexander Pope's *The Rape of the Lock*). A fourth kind of metafiction is the "knowing variation on a folkloric theme," such as J. M. Coetzee's *Foe* (there is another castaway, a woman, on Robinson Crusoe's island – an acquaintance of a novelist called Daniel Defoe). None of these works could themselves work without other literature of whose existence they constantly remind the reader.

timeline

1605–1615	1741
Cervantes' *Don Quixote* published	Henry Fielding's *Shamela* published

Metafiction or surfiction?

The novelist Raymond Federman prefers the alternative term, which carries with it the idea of "surfing" on the wave of literary history. Federman writes:

> "The only fiction that still means something today is that kind of fiction that tries to explore the possibilities of fiction; the kind of fiction that challenges the tradition that governs it: the kind
> of fiction that constantly renews our faith in man's imagination and not in man's distorted vision of reality – that reveals man's irrationality rather than man's rationality. This I call SURFICTION. However, not because it imitates reality, but because it exposes the fictionality of reality."

Metafiction is acutely aware of other fiction but also, characteristically, elaborately self-aware as well. It typically indulges a "narcissism" – a "look what I am doing" signal to the reader. Self-referentiality is raised to the status of an extended joke in a pioneer text in the high-metafiction canon, Laurence Sterne's *Tristram Shandy*. At one sublimely comic moment, well into the book, the narrator, Tristram, who has set out (like a horde of other "life writers") to chronicle his whole "Life and Opinions," discovers that the task he has set himself is impossible. His life is accumulating faster than he can write it down. The narrator's need to digress (describe situations, events, circumstances) hinders the need to progress. He will never catch up with himself. He's the sorcerer's apprentice, with no sorcerer to rescue him. Metafiction typically blends into metanarrative in this Shandyan way.

Of course novelists, like other narrators (those in film, for example, who have only two hours to work with), have developed strategies for circumventing the Tristram quandary – without troubling the reader on the subject. But Sterne *intends* to trouble the reader: it's the basic joke. "My next trick is impossible," as the conjuror says. Then he goes ahead and does it.

1759–1769	1966	2009
Laurence Sterne's *Tristram Shandy* published	Tom Stoppard's *Rosenkrantz and Guildenstern are Dead* first performed	*Pride and Prejudice and Zombies* published

One could go so far as to suggest that all fiction is metafictional to some degree. If you know you are writing a novel, you will also know you are working in the shadow of other novels. The novel can never be entirely novel. There are writers in the modern period – as the body of literature has multiplied unprecedentedly – who have used this fact, making generic impossibility their métier, or angle.

Donald Barthelme (1931–89) is one such metafictional virtuoso. Best known among his novels (or "antinovels") is *Snow White* (1967), a literary fantasia on Disney's cartoon of the original German fairy story. Barthelme's Snow White (the story begins with a corporeal inventory of her "beauty spots" – including a fine one on her buttock) misconducts herself disgracefully with her dwarfs in the shower.

Metafiction and originality Metafiction, one may say, focuses on the perennial literary problem – particularly troublesome for the modern writer – of how to achieve originality within a larger, inescapable unoriginality. All the literary space is occupied, all the stories used up. What can a writer do but chew the gum other writers have left
behind them?

One solution is to go back to those old stories and do them again – but differently, with modern inflections and twists. Chew the old gum differently. This literary recidivism has produced a rich crop, in recent years, of so called post-Victorian Victorian novels. It represents one of the more popular veins of contemporary metafiction, and would seem to have plenty of juice left in it.

The point of origin is a novel by Robert Graves, *The Real David Copperfield* (1933). Graves's novel mischievously switches perspective, narrating Dickens's version from a different angle. It introduces "grown-up" elements – no "happy ever after" for the hero with his Agnes, for example; his sexual desires are much more complex than those of Dickens's David (it is he, not Steerforth, who lusts after L'il Emily).

> **Metafiction? Boring ... all texture and no flesh and blood.**
> Raymond Carver

Following Graves, there has been a profusion of alternative angle PVVNs – *Wuthering Heights* from the point of view of Nelly Dean, *Jane Eyre* from the point of view of Bertha Mason (e.g., Jean Rhys's *Wide Sargasso Sea*). This genre has been hugely boosted by the millions" strong audience which television has recruited for Victorian period serial dramatization. Andrew Davies's adaptation of George Eliot's *Middlemarch* made that novel a Number One paperback bestseller in 1994. Trollope, Dickens, and Mrs. Gaskell have all enjoyed a similar posthumous success. It creates a vibrant reciprocity. The novel – say *Vanity Fair*, or Trollope's *The Way We Live Now*, is televised, then it is extensively read (often by reading groups – a fascinating modern phenomenon) and then it slips on to the prescribed reading of schools and universities. The author lives again.

A super-seller in the neo-Victorian genre is George MacDonald Fraser's "Flashman" series, which follows the outrageous career of the "cad" villain in *Tom Brown's Schooldays* through a dozen volumes. A *ne plus ultra* among PVVNs is Jasper Fforde's burlesque "Thursday Next" series. In one of the books (*The Well of Lost Plots*), the central characters of *Wuthering Heights* appear as plaintiffs before a tribunal of "jurisfiction" to establish which of them has legal ownership of their narrative. On a more serious plane are novels like A. S. Byatt's Booker Prize–winning *Possession*, John Fowles's *The French Lieutenant's Woman* and Sarah Waters's *Fingersmith*, which do Victorian fiction a century after the era is dead and gone. As the great corpus of literature grows, metafiction – novels about novels – will, to a certainty, grow too. Who knows, one day it may be the only kind of fiction available.

the condensed idea
Nothing new under the literary sun

29 Solidity of Specification

"One can speak best from one's own taste, and I may therefore venture to say that the air of reality (solidity of specification) seems to me to be the supreme virtue of a novel – the merit on which all its other merits ... helplessly and submissively depend." So wrote Henry James. It's the only time in his voluminous writings on writing that he uses the phrase. It is, none the less, central not just to his novels but to the whole fictional enterprise.

The realistic detail Consider the following episode from *Robinson Crusoe*. The hero has been miraculously (or, as he later comes to believe, for some divine purpose) shipwrecked on an island off the coast of South America. Of his former shipmates, presumed drowned, he says: "I never saw them afterwards, or any sign of them except three of their hats, one cap, and two shoes that were not fellows."

It's an incidental detail of no significance – but every reader I have met recalls those irritatingly mismatched shoes. But why does Defoe have Robinson mention them? They never come up again in the story. Virginia Woolf explains it as the novel's ingrained factuality. Defoe is a master of the art – he has "a genius for fact." By means of it, "he achieves effects that are beyond any but the great masters of descriptive prose. He has only to say a word or two about "the grey of the morning" to paint vividly a windy dawn."

timeline

1595	1849
Sir Philip Sidney's *Defence of Poetry* published, arguing for literary illusion	Charlotte Brontë in her prefac to *Shirley* argues for fiction a realistic as "Monday Mornin

In narrative, some descriptive details (such as the dog that doesn't bark in the Holmes story) are "motivated." That is to say, they will have a role to play in the eventual unfolding of the story. Occasionally, novelists over-motivate. Anthony Trollope (who liked a relaxed style of narrative) is very severe on his fellow novelist Wilkie Collins:

> **L'art d'ennuyer – c'est tout dire. (The art of boring is to say everything.)**
> Voltaire

"When I sit down to write a novel I do not at all know, and I do not very much care, how it is to end. Wilkie Collins seems so to construct his that he not only, before writing, plans everything on, down to the minutest detail, from the beginning to the end. . . . The construction is most minute and most wonderful. But I can never lose the taste of the construction. The author seems always to be warning me to remember that something happened at exactly half-past two o'clock on Tuesday morning; or that a woman disappeared from the road just fifteen yards beyond the fourth mile-stone."

Few novels (arguably not even Collins, his defenders protest) dovetail every detail in the way Trollope complains about. Fiction is usually replete with a wealth of unmotivated detail – milestones that will play no part in the plot at all: they are just there, like Defoe's mismatched shoes.

Henry James and solidity of specification Why are the milestones there? Henry James answers: "to give an air of reality." He insists that the narrative, however "solid," cannot be reality itself – leave that to the photographers. The aim is not to plug every hole in a narrative, but to supply just enough detail to capture that "air" of reality.

Some writers (Defoe, as it happens, is one) indulge in what the Victorians called "detailism." They fill in a lot of the physical background. Others don't. Notable among the detail-light narratives is Jane Austen. Ask any reader what, for example, Elizabeth Bennet looks like, and you'll get blank looks. Of course Keira Knightley (or, if it's a senior Austenite, Greer Garson) will jump into one's mind because Austen customarily leaves a total vacuum where personal description of her characters is concerned. And the mind, like nature, abhors a vacuum.

1880s	1908	1920s	2000–2010
Emile Zola leads the new school of fictional realists in France.	Henry James, in the preface to his collected works, makes the case for "solidity of specification"	Theodore Dreiser establishes realism as the dominant fictional mode in the US	"Hyper-realism" establishes itself as a current literary style

Does Shakespeare fail the reality test?

How old is Hamlet? It's not a small thing – every stage production has to come down definitely on the subject.

He's repeatedly called "young Hamlet." He's a student and a prince, both suggesting youth. In his verbal joshing with Rosencrantz and Guildenstern, he reminds us of every undergraduate we've ever known. Yet by the gravedigger's very precise reckoning (using Yorick's skull as his calendar), Hamlet is in his thirties. That's well into middle age in the early seventeenth century (Shakespeare himself died aged 52). Some solidity of specification would be very welcome on this point. But without a text in front of them (offering documentary validation), audiences are rarely troubled by the unsolidity.

Is this thinness of texture a failing in Austen? No, it isn't, because she gets her characteristic "air of reality" by other means (free indirect discourse, of which she is a pioneer, is one).

The concreteness of the worlds created by literary works depends on the richness of accidental detail. It's particularly necessary in historical novels, and future-historical novels – what we call science fiction. But too much researched detail can produce what Walter Scott, the father of the historical novel, calls "the repulsive dryness of mere antiquity." Tact is required – not too much, not too little. The aim, says Scott, should be to produce a "general coloring" (an idea close to James's "air of reality"). Hence such exchanges as the following from *Ivanhoe*:

> "Yet, bethink thee, noble Saxon," said the knight, "thou hast neither hauberk, nor corslet, nor aught but that light helmet, target, and sword."

Scott must know that many of his readers would not know a hauberk from a haddock. It's there simply to create an effect, not give a lecture on the accoutrements of the fourteenth-century knight at arms.

Orwell and the telling detail Distinguishing between motivated and unmotivated detail can be tricky. Take (again) the opening sentence of *Nineteen Eighty-Four*: "It was a bright cold day in April, and the clocks were striking thirteen." Orwell, it may be noted,

> **"Life is not a series of gig lamps symmetrically arranged; life is a luminous halo, a semi-transparent envelope surrounding us from the beginning of consciousness to the end."**
> **Virginia Woolf**

originally wrote: "and a million radios were striking thirteen," before changing it in the manuscript version.

Is the detail here motivated or unmotivated? On the face of it, what does it matter if it's noon, or one o'clock, or two o'clock? Not at all. It's simply a time-and-place thing, creating (along with the rest of the paragraph) the *mise en scène*.

But if one looks carefully, particularly having read the whole history of Winston Smith, motives do appear. "Thirteen" is unnatural, un-English. England, we later learn, has been swallowed up in the amorphous bloc, Oceania. Thirteen is proverbially the unluckiest of numbers. It is ominous. Radios would have been appropriate to the future Orwell was writing about – a future that has, as Lenin demanded, been wholly "electrified."

But on second thoughts, Orwell decided he wanted clocks – public clocks, like Big Ben. Why? Later, a nursery rhyme gets stuck in Winston's head – "Oranges and Lemons/Went the Bells of St Clements." The jingle then goes through all the time-chiming churches in London. But Winston can't, for the life of him, remember the last line. The Thought Police officer who sends him off to Minilove's horrific Room 101 reminds him what that last line is: "And here comes the chopper to chop off your head."

It is, one eventually works out, motivated. But how do we know until we have read the whole thing? One of the tasks alert readers must set themselves is to remember everything, in the event that it will "come in useful" later. Most detail won't. Some will.

the condensed idea
Where detail is concerned, enough is a feast

30 Structuralism

"I was asked for Dalgliesh's views on structuralism – or was it post-structuralism?" muses P. D. James. "I replied that he had given it careful thought for a number of evenings and had come to the conclusion that it was nonsense." Baroness James – the country's most eminent crime-writer – is wrong. The issues raised by structuralism/poststructuralism (the discussion of literature in terms of its inherent shaping) are well worth Detective Inspector Adam Dalgliesh's time. Who knows, they might even enrich his poetry.

Can literature be a "structure?" Literature is linear – lines. Lines on a page, in script; or pixelated, left to right, on a screen; or heard over two hours in a theater. Yet we routinely talk of a novel, a play or a poem spatially, with words like "form," or "structure." Writers, on their side, often "see" their work spatially. Wordsworth airily pictures his autobiographical poem *The Prelude* as the "ante-chapel" to the "cathedral" that will be the larger structure (never completed), *The Excursion*. So, too, Henry James's "house of fiction" – all those millions of lines coming together as one three-dimensional edifice: as solid as James's mansion in Rye.

So we *read* a novel as lines on the page and simultaneously *see* it as one might see a painting or a sculpture. There are, however, treacherous false analogies lurking in that comparison.

If a husband and wife, on holiday in France, look at the Venus de Milo in the Louvre, the man (as surveys confirm) will probably look at the statue's breasts first and the woman will first look at the face. If the couple have both brought the same book with them to read

timeline

*c.*332 BC	1906–1913
In *The Poetics*, Aristotle decrees that "plot" is the soul of tragedy	Ferdinand de Saussure del his lectures, later published *A General Course in Lingu*

Poststructuralism

The relationship between structuralism and poststructuralism is fuzzy. But "post" here – as elsewhere in critical terminology – might better be expressed as "beyond," with a suggestion of "anti" thrown in. The seductive attraction of structuralism was its being so clear-cut. It put things together so neatly. But this, poststructuralism asserts, is structuralism's shortcoming.

The contrariness of poststructuralism, its wilful awkwardness, originates in its vexed birth time. It was, recalls Terry Eagleton, "the product of that blend of euphoria and disillusionment, liberation and dissipation, carnival and catastrophe, which was 1968." The easiest way to pin it down is that it is structuralism with ragged edges. And in the last couple of decades, the term has largely been replaced in critical discourse with "deconstruction" – an idea (all ragged edges) that, genetically, grew out of it, as part evolution, part correction.

(say *The Da Vinci Code* – to keep up the Louvre theme), they will, both of them, start at page 1 and work through to page 2. Linearly. Mr. Tourist will not start at page 60 and work back and forward, and Mrs. Tourist at page 90.

In an important sense it is the reader who, following the long line of a literary text, "makes" it; or, put another way, makes sense of it; like Dalgliesh, or Sherlock Holmes, assembling their "clues" into a narrative. Works of literature are not there, fully made – even the shortest, most imagistic works, which can be gulped down in a single eye bite.

The reader's contribution The work of Literature is, largely, the reader's job. To read is to construct: investing black marks on a white surface with meaning and, as one goes on, shape. The sculptor

1920s	**1949**	**1970**	**1980**
"Russian formalism," precursor of structuralism, establishes itself	Lévi-Strauss's *Elementary Structures of Kinship* adopts structuralism as his guiding principle in anthropological investigation	Roland Barthes publishes *S/Z*, based on an extended structuralist seminar in Paris	Poststructuralism replaces structuralism as the dominant formalist practice

(unless they're very modern) doesn't give you a square block of marble and a set of chisels and tell you there's an interesting object somewhere inside. Authors routinely do just that.

Structuralism is unusually good at explaining itself to newcomers. Jonathan Culler (its high priest) offers an illuminating parable. If, while strolling through a grassy meadow, I happen on a spherical stone and kick it between a couple of logs that happen to be nearby, what does it mean? Nothing. Just that I wanted to swing my leg.

Supposing, on a field at Wembley, David Beckham shoots the ball into the net between the opposition uprights. What gives his kick the meaning "goal?" Not the grass, not the wooden uprights, not the netting, not the spheroid, not Beckham's genius left foot, but the rules of association football. If Beckham picked up the soccer ball and ran with it through the posts, that would be a foul. But why, a couple of miles away, might it be a "try?"

It is the "structuration" – the rules and all the invisible frameworks around these triumphs on the field – that construct the meaning.

Structuralism is a very exhilarating theory. When it burst on to the Anglo-American critical scene in the early 1960s, there was a sense of excitement: a "Eureka!" moment.

The most vivacious of the crew, Roland Barthes, when structuralism was *le dernier cri*, wrote a sparkling essay on, of all things un-French, "Steak and Chips." When we sink our teeth into that particular dish, he lyricized, we are not merely ingesting flesh: "Steak is part of the same sanguine mythology as wine. It is the heart of meat, it is meat in its pure state; and whoever partakes of it assimilates a bull-like strength." It is, in a sense, a communion act – sacred. But while steak (the majestic Texan 32 oz T-bone, for example) confers national glamor, chips, Barthes suggests, are nostalgic and patriotic (french fries).

> **For sale: baby shoes, never worn.**
> Ernest Hemingway's suggested "shortest possible novel"

Problems It's heady stuff. But there are a number of problems with structuralism, when applied to literature, which render it if not Dalglieshian nonsense, then not quite the perfect Cinderella-shoe fit one would like.

The theory of structuralism was developed initially in social anthropology to explain such things as gift exchange, totemism, and the distinction between "sacred" and "profane" objects – the communion wafer and a McVitie's chocolate digestive, for example. Texts, or literary genres, are harder to work with, as Barthes found when he moved from edibles like steak and chips to literary narratives.

A second issue is structuralism's immateriality. This is both a useful and a problematic aspect of the theory. Its usefulness is that it helps us get round the following awkwardness: if my Victorian ancestor is reading, in 1872, the first four-volume edition of *Middlemarch* and I, 140 years later, am reading the Penguin Classic, are we reading the same novel? Yes, says the structuralist (a beefsteak is a beefsteak is a beefsteak). But common sense (and historicist/new historicist thinking) argues that I and my great-grandad are having very different experiences.

This immateriality links to a third objection. Namely that structuralism is ahistorical. It abstracts literature from all its accidents of time and place. This runs counter to common sense, which tells us that *Middlemarch* was a different kettle of fish for a middle-class Victorian lady in 1874 from what it is for a twelfth-grader or A-level student today. Do the structures of Eliot's novel buckle and change – like Dali watches – with the passing of time?

The most forceful objection is that structuralism is essentially authoritarian in implying there is singularity, not multiplicity, in the meanings we find in any one work of literature, and that singularity is located in the work (or the author's "art"), not our response. A work of literature, closely examined, can no more have two structures than the person examining it can have two backbones.

the condensed idea
Meaning is conferred
by social structures

31 Deconstruction

"I'm a bit of a deconstructionist myself. It's kind of exciting – the last intellectual thrill left. Like sawing through the branch you're sitting on." So says Morris Zapp – a character widely presumed to be the American critic Stanley Fish – in David Lodge's comic novel, *Small World*. Few critical ideas have been more widely misunderstood or have been more aggressively cited as evidence of what has gone wrong with literary criticism over the last 40 years than deconstruction. Is the idea something every well-read person should be familiar with? Or is it something that should never leave the hot air of academic conferences?

Its arrival on the scene The emergence of deconstruction in the English-speaking world can be precisely dated. It happened on 21 October 1966, when Jacques Derrida gave his lecture "*La Structure, le signe et le jeu dans le discours des sciences humaines*" at the International Colloquium on Critical Languages and the Sciences of Man, at Johns Hopkins University in Baltimore.

Derrida had traveled from France with Roland Barthes and Jacques Lacan, two other foundational figures in the rise to dominance of what would thereafter be called (misleadingly) "theory." Initially derided as "higher Froggy nonsense," the new approach took off like wildfire among the younger American faculty. So much so that the high priest of deconstruction, Jacques Derrida, could assert in the 1980s, "America *is* Deconstruction."

As young *doctrinaires* progressed upward through the academic ranks, it became orthodoxy – and to the nonacademic world, scandal. The

timeline
1906–1913
Ferdinand de Saussure delivers lectures later published as *General Course in Linguistics*

essential tenet of deconstruction, as amusingly outlined in David Lodge's Zappism above, is that any encounter with literature involves arbitrarily constructing meaning, then promptly erasing that meaning, only to go through the process again with the reassembled text. There is no finality; every literary text is inherently indeterminate. The only conclusion, depressingly, is what the deconstructionists call "aporia:" total dead end, out of which there is no way forward, or back.

> **"Deconstruction, the first time you hear the word, sounds like what happens when your four-year-old has a temper tantrum with his erector set."**
>
> David Lehman

A pessimistic doctrine? Why, if the journey is so pointless, go on with it? At least when Penelope wove (by day) and unwove (by night) her absent husband's burial shroud, there was a reason. Why construct and deconstruct *Hamlet*, simply to go through the process again – ad infinitum?

Because, deconstruction explains, the making of meanings, however arbitrary, is the only lifeline we shall ever have across the abyss of unmeaningness. Writing literature (*écriture*) is an analogous activity. Deconstruction pictures authors and readers as like the Flying Wallendas in their high-wire act across the Grand Canyon. Why do it? Because it's walk the quivering high wire or plummet into the gulf of unmeaning below.

Deconstruction involved two quite opposite moves in its heyday (roughly the mid-1960s to the 1980s). One was a broadening of scope with a generous gulp of European (principally French) philosophy. At the same time, as it coalesced into a school in the Anglo-American academic establishment, there was a centring of power in the loftiest ivory towers (notably Yale in the US) and a handful of sages. The most powerful of them was the Belgian immigrant (and Yale professor), Paul de Man.

Examples of how it works De Man published little. His first book, *Blindness and Insight*, appeared when he was in his early fifties. But his influence was radioactive in its penetration (and, some would argue, malignity). Famously de Man demonstrated the deconstructionist doctrine with an example from the TV show *All in the Family* (the American version of *Till Death Do Us Part*):

1966	1962	1983	1987
Conference at Johns Hopkins University at which deconstruction is first introduced into the US	Jacques Derrida's *Of Grammatology* published	Paul de Man's *Blindness and Insight* published	Ortwin de Graef discloses de Man's wartime writings

"When asked by his wife whether he wants to have his bowling shoes laced over or laced under, Archie Bunker answers with a question: 'What's the difference?' His wife replies by patiently explaining the difference between lacing over and lacing under, but provokes only ire. 'What's the difference?' did not ask for the difference but means instead 'I don't give a damn what the difference is.' "

De Man then jumps, brilliantly, to the last lines of W. B. Yeats's poem, "Among School Children:"

O body swayed to music, O brightening glance,
How can we know the dancer from the dance?

Mrs. Bunker might understand this as "Please tell me the expert who can separate these two elements and come up with some names from the world of ballet." The more knowledgeable reader might understand it as "Dancer and dance are inseparable; they have merged into each other." This second is not, of course, to be taken as the *authoritative* meaning of Yeats's poem. There can be no such thing – meaning is forever, as Derrida put it, "deferred." What de Man was illustrating by his Bunker–Yeats conjunction was the insoluble fragilities of meaning.

The intellectual excitements offered by deconstruction are clear. It put a wrecking ball into the reader-critic's hand, particularly that of young

Derrida on deconstruction; the plain man on Derrida

In his seminal 1966 Johns Hopkins Lecture, Derrida explained what would come to be known as deconstruction thus: "The entire history of the concept of structure, before the rupture of which we are speaking, must be thought of as a series of substitutions of centre for centre, as a linked chain of determinations of the centre." The poem "Deconstruction," by Peter Mullen, puts it more trenchantly:

D'ya wanna know the creed'a
    Jacques Derrida?
Dere ain't no reada
Dere ain't no wrider
Eider.

> **I'm not against asking the audience to work, but I think what you have now is a sort of gratuitous deconstruction as a result of a fashion of literary deconstructionism indicating that there are no meanings.**
>
> Theater director and sage, Jonathan Miller

academics, eager for some Oedipal intellectual mayhem. There were those who viewed it as a benign "Sturm und Drang" interval – an exuberant clearing of the decks; an "everything must go!" moment before the shop is stocked with entirely new wares.

In 1987, four years after de Man's death, deconstruction was hit by its own wrecking ball. A young Belgian scholar, Ortwin de Graef (initially a disciple) turned up some 170 articles written by de Man during the Nazi occupation of Belgium – most of them for the country's leading newspaper, *Le Soir*. A handful of which looked suspiciously like party-line anti-Semitism, notably a piece published on 4 March 1941, "The Jews in Contemporary Literature," which concluded:

> "A solution to the Jewish problem that would lead to the creation of a Jewish colony isolated from Europe would not have, for the literary life of the West, regrettable consequences. It would lose, in all, some personalities of mediocre worth and would continue, as in the past, to develop according to its higher laws of evolution."

Even if he did not know the "solution" his current employers had in mind, de Man, it was pointed out, could surely not but have noticed the current persecution of Belgian Jews, who had recently been required to mark themselves for execution by wearing the yellow star.

In the wake of de Graef's revelations, other skeletons were hauled out of the deceased de Man's cupboard. Deconstruction was not destroyed by the revelation of de Man's wartime publications and other alleged malfeasance (bigamy, notably). But it was substantially deconstructed.

the condensed idea
Meaning is always deferred

32 Textuality

"Text" is a word that has come up frequently in the foregoing sections. But is *Hamlet* primarily a "text?" Or is it a play? Is *War and Peace* a "text," or a novel? Is *The Waste Land* a "text," or a poem? The answer depends which side of literary activity you are coming from: or, more accurately, where you choose to stand. And part of the answer is found in the fact that we can apply the word "text" to all these, in themselves very different, works of literature.

Text versus work Modern critics tend to address themselves to "texts." Writers, ancient and modern, never, or very rarely, employ that term about what they create. Dickens, for example, did not regard himself as composing a "text" when, in April 1836, he set about *The Posthumous Papers of the Pickwick Club*. He wasn't, as it happened, sure whether what he was embarked on was a set of sporting papers (which the publishers had asked for) or a novel (which is what he fully intended to write). But as far as the young Boz was concerned, "texts" were what parsons sermonized about on Sundays ("our text for today is taken from the Gospel according to ..." etc.).

Yet Dickensians fall quite naturally into such phraseology as "the text of *Pickwick Papers* presents unique problems for the reader." The widespread textualization of literature – a kind of prepping (as surgeons call what is done to patients before wheeling them into theater) – is a relatively recent phenomenon. Authors still see themselves, and wish to be seen, as what they have always been: the creators of novels, plays, poems, gathered together under the loose description "works of literature."

timeline

1906–1913
Ferdinand de Saussure delivers lectures later published as *A General Course in Linguistics*

1940–45
Paul Ricoeur develops his theory of textuality and hermeneutics

"*Il n'y a rien hors du texte.* (There is nothing outside the text.)"

Jacques Derrida, From inside the text *Of Grammatology*

Varieties Why, then, do critics prefer the alternative term, "literary text," in preference to "work of literature?" One obvious reason is that their work, as critics, is different and requires some redrawing of the rules. Textualization dissolves everything under investigation to a single *primum materium literarium* (primary literary material). In so doing it opens up a whole range of areas for critical analysis. For example:

1. *Intertextuality*: this term, invented by the French theorist Julia Kristeva, goes well beyond old-fashioned ideas of "influence" (e.g., "Dickens's *A Tale of Two Cities* shows the clear influence of Thomas Carlyle's *The French Revolution*"). Intertextuality presupposes not merely that writers draw on other writers, but that we, as readers, read texts in the light of having read other texts. If I have read every scrap of Tolstoy's published work, *War and Peace* will be a different text for me than it is for someone who comes to it as their virgin experience of the author.

2. *Paratextuality*: this term, associated principally with the French theorist Gerard Genette, considers items that are in the text but have traditionally been considered extraneous to it. Such things as the title, the epigraph, the dedication, stage directions (in plays), even typography are thus put into relationship with the body of the text.

3. *Subtextuality*: texts may have submerged countercurrents or repressed elements within them. The category of "subtextuality" means these can be clinically worked on, without having to delve into the psychopathology of the author.

4. *Contextuality*: this enables works of literature to be set in environments – not necessarily literary. New historicists often suggest that context has precedence over text.

1966	1967	1997
The structuralist critic Julia Kristeva coins the term "intertextuality"	Jacques Derrida, in *Of Grammatology*, decrees "there is nothing outside the text"	Gerard Genette publishes *Paratexts. Thresholds of Interpretation*

5. *Pantextuality*: this is one of the more daring leaps made by the textualizers. It presumes not just that literature is all text, but that the whole perceived world is text. We "read" reality. Pantextuality is assumed as a given by the father of deconstruction, Paul de Man, who declares (in his founding tract for deconstructionists, *Blindness and Insight*), "the bases for historical knowledge are not empirical facts but written texts, even if these texts masquerade in the guise of wars or revolutions." World War II, in other words, is not a historical fact, but a text.

Textuality and the work of criticism There is another, subtler issue involved in the textualization of literature. To classify *The Waste Land* as a "work of literature," as critics used to do, assumes, implicitly, that Eliot's poem is an *objet d'art*, something achieved, inviolable, complete in itself, to be reverenced.

"Text," on the other hand, suggests a field of activity, where the reader/critic is free to unmake, or remake, what is on the page. Put another way; one *appreciates* a work of literature. One is free to *analyse* a text.

Whose baby is it?

Authors tend to dislike critics who, by approaching works of literature as "texts" to analyse rather than finished objects to appreciate, presume to discover more about *their* (the writers") creation than *they* (the writers) ever know themselves. Some authors positively detest these lice on the locks of (their) literature. Nabokov, a prime detester, decreed that the textualists should be not merely resisted, but sabotaged: "An artist should ruthlessly destroy his manuscripts after publication lest they lead academic mediocrities into thinking that it is possible to unravel the mysteries of genius." Thankfully for the hosts of academic mediocrities, whose careers depend on the unraveling of the mysteries of genius, most writers do not follow the Nabokovian rule.

66 Is there a text in this class? 99

Artless student question, used by Stanley Fish
as the title of his best-selling book

Appreciation leads to what is called "critical belletrism:" often accompanied by an attempt to match the fine writing of literature in one's own commentary. It used to be a term of praise. Nowadays it is more often a term of contempt. Belletrism sees literature as installed, honorifically, in a kind of museum of the mind. One can admire what is on display but you may not touch. No one, for example, would get a ladder into the Sistine Chapel and start picking off Michelangelo's paint to see what previous efforts might lie beneath the surface. Textualism, by contrast, aims at something equivalent to the scientist's laboratory, where literature can be legitimately taken apart. And once it is taken apart, anatomized, and put back together again to whom does the object under examination belong? The author may own the work, the critic may well lay claim to the text.

"We murder to dissect," said Wordsworth: effectively putting up a "do not trespass" sign on his poetry (that "we" means "you"). Murder, you say? Indeed yes, retorts the arch-dissecter, Roland Barthes, who decreed that the author must be killed (metaphorically), in order that his/her literature can be better read. No more authorial sovereignty. It belongs with the sun-kings of the French *ancien régime*. Barthes replaced the term "author" (with its shadow implication "authority") with "scriptor" – as if the maker of the text were no more than a secretary, taking down dictation from some disembodied voice. Michel Foucault went one stage further than his compatriot. The author was, he decreed, merely an "effect" in the text.

the condensed idea
Literature is appreciated; a text is studied

33 Double Bind

"Double bind" is an idea used principally in psychology and communication studies. It has also had useful applications in literary discussion. A double bind refers to situations in which separate instructions clash, then mesh, creating (like other kinds of bondage) paralysis. Unlike "dilemma" ("Shall I take the blue pill, or the red pill?") the idea shifts attention from choice to the bondage scenario or "frame" in which choice is enforced.

Essential unfairness of the double bind situation A standard illustration of double bind is the mother who remonstrates with her child: "If you loved me, you wouldn't go out tonight." The child may, of course, go out and still love its mother. But the double bind (the insidious "if") kicks in to prevent that rational justification for a night on the tiles.

Double bind presumes inequality between a person or institution with power, who does the binding; and a victim, who is bound. Marvell's poem "To his Coy Mistress" illustrates the point. It opens, "Had we but world enough, and time/This coyness, lady, were no crime." She won't, that is, sleep with him. The poet goes on to say that if they had eternity, he would, of course, honor her maidenly reluctance:

> But at my back I always hear
> Time's winged chariot hurrying near;
> And yonder all before us lie
> Deserts of vast eternity.
> Thy beauty shall no more be found,
> Nor, in thy marble vault, shall sound
> My echoing song; then worms shall try
> That long preserv'd virginity,

timeline

1605
Shakespeare offers a classic definition
of moral dilemma in *Hamlet's*
soliloquy "to be or not to be"

1949
Orwell introduces the te
"doublethink" in his nov
Nineteen Eighty-Four

And your quaint honour turn to dust,
And into ashes all my lust.
The grave's a fine and private place,
But none I think do there embrace.

If you don't submit, you'll die withered up and unfulfilled. The "bind," as they usually are, is disingenuous. The term "mistress," with its ambiguous double meaning – "adored virtuous one" and "illicit bed partner" – gives the game away. As does the morally diminutive epithet "coy" (i.e., "shy"). If the poem were called "To the Virtuous Woman I Desperately Want to Screw but Don't Want to Marry," its motive would be clearer, if less poetic. As it is, the lady must be either promiscuous (unladylike), or a dried-up old maid. Double bondage.

The "authority" in this situation lies with the male suitor. She cannot answer him with another of the most brilliant poems in the English language. Or, apparently, with the riposte: "Marry me, then, if you want it that badly."

Is it useful in thinking about literature? The value of the double bind idea, in literary contexts, is that it switches focus from the drama (will she, won't she?) to the larger situation that enforces the dilemma: forces, typically, outside the work of literature. These forces – the "frame" – are socially and historically variable. The heroines in Richardson's *Pamela*, Kingsley Amis's *Take a Girl Like You*, and Sylvia Plath's *The Bell Jar* face the same submit-or-resist dilemma as Marvell's coy mistress. But the coercive situations are as different as the historical periods in which the narratives are set. It's easier to surrender your pearl without price in 1960 than 1760, for example.

The double bind is a staple of fictional plot. If Anna Karenina submits to Vronsky, she follows her heart (an imperative of the romantic world view, to which she is a convert). If she resists, she follows the

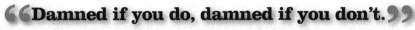

❝Damned if you do, damned if you don't.❞
Proverbial definition of double bind

1956
Anthropologist Gregory Bateson (thinking principally about schizophrenia) introduces concept of "double bind"

1961
Joseph Heller publishes his novel *Catch-22*

1973
Harold Bloom publishes *The Anxiety of Influence*, which analyses poets' condition of being simultaneously original and unoriginal

The double bondage of 1984

George Orwell makes institutionalized double bind central to the tyranny of *Nineteen Eighty-Four*. Winston Smith, a *Times* journalist, is professionally bound to report the facts. But as a party member, he must believe (wholeheartedly) the fact that Oceania has always been at war with Eurasia, when he knows that a few hours ago Eurasia was an ally against Eastasia. The only way through the double bind is "doublethink" – institutionalized schizophrenia. Sometimes, as Winston's torturer O'Brien patiently explains, two and two is five, sometimes four. The anthropologist commonly credited with inventing the term "double bind" in 1956, Gregory Bateson, specifically connected it with the conflicting messages experienced by schizophrenics, from the world outside, and from their inner voices. Both must be obeyed.

imperatives of wifely duty (to the obedience of which she has taken a sacred oath). Paralysis and self-destruction ensue.

Double bind and *Catch-22* Joseph Heller's *Catch-22* is a novel that pivots on the idea of double bind, and gives it a classically ironic definition. "There was only one catch," Heller's pilot-hero Yossarian discovers when he's thinking of getting a release from combat duties by feigning craziness:

> "and that was Catch-22, which specified that a concern for one's safety in the face of dangers that were real and immediate was the process of a rational mind. Orr was crazy and could be grounded. All he had to do was ask; and as soon as he did, he would no longer be crazy and would have to fly more missions. Orr would be crazy to fly more missions and sane if he didn't, but if he was sane he had to fly them. If he flew them he was crazy and didn't have to; but if he didn't want to he was sane and had to. Yossarian was moved very deeply by the absolute simplicity of this clause of Catch-22 and let out a respectful whistle. "That's some catch, that Catch-22," Yossarian observed. "It's the best there is," Doc Daneeka agreed."

> **And, like a man to double business bound, I stand in pause where I shall first begin.**
>
> Claudius, in *Hamlet*

In the larger literary sphere, there have been other fruitful applications. Postcolonial literature is a prime example of the double bind in action. Authors such as Chinua Achebe or Wole Soyinka assert their national independence and *négritude* in their fiction. But they use the language of the white master to do so. It is a problem that also afflicts Western writers, wholly at home with their literary heritage. How can the poet express "thoughts that do lie too deep for words" when all the poet has is words to express those deep thoughts with? Double bind again.

Harold Bloom, in *The Anxiety of Influence*, sees the whole of literature as wrapped in a double bind. Writers, given the communal nature of their activity, depend stylistically on their predecessors, but need – at the same time – to be free of that stylistic dominance; to be "themselves." Tennyson drew on Keats who drew on Spenser who drew on Chaucer. But each is deliberately *not* the poet(s) they drew on. The relationship, Bloom argues, is Oedipal. And, as with the Oedipus complex, it results in neurosis. Nor, as Bloom sees it, is there any easy way out. You can invent many things in literature – but the one thing you cannot invent is literature itself.

The consequences of the double bind for the maker of literature, Bloom argues, is a degree of psychic disorder, but one of the inescapable conditions of literary creation. For the reader of literature the idea is valuable in directing attention to the frameworks – the bigger picture. In that respect, it's a handy couple of words.

the condensed idea
There's no way out

34 Postmodernism

Postmodern – "pomo" in the mouths of the knowing – is an epithet, initially applied to subversive works of art, that has slipped its leash and is now found everywhere. There is postmodern legal theory, postmodern architecture, postmodern ("gonzo") journalism, even postmodern cuisine.

Authorial embrace There are some critical terms creative writers never use about themselves. No novelist, for example, would describe himself as a "heteroglossiac." Novelists such as William Gibson, by contrast, are happy not merely to be labeled, but to proclaim themselves "cyberpunk" and "postmodern" practitioners of SF.

Postmodernism; as a term in literature, and literary discussion, manifestly defines itself in relationship to "modernism." Like romanticism, modernism is a slippery term that can at the same time indicate both a specific period and a looser "school," or group style with shared characteristics, of no particular period.

Historians see "modernism" beginning around the period that used to be called the Renaissance. Literary historians have a different chronology and apply the term to a coterie of international avant-gardistes (Pound, Eliot, Yeats, Stein, Woolf, Joyce), active around 1890–1930 (the first writer to use the term "modernist" was the French poet Charles Baudelaire).

Modernists not only wrote, they theorized, endlessly, about what they wrote. In this they broke ranks with their predecessors. Charles Dickens would never have proclaimed, "I am a mid-Victorian realist." But modernists happily proclaimed themselves modernists. Their slogan was Ezra Pound's "Make it New!" – as stirring a call to arms as Lenin's "Electrify! Electrify!"

timeline

1863

Charles Baudelaire introduces the concept of modernism in *The Painter of Modern Life*

1910

Virginia Woolf declares tha "about December 1910 human character changed and the era of modernism began

Ultra pomo

In Beckett's minimalist play *Breath*, the stage curtain parts to illumine ("faintly") some rubbish. This shot is held for five seconds. There is a "faint brief" cry, the sound of breathing in ("inspiration") and a bit more light (Beckett's stage direction indicates precisely how much). This climaxes in ten seconds. The light then fades and the silence creeps back over the next five seconds, accompanied by the sound of breathing out ("expiration"). The curtain falls and the play is over.

What the modernists had in common was a resolve to break with the old Anglo-American styles and forms and – most controversially – to dispense with mass publics, whose very numbers exercised a coercive "bourgeois" pressure on the creative mind. "Mass Civilization, Minority Art" was another defining slogan.

"Modernist" implies that what is new is not merely *new* but better – and as necessary an improvement as, say, modern sanitation or faster trains. Literature does not merely change from generation to generation; it progresses. Avant-garde is always ahead of *ancien régime*. There is also sedition at the heart of modernism. Something is to be overthrown. A guillotine blade flashes, briefly. The seditiousness was given metaphoric expression in D. H. Lawrence's modernist manifesto essay, "Surgery for the Modern Novel: Or a Bomb." He was thinking of the hygienic explosives of the Russian anarchists. "Literary Bolshevist!" Alfred Noyes (author of the poem "The Highwayman") snarled at James Joyce (author of *Ulysses*). Society at large does not much like bomb-throwers, at least not when the cordite is still in the air. So too with modernism, in its early days.

The modern versus the contemporary The poet Stephen Spender – a second-generation modernist – draws a useful distinction between the merely "contemporary" and the truly "modern," in his

1922	1968	1971
Annus mirabilis of modernism: Joyce's *Ulysses* and Eliot's *Waste Land* published	Postmodernism arrives, riding the wave of youth radicalism and upheaval in Europe and America	Ihab Hassan publishes *The Dismemberment of Orpheus: Toward a Postmodern Literature*

polemical monograph *The Struggle of the Modern*. The first are writers such as Alfred Noyes or John Galsworthy, who successfully trudge along the ruts history has landed them in. The modernists – Woolf, Joyce, Eliot – leap out of the rut into the future. That leap involves combat.

Where, then, does this put "postmodernism?" Like its root-term, "modernism," it is double-edged, describing something that "comes after." But more than chronology is involved. The impact of modernism changes, mysteriously, over literary-historical time. The "new" no longer shocks. Modernism is tamed, defanged, neutered. *Ulysses* and *The Waste Land* are set for school examinations. The critic Fredric Jameson notes the paradox of cooling modernisms, that Picasso and Joyce, who shocked and appalled on their first appearance, "now strike us, on the whole, as rather 'realistic.' " For the younger generation, they are nothing more than "a set of dead classics:" the stuff you have to study at school.

Postmodernism, or Pomo It is in this context that postmodernism came about. The historical starting point is 1968: "the Year of the Young Rebels," as Stephen Spender grandiloquently termed it.

Postmodernism defined itself not merely as modernism's heir, but its violent nemesis. It was a willed break (the French word *coupure* was often preferred) with what had gone before. And breakage brought with it deliberate fracturing, or brokenness.

What, then, is "Postmodernist Literature?" Ihab Hassan, who first popularized the term in the early 1970s, invokes the image of Orpheus, the divine singer, torn to pieces by maenads, but whose head continues singing, his lyre broken into a hundred pieces by his side.

> **Modernism released us from the constraints of everything that had gone before with a euphoric sense of freedom.**
>
> Arthur Erickson

The essence of postmodernism's quarrel with its parent was that for all its exciting novelties, modernism was essentially *rational*. Beneath the rippled narrative surface of Virginia Woolf's *Mrs. Dalloway* was a "stream of consciousness" doctrine. You could argue, as Woolf eloquently did, that the doctrine made better sense of what was happening on "the floor of the mind" than the old classic realist techniques – that it was truer to what actually goes on in the human mind. But the objection was to that very phrase, "making sense."

> **❝It used to be that the great literary modifier was the word beyond.... But we seem to have exhausted the beyond, and today the sociological modifier is *post*.❞**
> **Daniel Bell**

Postmodernism's quarrel went past modernism to Enlightenment itself. Adorno's maxim, "Enlightenment is totalitarian" is cited. The French Revolution and its irrational Terror sprang from rational principles (Liberty, Equality, Fraternity). The Holocaust was framed as something eminently rational – "a final solution" – as was the Gulag Archipelago ("resettlement of population").

Postmodernism's "break" was radical. All structure, anything that could be "made sense of," or rationalized, was suspect. Continual "disarticulation" and fracturing was, paradoxically, the only way forward. But what does "forward" mean? Ihab Hassan sees two "pure" manifestations of postmodernism: the silence of Beckett, and the infinite, meaningless permutations of lust in the pornographic extravaganzas of the Marquis de Sade.

One could add to Ihab's example vandalism – the Duchamp moustache on the *Mona Lisa* and the new, illogical lateralities of the World Wide Web come to mind. It is hard to see what "post," "after," or even "next" means in this new-tech context. Most probably a withering of pomo as it works itself out to its logical, splintered, conclusions and some kind of return to the mainstream. It will have been an exciting interlude.

the condensed idea
Make it new, then make it newer. Differently

35 Heteroglossia

The daunting term heteroglossia – meaning roughly "many-voicedness" – entered into Anglo-American critical discourse with the growth of interest in a Russian critic with an equally daunting name, Mikhail Bakhtin. Bakhtin (1895–1975) was, as it happened, wrestling with the question of literary ambiguity at the same period as William Empson, during the English critic's Cambridge years. Bakhtin's lodgings were, however, less comfortable. He had been arrested by the secret police in 1929 and charged with being a clandestine Christian. "Compassionately" (his health was poor), he was sentenced to a mere six years" internal exile in Kazakhstan.

The inventor of the idea During his enforced rustication in Russia's back country, Bakhtin, as much a philosopher as a literary critic, pondered the nature of prose fiction. Around 1935 he came up with his idea of heteroglossia. Not all his writing from this period has survived. *In extremis* he was obliged to cannibalize his working notes for cigarette paper.

After an obscure career as a teacher in the provinces, Bakhtin died of natural causes in 1975. He was lucky. His closest literary collaborator, Pavel Medvedev, was executed in one of Stalin's crazed purges in 1938. The work of the so-called "Bakhtin Circle" permeated the Western academic communities, via translation and conferences, in the mid-1970s, spreading like wildfire among the PhD-writing classes in the following decades.

Heteroglossia literally translates as "many-voicedness." It accompanies another, nearly synonymous, term used by Bakhtin, "polyphony." T. S. Eliot, famously, originally intended to call *The Waste Land*,

timeline

1300	1865
Composers of sacred music in Europe develop the practice of polyphony in chants	Publication of Charles Dick[...] *Our Mutual Friend* in whic[...] Sloppy "does the police in different voices"

"He Do the Police in Different Voices." It alludes to an aside in Dickens's novel, *Our Mutual Friend*, where a literate working-class lad, Sloppy, reads out from the sensational *Police News*, doing the stilted police report of crimes in a cod "official" accent.

❝I hear Voices in my Head.❞
Randy Orton

Dickens was, with Dostoevsky, one of Bakhtin's principal exemplars of polyphony. He seems not to have known Eliot – whose 1922 poem is polyphony versified (famously V. S. Pritchett called Eliot "a company of actors inside one suit, each twitting the others").

Heteroglossia versus polyphony Heteroglossia is not quite the same as polyphony moving, as it does, beyond voice, into analysis of the social pedigree of the voice. There is in language, and in the words that make up language, what Bakhtin saw as fascinating social mixtures.

Take, as an example, the line in *Hamlet* in which the hero encounters Ophelia, prayerbook in hand. As they talk, courteously, Hamlet suddenly apprehends that she has been "loosed" on him, like a streetwalker, by her father and Claudius, to elicit what plots he might be hatching. "Get thee to a nunnery, go!" he tells her angrily.

Carnivalesque

In his later years Bakhtin pondered the idea of "carnival" and its principal literary exemplar, Rabelais. What fascinated him was the quasi-revolutionary nature of carnival. There were "no footlights" or class divisions: "carnival does not acknowledge any distinction between actors and spectators." As such, it is both the epitome and a forecast of socialist utopia, without transitional political ordeal. Along the same lines, Bertolt Brecht imagined a theater in which the audience reacted like their counterparts at a boxing match – smoking, shouting, cheering, hooting, booing, throwing scrunched-up programmes or even chairs. In so doing, they are no longer passive consumers, but part of the act.

1922	1965	1975
Publication of Eliot's *The Waste Land*, originally entitled "He Do the Police in Different Voices"	Mikhail Bakhtin introduces his idea of the carnivalesque in *Rabelais and his World*	Publication of Mikhail Bakhtin's *The Dialogic Imagination*, in which he articulates his theory of heteroglossia

Hamlet's dismissal can be construed in two ways. "You are still a pure young girl, Ophelia – escape this corrupt world of Elsinore." Or, drawing on a slang use of the word "nunnery" (house of ill repute): "Go back to your brothel, you slut." Or both.

In terms of its heteroglossia, there is, Bakhtin might argue, a centripetal or "official" meaning in the key word "nunnery" (houses of extremely good repute). There is another, centrifugal meaning, which would more properly come from the mouth not of a courteous prince, but a of whoremongering proletarian slob. The difference is social. The word is at war with itself.

Is literature inherently revolutionary? The tendency of authority (Church, state, institutions) is, Bakhtin observes, to "monologize," to iron out social friction. To "own" language, and make it mean one thing only. *Roma locuta, causa finita*, the Vatican pontificates (Rome has spoken, the matter is concluded). Language inherently resists that ownership, and literature raises that resistance to art.

The attraction of heteroglossia is that it reinserts the literary text back into the real world. No longer is reading an Empsonian juggler's stage trick – pulling rabbits out of hats, or seeing who can squeeze most juice out of the lemon. The astute literary critic can now preen in the borrowed feathers of a political scientist, a historian, a social philosopher.

All language, Bakhtin observes, comes to us contaminated by previous usage, saturated with ideology, class association and history. Only Adam had it unsullied. Why, Walter Scott asked in *Ivanhoe*, do the French have one word for the animal and the meat of the animal – *boeuf* – whereas the English have two words, bull/beef (bully beef, in the slang compound)? Because, as the novel wittily makes clear, the Normans sat at table scoffing steak while the Saxons toiled in the fields among the cowpats. Every time we order a rib-eye in our favorite restaurant, we are honorary Normans.

> **The novel can be defined as a diversity of social speech types ... and a diversity of individual voices, artistically organised.**
> **Mikhail Bakhtin**

And before the Normans, it was the Romans who put their heels on the luckless Saxon neck. Hence our English reverence for Latin, where medicine is concerned. The Germans (always more resistant to Rome than us) call it "the crab" (*Krebs*). We, more deferentially, call it cancer, or carcinoma, and die with a deferential bow toward our long-distant toga-wearing conquerors.

It could be argued that we needed no Russian, returned from the steppes, to tell us these things. A quarter of a millennium ago, Dr Johnson, that epitome of English common sense, defined heteroglossia in one of his essays on Shakespeare when he poured scorn on Macbeth's invocation:

> Come, thick night!
> And pall thee in the *dunnest* smoke of hell.

Why, Johnson asked, did Shakespeare "insert an epithet now seldom heard but in the stable?" To pollute the high-flown soliloquy of a king with this low, *smelly* word was worse than indecorous; it was "contemptible." It would be like Macbeth putting a horse collar round his neck, rather than a crown on his brow. Nor can one suppress the suspicion that part of the offence for Johnson was the unhappy resonance of "dun" and "dung."

We probably think Johnson wrong; our nostrils are less easily offended by words – particularly words we rarely use. But it's clear the Great Cham could sniff out heteroglossia, and the class associations of words, some two centuries before Bakhtin gave it a name.

the condensed idea
Not Babel but literature

36 New Historicism

"New Historicists seize upon an event or an anecdote – colonist John Rolfe's conversation with Pocahontas' father, a note found among Nietzsche's papers to the effect that "I have lost my umbrella" – and re-read it in such a way as to reveal through the analysis of tiny particulars the behavioural codes, logics and motive forces controlling a whole society." This according to H. Aram Veeser is the character of new historicism – a school of criticism that emerged in the 1970s and has since become a dominant voice in literary discussion both inside and outside the academy.

Historicism versus new historicism One's everyday reading is conducted in a constant state of tension between the historical and the ahistorical (critics, averse to using simple words when technical ones are to hand, use the terms synchronic/diachronic for this tension). What works best? Should one create an imaginary time machine, twirl the lever, and whisk back to the period in which the work of literature was created? Or drag the work of literature into the clinic of the present, as something outside time, place and historical accident?

Common sense instructs us that historicism is a fact of any reading. If you find an old newspaper lining an antique chest of drawers, you look at the headlines ("*Titanic* Sinks: Many Casualties") differently from this morning's hot-off-the-press *Guardian* or *New York Times*. But why? They are all newspapers.

Historicism has always been regarded as one of the handier tools in the critic and reader's toolbox. Can one respond to *Moby-Dick* unless one knows something of the early nineteenth-century whaling industry?

timeline

1755	1848
Samuel Johnson publishes his dictionary on historical principles, tracing the modulations of words through time	Thomas Macanlay publis͏ his *History of England*

The danger, though, is that historicism explains things too glibly. If, for example, one reads Jacobean tragedy in terms of the gloom that descended on the country after the death of Elizabeth (exacerbated by the rampant epidemic of "pox," or syphilis), it closes the case too efficiently. Historicism won't explain the crucial individual differences between the drama of John Webster, Thomas Middleton and late Shakespeare.

New historicism's nonreductive approach Historicism leads to reductive readings – as if literature were merely a by-product. New historicism is consciously un-reductive. It complicates rather than simplifying. Primarily it does this by *reading* the historical circumstances of literature as if they too were textual. A favored slogan of the school is "the historicity of texts and the textuality of history" (don't, incidentally, use it if there's a bona fide historian in earshot).

How would a new historicist approach the plays – or, more accurately, the "theater" – of Elizabethan England? They might well begin by pointing out where the Globe (Shakespeare's theater) was situated – south of the river, in Southwark. In the seventeenth century this, on the city boundary, was also where the taverns and brothels tended to be. What comes to mind is the red-light area in New Orleans that gave birth to jazz.

This "liminality" – urban edginess – explains the subversive nature of the drama of the period, new historicists suggest. Parliament, the Inns of Court, Westminster Cathedral were across the water. Visible, but within the pale. The theater were neither in, nor out, but on the fence. In short, the new historicist would say, a ride on the 68 bus across Waterloo Bridge (our new historicist could make much of that imperialist structure, as well) will be as useful as a whole page of notes in the Arden edition of Shakespeare.

**❝Die Weltgeschichte ist das Weltgericht.
(The history of the world is the wisdom
of the world.)❞**
Friedrich Schiller

1957	1966	1980
Political scientist Karl Popper publishes *The Poverty of Historicism*	Michel Foucault introduces his idea of the "episteme," in *The Order of Things*	Stephen Greenblatt's *Renaissance Self-Fashioning*

The theater pit and the bear pit

When Macbeth says, as the enemy closes in, "They have tied me to a stake; I cannot fly/But bear-like I must fight the course," the protestation was the more powerful for there being nearby pits in which – for the amusement of the same clientele who patronized the theaters – mastiff dogs were set upon bears tied to posts (sometimes blinded, to make the "baiting" more exciting). The bear-baiting lobby had political clout, and in 1591 succeeded in getting the theaters closed on Thursdays, so as not to steal too many of their paying spectators. Modern – ahistorical – commentators have mocked the scene, in *A Winter's Tale*, that ends: "Exit, pursued by a bear." But bears were close enough during the first performances of that play almost to smell when the wind was blowing the animal stink the wrong way.

A Shakespearian illustration When Hamlet instructs Ophelia to "get thee to a nunnery, go" (punning on the nunnery/brothel street slang), his brutality gains resonance from the fact that there were brothels next door. One particularly famous house of ill repute – doing good business during Shakespeare's day – was the Cardinal's Cap and the Bell (it was allegedly patronized by the star actor Edward Alleyn – who was also a brothel owner).

All this risky business – together with the wildest taverns and a lot of crime – happened south of the river (the "wrong side of the tracks" in post-railroad slang). What distinguishes new historicism from old historicism is its interest in the (actively) subversive rather than the (passively) reflective aspects of culture. Like taverns and brothels, Elizabethan/Jacobean drama is inherently dissident and antiauthoritarian. Hence the strict censorship under which the British playwright worked until, incredibly, the abolition of the Lord Chamberlain's Office in 1969.

The critic who founded new historicism, Stephen Greenblatt, recalls being inspired to do so while teaching a course on Marxist aesthetics.

66 New Historicism is a label historians don't like very much. 99
Michael Warner

One detects a sophisticated version of the familiar base/superstructure model. One of the more influential new historicist interpretations (associated with Greenblatt) is to read *The Tempest* as a subversive critique of imperialism – a twist that, perversely, ennobles Caliban (something routinely reflected in contemporary productions of the play), aligning Shakespeare with Frantz Fanon (advocate of radical *négritude*). In a 1974 National Theatre (London) performance, Caliban was made up, Janus style, with one side of his face a version of Rousseau's noble savage, the other side a repulsive ape. The effect was unsettling.

Neo-Marxism (often watered down) is one distinguishing mark. The other salient feature distinguishing new historicism from traditional historical approaches is its characteristic focus on small, in themselves, incidental elements in the literary design. The old historicists massed as much contextual data as they could. For the new historicists, a single datum can have as much, or more, illustrative value as a mountain of data.

The guiding light here is not Marx, but the anthropologist Clifford Geertz, and his essay on a cockfight, from which he deduces large interpretations about Balinese culture. In literature there are also apparently incidental aspects that are illustrative.

The objection lodged against new historicism (particularly by historians) is that it is lazy, unsystematic history.

Its approach to the past is that of the magpie to nest-building – a piece here, a piece there, nothing comprehensive. The objections from cultural conservatives target its leftist liberalism (or worse). It is the literary criticism of the revolution. New historicism remains, however, one of the most accessible and illuminating of recent critical innovations.

the condensed idea
Sweat the historical
details

37 Postcolonialism

The imperial prejudices of reading and criticism survived some time after the British Empire itself. It was common until well into the 1960s for English academic curricula to see American literature as "English Literature published in America." Postcolonial literature depends on the decay of such confident prejudices. Former empires have the sad privilege of possessing this particular kind of literary product. The USA is a democratic republic – or a ruling imperial power, depending on where you are standing – and does not have a corpus of postcolonial works of its own (yet?). There is, however, some seepage into the national literature, particularly that written by African Americans – via such concepts as "*négritude*," and "alterity" ("otherness") – ideas current in postcolonial critical discourse.

Imperial, Commonwealth, or postcolonial? The British Empire – over which the sun, famously, never set, and which colored a third of the world atlas red at its height – produced very little indigenous "native" literature. Chinua Achebe – author of "the most read novel to have come out of Africa" – recalls that the first novel he read was *Pilgrim's Progress*. In early reading of adventure writers such as Rider Haggard, Achebe "took sides with the white men against the savages."

It was only with the winds of change, and the wave of decolonization after World War II, that "Commonwealth" (as it was first called) writing began to appear as something to be taken notice of. It was a

timeline

1789

Olaudah Equiano publishes narrative of transportation from Africa to slavery in North America

1845

Frederick Douglass publishes the narrative of his life as American slave three-pronged thing. The British publishing industry began, actively, to recruit writers from the soon to be independent, or recently independent, colonies.

Achebe's great novel, *Things Fall Apart* (1958), was published as something of a gamble by the London publisher Heinemann in a series called "New Voices" (Achebe, indignantly, pointed out that Africa had some very old voices).

The second prong was the status of postcolonial texts as objects of academic attention. It was largely demographic. University teachers in Africa, India, and the West Indies had, preponderantly, been white. They returned to the UK, bringing with them first-hand experience. Alex Rodger, for example, the professor who taught Achebe Yeats (the allusive source of the title *Things Fall Apart*) at Ibadan University, returned to work at Edinburgh University, where he started up one of the first courses in Commonwealth literature in the UK.

Postcolonialism and colonial guilt Thirdly, there was a *mauvaise honte* – a diffused guilt – among younger readers particularly, about the "crime" of colonialism. The novel that to everyone's surprise took off as a "campus best-seller" in the early 1960s was *Lord of the Flies*. In it, William Golding reverses R. M. Ballantyne's *The Coral Island* – that parable of Victorian colonialism, in which three marooned English public school boys civilize the desert island on which they find themselves. In the climax, they are in dire peril from bloodthirsty cannibals. They pluckily save themselves, and their "English" decencies. In Golding's version, it is the English schoolboys who, marooned on their island, revert to savagery.

Postcolonialism, as a literary phenomenon, has taken root in three ways:

1. There has been patronage and encouragement for "New Voices." This is clearly reflected in Britain's premier literary prize, the Man-Booker. Since V. S. Naipaul won in 1971, over half the subsequent winners have been of Commonwealth origin (including Canada, the Caribbean, Australasia, the Indian subcontinent, Africa, and – perhaps more controversially – Ireland).

1952	1958	1981–2008	2001
Amos Tutuola pioneers colonial fiction with *The Palm-Wine Drinkard*	Chinua Achebe publishes *Things Fall Apart*	Salman Rushdie wins the Booker Prize with *Midnight's Children*	V. S. Naipaul wins the Nobel Prize for Literature

2. There has been new prominence, and respect, for the postcolonial writers on academic curricula. It is unlikely that anyone now gets through three years of an honors English course without contact with postcolonial literature.

3. There has been a new stress on authenticity. An example, from the US, is William Styron's *The Confessions of Nat Turner*. Nat Turner was the leader in 1831 of "the only effective, sustained revolt in the annals of American Negro Slavery," not far from where Styron had been born. The rebellion was put down. Turner was hanged. Styron's novel was published in 1967, just three years after the Civil Rights Act and a few months before the assassination of Martin Luther King. It was OK for a white lady abolitionist to create Uncle Tom, in 1852. It was not all right for a rich white Southerner to get inside a hero of the Black Struggle a hundred years later. Nat Turner's "Confessions" went straight to the top of the *New York Times* best-seller list while attracting an extraordinary amount of opprobrium from the people who mattered most to Styron – notably American blacks.

Postcolonialism and the syllabus

In a lecture at Amherst College, on 18 February 1975, Chinua Achebe delivered his canon-busting lecture, "An Image of Africa: *Heart of Darkness*," in which he denounced Joseph Conrad as "a bloody racist." Why, he asked, should his people, his continent, the plight of hundreds of millions of Africans be cast as the mere anonymous, depersonalized "backdrop" to a European's "nervous breakdown." Conrad, Achebe alleged, "had a problem with niggers." Achebe's blast was hugely influential in reassessing texts, such as Conrad's, complacently viewed in the West as liberal. The effect in classrooms in Britain and America was drastic. From being a "set" book, *Heart of Darkness* became a nonbook, as far as course designers were concerned.

Postcolonialism has not merely brought new titles into the canon; it has rewritten classic works of literature already installed there. Edward Said, for example, has directed attention to the question: where does the money come from in *Mansfield Park*? From Sir Thomas Bertram's slave-worked sugar plantations in the West Indies, the careful reader will deduce. In the pre-post-colonial period, no one asked that kind of question. One does not, of course, have to see it as all-important. But nowadays readers of Jane Austen do *see* it, as earlier generations did not. Similarly *Wide Sargasso Sea*, Jean Rhys's version of *Jane Eyre* from the viewpoint of the mulatto first Mrs. Rochester, Bertha Mason, has effectively rewritten Brontë's narrative, with the force of a historical reverse shot.

Small details, hitherto passed by or over, became meaningful in the light of postcolonial analysis. Why, in Kipling's novel *Kim*, is there no reference to the Indian Mutiny of 20 years earlier?

Problems for the postcolonial writer Postcolonial writers have achieved considerable profile, and have changed the ways in which literature is read. But, inevitably, they are not wholly unchained. In general, they use English – with whatever dialect variations (Hindi words in Rushdie, for example) the largely white readership they have can take on board. How to repossess the "poisoned wells" of language, Rushdie laments, is a continual postcolonial struggle.

The best-known and best-selling postcolonial writers are necessarily indentured to Anglo-American publishers (who else can come through with handsome advances?). What does it mean when writers of impeccable postcolonial sentiment such as V. S. Naipaul, or Salman Rushdie, go down on their knee, to be dubbed knight by the English queen? Or when Wole Soyinka receives the Nobel Prize? Is "marginality" – the sense of being on the edge, or outside – the sine qua non for postcolonial authenticity?

the condensed idea
The empire strikes back

38 Semiology

Picture the international road sign that shows a stick person crossing a road. Picture the same sign, but with a diagonal red line through it. I use the term "same sign" – but is it? It "signifies" entirely opposite things. "Walk/Don't Walk." How does a small mark perform that trick? This big idea, semiology – the "science" of semiotics – helps. It's not, to be honest, the biggest idea. Semiology of itself has not proved an outstandingly rich vein of literary explanation. It has, however, served as a starting point for much new thinking on how literature works.

Origins of the idea Literally the word points us to the (simpler) Greek for "sign." Communication, semiology presupposes, depends on signification: the encoding, transmission and decoding of signs. The founder-figure of semiology in its literary applications was a Swiss linguist, Ferdinand de Saussure. An obscure scholar in his own time, Saussure's theories survive, like many of Coleridge's, primarily in lecture notes taken by his students. His "courses in general linguistics" were not substantially translated into English until the 1960s, when his ideas took off like so many rockets, leaving a trail of theory behind them.

Saussure laid down a set of binary (two-sided) axioms from which much modern theoretical practice kicks off. The "difference" between them was where meaning was located (e.g., the difference between the two signs above). Saussurian binarism accounts for the typographic fad for the dividing slash (as in Roland Barthe's monograph S/Z) in recent decades. Until he came along, it was not a heavily pounded key on the QWERTY board.

timeline

1690	1860s
John Locke investigates "semeiotics" in Book IV of his *Essay Concerning Human Understanding*	American philosopher Charles Sanders Peirce begins investigating the logic of semiotics and sign-relations

Keep your eye open for small signs; they can mean a lot

An awareness of the semiotic dimension means we are more likely to *see* what we are looking at, rather than merely *read* it. Words, semiology asserts, only *mean* in relation to other words, and the differences between them. In the first published version of his poem "Gerontion," T. S. Eliot wrote of "the jew" (a landlord) squatting on the narrator's windowsill. In postwar versions of the poem, Eliot (a publisher, who minutely superintended the production of his work) altered "jew" to "Jew." Semantically the word means precisely the same. If the poem were recited (as it often is), the ear wouldn't know. But "Jew," although essentially the same sign, takes on its later significance (respect, not contempt) from it's not being "jew" and our being aware that it isn't. It's "jew" with a red line through it.

Among Saussure's most influential binarisms are:

synchronic/diachronic
langue/parole
signifier/signified

The first binarism (S/D) observes that there are two ways of looking at language: historically or ahistorically. Saussure was exclusively interested in synchrony. How it works, not where it came from.

The second (L/P) sees a vast, imaginary linguistic potential – the language system – that can generate an infinite number of individual speech or writing acts. However many *paroles* are generated, *langue* will never be exhausted.

The third binarism (S/S) observes that there is no equational or (necessarily) logical relationship between signifier and signified. Consider the following favorite example among semiologists: a man gives a woman a bunch of red roses. What those flowers signify is

<table>
<tr><td>**1906–1913**</td><td>**1964**</td><td>**1981**</td><td>**1983**</td></tr>
<tr><td>Ferdinand de Saussure delivers lectures later published as *A General Course in Linguistics*</td><td>Roland Barthes publishes *Elements of Semiology*</td><td>Jonathan Culler publishes *The Pursuit of Signs: Semiotics, Literature, Deconstruction*</td><td>Umberto Eco publishes *The Name of the Rose*</td></tr>
</table>

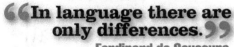

> ## In language there are only differences.
> **Ferdinand de Saussure**

nothing horticultural. A bunch of red radishes would signify something quite different, although a Martian might have difficulty distinguishing between the two acts.

A basic tenet is the essential arbitrariness of linguistic signification. Imagine the following. A woman is found disoriented in Central Park. "Who did this to you?" asks a policeman. "Therapists," she bleakly replies. Writing up his report on the precinct computer, the cop's hyphenation program divides "therapists" to read at the line break "the-rapists." There is no logical explanation for why the same set of letters should convey such radically different messages.

Literary applications Semiotics has an obvious problem with literature. It's not pictorial, but phonetic, alphabetic and scriptive. It is, in the main, transmitted by a code – print: thicker than Morse code but thinner than what the artist's brush and palette supplies.

Literature does, of course, have a physical form: words on the page and books on the shelf. But in general, authors surrender their creative rights over things like typography (font), layout and jacket design to printers, publishers and editors. They commonly retain rights over punctuation, paragraphing, capitalization and italicization. These have signifying potential, but not a lot.

Interest in semiotics has, observably, made readers more alert to such things as James Joyce (who was a tyrant over his proofs) deciding to use the "continental" method of signifying speech in *Ulysses*. Thus

> "The mourners moved away slowly, without aim, by devious paths, staying at whiles to read a name on a tomb.
>
> — Let us go round by the chief's grave, Hynes said. We have time.
> — Let us, Mr Power said."

Conventionally, this exchange would be speckled with quote marks (e.g., "Let us go round by the chief's grave," Hynes said. "We have time."). Is there a difference in signification between these alternative punctuational systems? Yes, there is. The continental system, without its rupturing inverted commas, conduces to flowingness – stream of consciousness, free indirect discourse.

> **Every act of communication to or between human beings presupposes a signification system as its necessary condition.**
>
> Umberto Eco

Umberto Eco – virtuoso of semiotics A spectacularly experimental play with the insights of Saussurian semiology was made by Umberto Eco, the author of the 1979 manual, *A Theory of Semiotics*. Few critics write fiction; very few write distinguished fiction; fewest of all write best-selling fiction. But that is what Eco did with his 1983 novel, *The Name of the Rose*.

The title is itself a misnomer – a sign pointing nowhere, but drawing on the infinite significations of the rose. In his semiological manual, Eco refers to the "well known verse by Gertrude Stein: *A rose is a rose is a rose*." On the face of it, the sentence conveys "the most elementary kind of information." Nevertheless, as it echoes in the mind, "the message gives the impression of saying something that is semantically rich and therefore highly ambiguous." It contains a multitude of "informational possibilities." Signposts pointing everywhere but leading us nowhere.

The action of Eco's romance is set in an Italian monastery, in 1327. A monk detective, with the unlikely but signposting name, if we know our Conan Doyle, William of Baskerville, has been summoned to solve a murder. A manuscript, Aristotle's discourse on comedy (mentioned in *The Poetics*), which does not (may not?) exist, is central to the mystery – which is never solved. No Sherlock is around in 1327.

The Name of the Rose allegorizes the semiotic plight – the search for the "really" signified, which will always fail because we can never get beyond the nominal/signifying universe of understanding that is the human condition.

the condensed idea
Signification makes meaning

39 Reception Theory

"It is apparent," writes Jane P. Tompkins (a leading exponent of the approach), **"that although theorists of reader-oriented criticism disagree on many issues, they are united on one thing: their opposition to the belief that meaning inheres completely and exclusively in the literary text."** Reception theory (also called "reader response theory") looks at the destinations of literature – the end of that long line that begins with the moment of creation.

The subjectivity problem There's an obvious problem, of course. A work of literature normally only has one creator working in one time frame and in one place – Shakespeare's "onlie begetter." The same work of literature can have tens of millions of recipients across time and all over the place. How many people(s) have watched *Hamlet*? It would fracture a calculator. You could fracture another calculator with how many have read the play.

Historically, the bundle of ideas that make up reception theory coalesced into a critical "school" in West Germany in the late 1960s. Hans Robert Jauss and Wolfgang Iser are pioneer figures in the school. Plausibly, it originates in uneasiness about the legacy of the Third Reich, and its ruthless insistence on "*Gleichschaltung*" – ideological uniformity.

As it has taken root in critical thinking in the English-speaking world, reception theory concentrates on three principal areas: (1) the means – or media – by which literature is delivered to the reader; (2) the "implied," or "textualized" reader, as opposed to the "real" reader;

timeline

1782
In his *Life of Thomas Gray*, Samuel Johnson declares: "I rejoice to concur with the common reader"

1896
First best-seller lists appear in the American *Bookman* magazine.

1912
Authoritative best-se lists establish thems in *Publisher's Week*

(3) the relationship of the individual reader and the larger "reading public."

Reader response and the history of the book It is no accident that reception theory has been accompanied by the emergence, since 1970, of book history as an academic discipline. Literature is not "discovered;" it is delivered in various material packages. The nature of book trades, retail (shop) and circulation (library) systems has a formative effect on reception/response.

> **_Quot homines tot sententiae. (There are as many opinions as there are men.)_**
> Terence

One small example will make the point. In November 1848, the firm of W. H. Smith was given a monopoly on the distribution of reading matter at Euston railroad station. The authorities were worried about salacious materials being sold by pedlars. The instruction was given to Smith's to "purify the sources of entertainment and instruction" for the millions traveling on the railroads, which they did, and still do. What was "received" by the traveler was materially altered.

One talks of "reader response," but there are, of course, many readers of a literary text. They will not, self-evidently, have the same response. Some reader response, for example, is "textualized." When Jane Eyre leaps off the page to announce: "Reader, I married him," Charlotte Brontë, writing in 1847, had a certain shadowy fellow Victorian in mind on the receiving end of Jane's statement. Reading the novel 160 years later, one has to juggle that historical figure with one's very un-Victorian self.

There are also, Wolfgang Iser points out, "ideal readers" whom the author will optimistically aim at. Look, for example, at the prefaces of Henry James, devised for the great reissue of his collected work in 1908. James addresses a reader he clearly conceives as an intellectual equal. Cynics might say he is addressing another Henry James.

Outside Germany, reception theory has taken on different inflections. In France, it pops up as Roland Barthes's binary distinction between texts that are *lisible* ("readerly") and those that are *scriptible*

1925	1980	1982	1989
Virginia Woolf publishes *The Common Reader*	Jane P. Tompkins publishes *Reader-response criticism: from formalism to post-structuralism*	Hans Robert Jauss's *Toward an Aesthetic of Reception* first published in English translation	Wolfgang Iser's *Prospecting: From Reader Response to Literary Anthropology* published in English translation

("writerly"). The "writerly" text (of main interest to Barthes) is "open;" it resists closures and wrap-it-up meanings. The French *roman nouveau* would be an example (as Bunyan's *Pilgrim's Progress* would be an example of the "readerly" text, which insists on being understood one way only). The reader is, by contrast, free to supply his/her own meaning to these open texts. None, of course, will ever satisfactorily close the text.

Different national theorizations In Britain, the sociologist Stuart Hall has proposed a somewhat different variant of the Barthesien model. Readers do not, Hall says, "receive" in the way, say, that a telephone receives a message. There are, he proposes, three ways of answering literature's incoming call. One is to submit to the "dominant" – typically authorial – instruction. The second is to "oppose," or quarrel with, the text as an equal. The third way is to work out some kind of compromise, or "negotiated" reading.

A young Victorian woman might wholly approve of Jane Eyre's resolving to marry Rochester. A twenty-first-century woman reader might think that enslaving yourself to a brute prepared to lock up his

Best-seller lists: maps of reception

"I rejoice to concur with the common reader," said Dr Johnson. But in the eighteenth century it was difficult to know what *was* the common reader's current preference. The practice of systematically identifying, and listing, certain books as noteworthy for the speed and volume of their sales – and absolutely nothing else – began with the American monthly magazine *The Bookman,* and its editor, Harry Thurston Peck, in 1896. Peck's magazine was the first to list a selection of new titles "in order of demand" –

that demand being measured by units of sale. The earliest recorded use of the compound noun "best-seller" occurs in 1902. In 1912, the American trade magazine *Publisher's Weekly* began issuing a best-seller list. In the present day, EPOS (electronic point of sales) systems for the capture of retail sales data have made retailing apparatus infinitely more sensitive. It is now, literally, possible to identify "books of the day." Or even of the hour. We know precisely what the common reader is up to.

> **Hypocrite lecteur, – mon semblable, – mon frère! (Hypocritical reader, my lookalike, my brother!)**
> Charles Baudelaire, "To the Reader"

wife in an attic and commit bigamy would be a big mistake. Most readers work their way through the two positions so as to live happily with the novel.

The principal US variant of reception theory seizes on the "democratic" implications of readers being the ultimate trustees of meaning. Associated principally with critics such as Jane Tompkins (and the English Department at Duke University), it applauds the move from author's sovereignty to reader's rights: not just in "open" texts, but all texts. It is less the continuous power struggle that Stuart Hall pictures than reader emancipation.

The danger, self-evidently, is rampant subjectivism. Some readings are clearly stupid, blinkered or perverse. Leon Feuchtwanger wrote his novel, *Jüd Suss*, as a plea for racial harmony. The Nazis (via film adaptation) used it as anti-Semitic propaganda. Is Josef Goebbels's interpretation to be valued equally with that of the author, or Feuchtwanger's more congenial readers?

A way through this was suggested by Stanley Fish, Tompkins's colleague (and husband) at Duke (where the American variant of reception theory has found a warm home). Meanings should not be the property of the individual, Fish suggests, though they might well start there. Readings should be stabilized by "interpretive communities." The practical effect of this is to prioritize the seminar, which – after lively discussion – arrives at something bearably consensual.

But not, necessarily, permanent. The interpretive community, so to call it, which made up the audience of Shakespeare's Globe, saw Shylock as a bloodthirsty villain. A modern production would more likely see him as a victim of prejudice – even a hero. Literature lasts, interpretive communities don't; and with their changes, the meanings of literature also change.

the condensed idea
It's the readers who matter

40 Sexual Politics

Universities began as monastic institutions. There was no scholarship in medieval convents: no scriptoria, no illuminators, no libraries, little literacy. The female point of entry into higher education in Britain and America was the English Department. Despite the fact that English was traditionally disdained as a "soft" subject (unlike, say, theoretical physics), there was, by the 1960s, a sizeable presence among the younger ranks of scholars to respond enthusiastically to initiatives such as the foundation of the National Organization for Women (under the leadership of Betty Friedan, author of *The Feminine Mystique*) in 1966.

The angry origins It was no accident that feminism arrived on the scene when it did. The 1960s was a decade of "political liberation," with the Civil Rights Act of 1964, and political protest (principally against the Vietnam War).

The term "sexual politics" was the title of a book published by Kate Millett in 1970. It began as a doctoral thesis at Columbia University in New York. Millett was a student during the "Years of the Young Rebels."

She took her data from across the canon of literary studies – all of her principal examples being male. Millett opened her monograph with "instances." The first instance was from Henry Miller's "raunchy" memoir *Sexus*. This was a work that had been banned in the US until the "liberalizing" *Lady Chatterley* court cases of 1959–60, which made "raunch" legal.

timeline

1790	1848
Mary Wollstonecraft publishes *A Vindication of the Rights of Woman*	The first women's rights convention held in the United States

Bertha Mason: monster or symbol of oppressed womanhood?

This is how Jane Eyre reports her first clear sight of the woman who has been roaming Thornfield at night, and who eventually destroys the building by fire.

"What it was, whether beast or human being, one could not, at first sight, tell: it grovelled, seemingly, on all fours: it snatched and growled like some strange wild animal: but it was covered with clothing; and a quantity of dark, grizzled hair, wild as a mane, hid its head and face ... the clothed hyena, rose up and stood tall on its hind feet.... The maniac bellowed: she parted her shaggy locks from her visage, and gazed wildly at her visitors."

Madwoman or victim?

The passage Millett chose to open her case describes Miller lying in his bath, summoning his paramour, and brutally screwing her:

"I left the stockings on – it made her more lascivious looking, the Cranach type. I lay back and pulled her on top of me. She was just like a bitch in heat ... as I pulled away I left the mark of my teeth on her beautiful white ass. Not a word spoken."

What, precisely, had been "liberated?" enquired Millett. She went on to answer with a single word: "patriarchy" – a system of female oppression stretching as far back as literary (and biblical) texts could take us. The issue was not obscenity, but "politics" – who was in charge in the scene above?

Sexual relationships were not, as Millett saw it, biological, but rooted in "power" – or, as she preferred to call it, "force" (a word with closer relation to "rape"). "The history of patriarchy," she grimly asserted, "presents a variety of cruelties and barbarities: the suttee execution in India, the crippling deformity of footbinding in China, the lifelong

1917	1963	1970	1970
Women over the age of 30 are enfranchized to vote in the UK	Betty Friedan publishes *The Feminine Mystique*	Kate Millett publishes *Sexual Politics*	Germaine Greer publishes *The Female Eunuch*

ignominy of the veil in Islam, or the widespread persecution of sequestration, the gynacium, and purdah." Literature (predominantly written by men) was patriarchy's mirror, its apology, and an argument for its continuation.

Sexual politics and British literary criticism In the UK, at the same period, a young English lecturer at Warwick University (an institution, like Columbia, that the newspapers liked to label a "hotbed") published *The Female Eunuch*. Germaine Greer's doctorate had been on Shakespeare's comedy. *A Midsummer Night's Dream* was a play of particular interest to her. Traditionally "the Dream" had been regarded as the most charmingly harmless of Shakespeare's fantasies. Greer read it differently. The action opens with the impending marriage of Theseus (ruler of Athens) and Hippolyta – formerly Queen of the Amazons. She has been abducted, literally "raped." The preparations are interrupted by the case of a girl who refuses to marry the man her father has chosen for her. She is casually condemned to death. Among the fairies, Oberon is angry with his wife Titania. He dopes her, and laughs as she submits to be (publicly) ravished by a donkey – traditionally seen as a beast with a monstrous penis.

The English school, represented by Greer, tended to see their ancestress as Virginia Woolf: a commentator who was commonsensical rather than ideological. In America it was Friedan (and behind her, Simone de Beauvoir).

Anger such as Millett's was the kindling. A more programmatic polemic was framed by Elaine Showalter. Showalter recalled, as an undergraduate, being instructed by a male lecturer that Woolf's *Mrs. Dalloway* was the study of an inadequate wife. As a professor of English at Princeton, Showalter edited the novel. She discerned – from hints carefully embedded in the narrative – that it was the study of a woman going through menopause.

> **All oppression creates a state of war.**
> Simone de Beauvoir

Keep out, men? Women, it was implied, had a privileged access to texts written by women. Showalter elevated this insight into a panoramic survey of women novelists, *A Literature of Their Own* ("our own," that is). Presses in Britain and America (notably the women-run collective, Virago) set out to "recover" this literature, bringing it back into print and thus more readily into the curriculum. Literary feminism ("gynocriticism"), argued Showalter, progressed through three phases: feminine/feminist/ female.

❝Outside in the Teaching Machine.❞
Woman's paradoxical place in academic life, according to Gayatri Chakravorty Spivak

A similarly wide-ranging conspectus was attempted by Sandra Gilbert and Susan Gubar in their manifesto work, *The Madwoman in the Attic*. Their title alludes to the first Mrs. Rochester ("Bertha Mason"), in *Jane Eyre*. As conventionally perceived, in the century after the novel's publication, she was a figure of Gothic horror, a monster.

Read with modern subtlety (aided by post-Freudian insight), Bertha took on two new characters. She was the oppressed woman of history who – when she rebelled – was thought merely mad. Secondly she was the raging protest within Jane that, all her life, Jane had been "manfully" suppressing. Jane was the eunuch, Bertha the woman *furiosa*. Bertha Mason in her attic (odd that she is rarely called "Bertha Rochester") was a prime example, but read carefully, all great literature – from Chaucer to Anna Karenina – demanded new reading and reinterpretation along these lines. That, in turn, required academic/critical power. It happened as women assumed equal professorial status. Showalter, to take one example, became head of the department at Princeton, where her colleagues were Toni Morrison and Joyce Carol Oates. In 2010, over half the literary editors in the dozen or so opinion-forming review pages in the UK national press were women (50 years earlier, the figure was precisely zero). In the publishing world women assumed for the first time CEO roles in multinational companies. They might still, as Spivak puts it, feel themselves somewhat "outside" but they were, undeniably, in the literary machine, at last. Even running it.

the condensed idea
There is a "female" literature

41 Plagiarism

When intertextuality gets too intertextual, allusion too allusive, or influence too influential, the "p word" is invoked. Literally the word plagiarism means "kidnapping" – taking someone else's child. Taking a literary brainchild is not quite "stealing," because the original remains still in place, undamaged. These quibbles aside, plagiarism is the Murder One in literature's criminal code. It is also an offence in civil law – damages are awarded, and penalties (such as court-ordered pulping) often ordained. Jail is not a risk, however, even for the most hardened literary kidnapper.

What is free, and what protected? The stern prohibition against plagiarism nestles uneasily with literature's primal liberties. As the law puts it, with biblical authority, an author may reap where he/she has not sown. Or, as book lore says: "there is no copyright in ideas." It is this permission (see pp. 65 and 79) that makes possible the me-tooism on which literature thrives.

If a writer like John Polidori comes up with the original idea of a glamorous "vampyre" (in 1816), there is nothing to stop a writer like Bram Stoker (*Dracula*) making a lot of money out of the same idea, or a writer like Anne Rice (along with innumerable others) making a whole, very profitable, career out of vampirology. There is no patent law, design or trademark protection in literature (so far – see p. 167). Copyright merely extends to the form of actual words (although not, interestingly, titles – in which, again, there is no copyright. I could, fancifully, call this book *The Da Vinci Code II*, if I wished).

timeline

1710	1817
The Queen Anne copyright act comes into law	Samuel Taylor Coleridge publishes *Biographia Literaria*, like other of his works plentifully laced with unacknowledged borrowings

After the Queen Anne copyright act of 1710, the definitions of literary property became sharper. But as literature became more accessible, and larger in mass, plagiarism boomed. There was so much more to kidnap.

Recent examples In his study of the offence, *Stolen Words*, Thomas Mallon anatomizes different kinds of plagiarist, and the explanations they offer. The "notebook" defense is commonest: "I copied it down and later forgot where it came from."

This was, effectively, the exculpation offered in the highest-profile case of recent times, that centered on Alex Haley's international bestseller, *Roots*. It was particularly sensitive since Haley's book purported to be a truthful family memoir that, over the generations, chronicled the history of black slavery and emancipation in the US.

> **Immature poets imitate; mature poets steal.**
> T. S. Eliot

Should plagiarism be decriminalized?

In the olden days, literature used to be wholly free and easy about *meum* and *tuum*. Shakespeare's *King Lear* plunders the pre-existing play *King Leir*. It wasn't just the title he "borrowed" but whole speeches. In *Antony and Cleopatra*, the bard also echoed whole sections of Plutarch's Roman history verbatim. And when John Dryden "improved" *Antony* and *Cleopatra* as *All for Love*, he in turn lifted great chunks of Shakespearian material, again almost verbatim, polishing up what he saw as the regrettably barbaric roughness in his source text. The absence of any objection (legal, moral or aesthetic) made some great literature possible. Would a loosening of the law do the same today?

1978	2006	2006–7
Alex Haley's *Roots* published; it is later indicted for plagiarism	Dan Brown acquitted of plagiarizing *The Holy Blood and the Holy Grail* by Baigent and Leigh	Ian McEwan defends himself against allegations of plagiarism from *No Time for Romance*

Large sections of the work were, a 1978 lawsuit determined, lifted without attribution not from Haley family lore (as the author asserted) but from an obscure novel, *The African*, by Harold Courlander, who sued. He was paid $650,000 in an out-of-court settlement. Haley protested that the passages he had transcribed "were in something somebody had given me, and I don't know who gave it to me. . . . Somehow or another, it ended up in the book."

Plagiarism where well-known authors are concerned is headline-making. In November 2006, the *Daily Mail* asserted that a central section of Ian McEwan's best-selling (and recently filmed) novel *Atonement* was lifted from the memoir *No Time for Romance*, by Dame Lucilla Andrews, about nursing wounded troops in World War II. Andrews had made her name writing "hospital romance." McEwan took the front page in the *Guardian* the following day to inform the world: "I am not a plagiarist." He made the point that he had credited Andrews in his afterword and – more importantly – that he had *used*, not *misappropriated*, her excellent memoir. He was supported by his fellow Booker laureate Thomas Keneally (whose *Schindler's Ark* had itself made ample use of primary documents). Keneally argued:

> "If it is sufficient to point to a simultaneity of events to prove plagiarism, then we are all plagiarists, and Shakespeare is in big trouble from Petrarch, and Tolstoy stole the material for *War and Peace*. Fiction depends on a certain value-added quality created on top of the raw material, and that McEwan has added value beyond the original will, I believe, be richly demonstrated.... If not, God help us all."

It will be seen that Keneally is falling back on the "reap where they have not sown" defense. McEwan rode out the storm.

The uncertain future More storms of the former kind are in prospect. Laws are not immutable, and the "no copyright in ideas" freedom is under continuous assault. In April 2006, Michael Baigent and Richard Leigh brought suit against Dan Brown and his publishers in the English courts on the grounds that *The Da Vinci Code* "appropriated the *architecture*" of their book *The Holy Blood and the Holy Grail* (1982).

The action failed. The judge gave it as his opinion that "Even if the central themes were copied they are too general or of too low a level of abstraction to be capable of protection by copyright law." It was a

> **The secret to creativity is knowing how to hide your sources.**
>
> Albert Einstein

robust vindication of traditional definitions ("no copyright in themes"). But for how long in the future?

The other factor making for change is the Internet. Plagiarism, via the net, has reached the proportion of a twenty-first-century plague, which is rotting the intellectual fabric of higher education. Surveys reveal well over half the Anglo-American student population confessing to plagiarism by download (and, one suspects, the other half not confessing to the same practice). Having an Internet connection is like being in a supermarket with the lights out, the doors open and the security guards napping.

This corrosive effect will, inevitably, seep into the artistic fabric of modern life. There are signs that among younger authors, old inhibitions are melting. In 2010, a 17-year-old German author, Helene Hegemann, published a novel, *Axolotl Roadkill*, chronicling the depraved Berlin nightclub scene, which became an overnight sensation. Within days a blogger demonstrated that large sections of *Axolotl Roadkill* were lifted, without acknowledgment, from a blog fiction, *Strobo: Technoprose from Berghain*, by "Airen." Hegemann's defense was aggressive. She was defiant in confronting "this whole copyright excess." She had "stolen nothing." "Airen" – a web pseudonym – did not want his identity disclosed, nor did he make any legal objection. One saw, in embryo, a new world emerging. Plagiarism? So twentieth century.

> **The greater the plagiarism the greater the work of art.**
> Hugh MacDiarmid

the condensed idea
Published literature is private property

42 Obscenity

No one is too clear about the etymological origin of the word "obscene." But its application, over the course of literary history, is crystal clear. It is a nonliterary label attached to literary work that happens to be morally objectionable to nonliterary people because of its sexual content. Obscenity is to be distinguished from pornography (etymologically, "writing about prostitutes"), in that obscenity is the charge commonly leveled at high, or experimental, literature, and it is, by legal definition, a criminal offence. Writers can bear the term with pride. Many have been imprisoned in the cause of "justified obscenity."

Literature at bay The charge of obscenity traditionally brings the author into conflict with authorities outside literature – not "critics," but police, the courts, and the court of public opinion that the Victorians called "Mrs. Grundy" and the 1960s knew as "Mrs. Whitehouse."

Question: What three things do the following works of literature have in common?

Ulysses (James Joyce)
Lady Chatterley's Lover (D. H. Lawrence)
Lolita (Vladimir Nabokov)

Answer: (1) They have all been banned, in their early years, in their home countries, on grounds of "obscenity;" (2) They were all first published in a foreign country, where they were judged to be not obscene; (3) They are now securely canonical and are taught in every course of higher literature in the Western world.

timeline

1857	1873	1889
Lord Campbell Obscenity Act passed into law, the first such legislation in England	Anthony Comstock founds the Society for the Suppression of Vice in the US	Publisher Henry Vizetelly is fined £100 for publishing "obscene libels" – translation of Zola's novels in English

Dirty book - for 250 years, and still going strong

Fanny Hill; or, Memoirs of a Woman of Pleasure as published in 1748–9 takes the form of a confessional letter describing the heroine's "progress," and was clearly designed to contradict the joyless moralism of Hogarth's *Harlot's Progress* (1732) and to show up the timidly parsimonious reference to sex in Defoe's "whore's autobiography" *Moll Flanders* (1722), both of which aims it achieves triumphantly. The name is a somewhat labored pun on *Veneris mons* – Venus's hill. It is not clear whether "fanny" was then, as now, street slang for a woman's private parts. Knowing Cleland, probably yes.

These books have not changed textually – they have not been "expurgated" or "bowdlerized" in order to "come home." The world, we presume, has changed in terms of its sexual mores and its sense of what is permissible. But why? Human beings have not changed biologically.

Obscenity, as the above example suggests, is a "moving target." It shifts in three senses. At any single point in time this man's obscenity is that man's erotica, and the criterion varies – often 180 degrees – over time and place. In American terms, what is "Banned in Boston" (or "Burned in Podunk") may be "Book of the Day in Manhattan."

Fanny Hill – obscene and not obscene An early, and formative, legal action on grounds of obscenity was that taken against *Fanny Hill* in the mid-eighteenth century. John Cleland is reputed to have written the book, the supposed memoirs of a nymphomaniac courtesan, as a wager that he could write a supremely erotic novel without ever resorting to "low" language. He actually wrote it in prison for debt (which the book somewhat relieved).

1915	1928	1957	1959	1960
D. H. Lawrence's *The Rainbow* prosecuted (successfully) for obscenity	Radclyffe Hall's lesbian romance *The Well of Loneliness* prosecuted (successfully) for obscenity	Allen Ginsburg's poem *Howl* cleared of charges of obscenity in San Francisco	Roy Jenkins's Obscene Publications Bill passes into law.	*Lady Chatterley's Lover* (first published in 1928) acquitted of the charge of obscenity at the Old Bailey in London

When the authorities took action against the disgraceful novel, Cleland disowned it as "A Book I disdain to defend, and wish, from my Soul, buried and forgot." No novel has been less buried and forgot than *Fanny Hill: Memoirs of a Woman of Pleasure*. According to his obituary in the *Gentleman's Magazine*, Cleland (who had the reputation of being, privately, a "sodomite") was awarded a pension of £100 a year from the public purse, on condition that he write no more corrupting works.

Fanny Hill was the first book to be (successfully) prosecuted for obscenity in America. It continued to sell like hot cakes underground. Following the acquittal of *Lady Chatterley's Lover* in 1960, a British paperback publisher put out an above-ground edition of Cleland's novel in November 1963. Copies were seized. Fanny, like many other ladies of the night, went on trial at Bow Street Magistrates" Court in February 1964. The book was again deemed an offence to public morals and the seized stock ordered destroyed.

Oddly, no successful defense of *Fanny Hill* has ever been mounted. It crept back into the bookshop shelves, and now has a learnedly annotated existence as an Oxford World's Classic. A BBC TV version, adapted by Andrew Davies in 2007, attracted an audience of seven million. It remains, technically, banned. The history of obscenity yields many such absurdities.

The obscenity laws, which had hobbled literature, were themselves eventually crippled by the ditching of the old "deprave and corrupt" tests and the admission into defense of the "redeeming merit (social or literary)" of the work in question. Expert witnesses could testify to the redeeming merit of anything, and did.

> **I acknowledge Shakespeare to be the world's greatest dramatic poet, but regret that no parent could place the uncorrected book in the hands of his daughter, and therefore I have prepared the Family Shakespeare.**
>
> Dr Thomas Bowdler,
> justifying his "bowdlerized" edition

1960: the critical literary historical
moment The threshold test of the new standards were the trials of D. H. Lawrence's long-suppressed novel, *Lady Chatterley's Lover*, in 1959/60. It was an easy work of literature to defend, since Lawrence's motives were so clearly moral (in the November 1960 Old Bailey trial, the Bishop of Woolwich likened the adulteries of Mellors and his aristocratic paramour to "an act of communion"). The case for the prosecution was not helped by the opening address to the jury by leading counsel Mervyn Griffith-Jones:

> "There cannot be a limit on the writer."
>
> John Mortimer, defending counsel for *Lady Chatterley*

> "You may think that one of the ways in which you can read this book, and test it from the most liberal outlook, is to ask yourselves the question, when you have read it through, would you approve of your young sons, young daughters – because girls can read as well as boys – reading this book. Is it a book that you would have lying around in your own house? Is it a book that you would even wish your wife or your servants to read?"

He had forgotten, or perhaps never knew, that it was 1960.

By the end of the decade, obscenity was, effectively, a dead letter. Some writers, such as Kingsley Amis, regretted its passing not on grounds of public decency but because it had forced writers to be cleverer than those blunderheads who would oppress them – as the great Russian writers (Dostoevsky, Turgenev, Chekhov, and Pushkin) had been obliged to wriggle their work past the Tsarist censor. Censorship kept writers on their mettle.

There remain sporadic bannings from libraries and schoolrooms on grounds of obscenity in the US, in townships where local communities have censorial power. But in the metropolitan areas of the English-speaking world, obscene literature is as nonsensical a formulation as obscene music (as, in the distant past, jazz and in the more recent past gangsta-rock have been defined).

the condensed idea
It's a moving target. And the law is never quick on the draw

43 Libel

Literature has a problem with real living people (RLP). It's made by RLPs, and read by RLPs. But depicting RLPs in literature has always been legally fraught. Fictional people, and dead people are no problem whatsoever. "Libel" literally means "that which is written" (hence the compounds "criminal libel" and "obscene libel"). It's different, in that respect, from "slander," or "defamation," or – vulgarly – slagging off, which is oral; a thing of the mouth, not the pen.

How can literature deal with those who can sue (or worse)? Slander – although it is actionable – is freer. I can say pretty much whatever disobliging things I want about anyone I want, so long as the company is not offended by my sounding-off. Stand-up comedians do it every night. Writing and publishing is something else. Newspapers and large (i.e., rich enough to sue) publishing houses nowadays have everything "legalled" – that is, examined by an expert for possible libel.

Despite the obstacles put in their way, writers remain fascinated by RLPs. In the distant, preliterary past, things were more robust. When John Dryden penned a satire on Lord Rochester, the nobleman hired three thugs to beat up the poet in Rose Alley, off Drury Lane. Nowadays it is the dulcet-voiced thugs in gowns and wigs who do the necessary pummeling.

The so-called *roman-à-clef* ("novel with a key" – the term does not translate well) is one way through past the libel obstacle. A name change, a few altered details and a ritual protestation about resemblances being coincidental will often suffice.

timeline

1679

John Dryden libels the Earl of Rochester (allegedly) and is set upon by three hired ruffians

1735

Alexander Pope libels Lor Harvey in "The Epistle to Arbuthnot," and is not bea

> ❝He who steals my purse, steals trash.
> But he who steals my good name,
> steals all that I have.❞
>
> Iago, in *Othello*

But the trick is to fudge legally actionable identification while allowing the reader to make that identification. They can't always be trusted. In the 1820s, when the "silver fork" novel about figures in high life was all the rage, publishers would routinely include loose-leaf "keys" with their volumes – disowning, of course, all responsibility for the thing. It would, however, have been a very sleepy reader who did not apprehend in Lady Caroline Lamb's revenge *roman-à-clef* novel, *Glenarvon*, that the "mad, bad, dangerous to know" hero was Lord Byron (not for Byron the limp *roman-à-clef* label; he called *Glenarvon* a "fuck and tell novel").

Saul Bellow: cunning libeller Modern writers like Saul Bellow have specialized in the transparent *roman-à-clef*. One reviewer of *Ravelstein* (2000) observed, wittily, that the standard disclaimer should be "any resemblance my arse," so transparent were Bellow's depictions of friends, enemies and former wives (his bitterest enemies).

The *roman-à-clef*'s cloak of invisibility does not always work, and when it fails, the results can be painful. Jake Arnott, the British "true crime" novelist, published *Johnny Come Home* in April 2006 only for his publishers to be obliged to pulp the entire first edition of the novel in August. In his narrative, set in London's Tin Pan Alley (not too far from Rose Alley) in the 1970s, Arnott introduced a character called "Tony Rocco:" a one-time big-band singer, now an impresario and a big-time pervert. Alas, out of obscurity, escorted by his learned friends in wigs, emerged the real-life Tony Rocco: former big-band singer and a figure of unimpeachable respectability. Exit the book. Exit, also, many thousands of pounds from the coffers of Arnott's publishers.

Where real names are involved, an author cannot hide behind that all-purpose shield: "any resemblance is purely coincidental." Nor do the

1903	**1816**	**2000**
The Protocols of the Elders of Zion, a "blood libel" on the Jewish people, published in Russia	Lady Caroline Lamb publishes her malicious portrait of Byron as the hero of her novel, *Glenarvon*	Saul Bellow publishes unmistakable portraits of friends, enemies and former wives in his last novel, *Ravelstein*

Al Gore "libeled?"

When Erich Segal, the author of the best-seller ("love means never having to say you're sorry") *Love Story*, died in 2010, the long-running rumor that the hero, Oliver Barrett IV, was based on Albert Arnold "Al" Gore. was again aired (Segal was teaching at Harvard when Gore was a student there; Gore's Harvard room-mate, Tommy Lee Jones, had a supporting role in the 1970 film). If true, Gore would have been in the teasingly paradoxical situation of being able, simultaneously, (1) to boast about a depiction that made him look glamorous, and (2) to sue the publishers for defaming him. He chose to do some discreet boasting, mainly to reporters, late at night.

courts accept ignorance as a defense. If it can be shown that by using a real-life name, you have injured a real-life reputation, then you will pay. The law is right alongside the Bard, as quoted above on the question of purses and good names.

The author is safe if the named victim has no good name to lose. When Giles Foden lampooned Idi Amin in *The Last King of Scotland*, he was quite safe – even though the exiled Amin was still alive in Saudi Arabia. Had Foden ventured to undertake an author's tour in Uganda, when Dada was in power, the Foden liver would probably have ended up with the others in the Amin family refrigerator. There are worse things than court judgments. Ask John Dryden.

> **Wart hogs should sue for libel. It is a terrible name and they are fine fellows and devoted family men and it is rare to see on by himself; the little woman and the kiddies are usually close at hand.**
>
> Ilka Chase

The future of libel law There is evidence that libel law is fraying somewhat, allowing writers a bit more slack. The TV-led docudramas of Peter Morgan (*The Deal, Frost/Nixon, The Queen*), which feature living politicians – not always flatteringly – indicate some redrawing of the lines. *The Queen* is particularly indicative, since *lèse majesté* (taking the monarch's name in vain) has been, traditionally, one of the more life-threatening forms of libel (for the libeller).

Comedians have a licence that can carry over from the microphone to the page. Rik Mayall, the alternative comic, published a spoof autobiography, *Bigger than Hitler, Better than Christ*, in which he modestly confides a relationship with a Tony and Mrs. Blair, describing Cherie as biting the pillow in the ecstasy of their "adulteree" afternoons (with a mouth her size, "Rik" adds, she can "bite a lot of pillow").

Any "serious" allegation of this kind (about a QC, no less, married to a barrister) would have been ruination. The comedian – so long as we know he's a comedian – can get away with it.

The one RLP novelists can introduce into their fiction, *in propria persona* (none of that *roman-à-clef* awkwardness) is themselves. Writers like doing it, with a knowing nod and a wink, and the practice can be traced back at least as far as Tobias Smollett. It has become rampant in modern times. Martin Amis has great fun with a satirical self-portrait of "Martin Amis" in his 1984 novel, *Money*.

Libel remains one of the more dangerous yet interesting minefields surrounding the literary enterprise. Wise authors trip through it carefully.

the condensed idea
Literature can be as realistic as it likes – but not with real living people

44 Blasphemy

The law of blasphemous libel was abolished in Britain in May 2008. Over the previous three centuries, authors had enjoyed a fairly easy ride from its strictures. Traditionally it was directed against dissenters, the crazed and (most harshly) free thinkers – whose ranks supply many martyrs. The law, thought a dead letter well before 2008, was ingeniously revived for sectarian purposes to persecute (and successfully prosecute) minorities – notably gays and, in one landmark case, their literature.

Horrible origins One of the most horribly martyrized "blasphemers" in English history was the Bristol Quaker James Naylor, who rode into his home town in 1656 perpetrating what was construed to be a blasphemously satirical impersonation of Christ's entry into Jerusalem.

Despite Naylor's protesting that his act was "symbolic," he was hauled before the House of Commons and found guilty of blasphemy. Some MPs wanted him stoned, as Leviticus (24:16) instructed. By the generosity of the House (and six votes) he was spared death and the following sentence was passed instead:

> "James Naylor … shall be whipt by the hangman through the streets from Westminster to the Old Exchange, London … wearing a paper containing an inscription of his crimes; and that at the Old Exchange his tongue be bored through with a hot iron, and that he be there also stigmatised in the forehead with the letter 'B.' "

Naylor was flogged 318 times; he did not flinch as the brand was put on his forehead and the poker to his tongue. What was left of him was left to rot in solitary confinement at the pleasure of Parliament.

timeline

1656	1841	1886
James Naylor is corporally punished for the blasphemous representation of Christ riding into Jerusalem	Edward Moxon successfully prosecuted for blasphemy for republishing Shelley's poem *Queen Mab*	George William Foo imprisoned for blasp for articles publishe journal *The Freethin*

Such savagery abated over the years, although the authorities always retained the charge of blasphemy somewhere deep in their arsenal. It was invoked, typically, during periods when civil unrest was abroad. In 1841, Edward Moxon was found guilty of blasphemous libel for publishing Shelley's *Queen Mab*. Shelley was dead, and the poem was a juvenile effusion. None the less, wild lines by a hot-headed undergraduate could still rile the rulers of the realm.

> **Here I swear, and as I break my oath may ... eternity blast me, here I swear that never will I forgive Christianity!**
>
> **Percy Bysshe Shelley**

Blasphemy was dusted off by the authorities again in the 1880s, like the "hungry forties" a politically troubled decade. The editor of the *Freethinker* newspaper, George William Foote, was imprisoned for a year (in 1886 he published a fine memoir of the experience, *Prisoner for Blasphemy*).

The last successful prosecution, as it was fondly thought, was that of John William Gott, trouser salesman and free thinker, who got nine months' hard labor in 1922 for writing that Jesus entered Jerusalem (echoes of Naylor) "like a circus clown on the back of two donkeys." The hard labor killed him. He died a few days after his release.

The false end of blasphemy The tide of tolerance moved on, slowly. Not everyone was pleased. Mrs. Whitehouse, founder of the Viewers' and Listeners' Association, particularly lamented the liberating Theatre Act of 1968, as did her fellow moralists. The Lord Chamberlain's office of stage censorship had been very hot on blasphemy. Whitehouse sprang into action in June 1976 when *Gay News* (itself a child of the liberating Sexual Offences Act of 1967) published a full-page poem entitled "The Love that Dares to Speak its Name."

Tony Reeves's accompanying illustration was a main article of offence. It depicts a conventional Deposition from the Cross, with the difference that the lowering is being done by a Roman soldier endowed with what Philip Larkin would call "a tuberous cock and balls." The Roman goes on to sodomize himself with Christ's still erect member.

1977	1988	1989	2008
Gay News publishes "The Love that Dares to Speak its Name" and is successfully prosecuted for blasphemy	Salman Rushdie forced into hiding after publication of *The Satanic Verses*	Joss Marsh publishes *Word Crimes* a study of blaspherry and literature	The offence of blasphemy is removed from English law; it remains on the statute books in southern Ireland

Percy Bysshe Shelley, blasphemer

The following are the offensive lines from *Queen Mab*. They still pack a powerful punch:

I was an infant when my mother went
To see an atheist burned. She took me there.
The dark-robed priests were met around the pile;
The multitude was gazing silently;
And as the culprit passed with dauntless mien,
Tempered disdain in his unaltering eye,
Mixed with a quiet smile, shone calmly forth;
The thirsty fire crept round his manly limbs;
His resolute eyes were scorched to blindness soon;
His death-pang rent my heart! the insensate mob
Uttered a cry of triumph, and I wept.
"Weep not, child!" cried my mother, "for that man
Has said, 'There is no God.' "

Mrs. Whitehouse initiated a private prosecution for blasphemous libel in November, which was heard in July 1977. Defending counsel John Mortimer vainly protested that it was "as if we had been whisked in a time machine back to the middle ages."

In vain. The jury, by a ten-to-two verdict, found the defendant guilty. The judge, in sentencing the editor of *Gay News* to a hefty fine (which effectively killed the paper), gave his opinion that "this poem is quite appalling and is the most scurrilous profanity." Appeals were unsuccessful. Temporarily, at least, medievalism ruled.

In 2002, a public reading of the "The Love that Dares to Speak its Name" was carried out on the steps of St Martin-in-the-Fields church in Trafalgar Square. No action was taken by the authorities. But whatever deductions might have been drawn from the defiant act, blasphemy was anything but a dead letter.

> **❝I would like to inform all intrepid Muslims in the world that the author of the book *Satanic Verses*, which has been compiled, printed, and published in opposition to Islam, the Prophet, and the Qur'an, and those publishers who were aware of its contents, are sentenced to death.❞**
>
> The fatwa issued against Salman Rushdie

Blasphemy and Islam In 1989, British citizens in Bradford agitated – while publicly burning Salman Rushdie's *The Satanic Verses* – to have a charge of blasphemy brought against the novelist. Since Islam was not the established religion of the UK, the demand went nowhere. But violence ensued and blood was spilt across the globe. Rushdie's offence had been to suggest that the Koran might be, in places fictional (as, for example, in certain passages falsified by a scribe called "Salman").

The Satanic Verses was anathematized – a judgment upheld throughout much of the Islamic world, notably Iran. Drastic remedies were required to keep Rushdie safe from assassination.

Although blasphemy was abolished in the mainland UK in 2008, it still remains unabolished in Northern Ireland. And in 2009, southern Ireland, under intense lobbying by the Catholic Church, introduced a Defamation Act, which enshrined the offence "blasphemous libel." As the clash of civilizations heats up and multiculturalism (more significantly, multifaithism) takes deeper root, blasphemy – whether technically an offence in law or not – will, for a certainty, figure prominently in future literary history. The red-hot poker still glows.

the condensed idea
Natural selection forms new species

45 Permissiveness

The image that haunted moral conservatives of the 1960s and early 1970s was that of "floodgates" being thrown open to let in a tidal wave of filth. The permissive rot began with the obscenity-liberating "Jenkins Act" of 1959 (partnering the "Roth" legislation in the US), the Sexual Offences Act of 1967 (which decriminalized homosexual acts), and the abolition of the Lord Chamberlain's censorship of the English stage, in 1969. It seemed, by 1980, a clear victory for literary-cultural emancipation. "The permissive society," as Roy Jenkins complacently put it, "was the civilized society." The country, too, felt pleased with itself. It was good to be "civilized."

Brief heyday Viewed in the longer term, the civilization issue is less clear-cut than Jenkins would have had us believe. As visible external legal control was lifted, control was subtly internalized into the machineries of culture – often invisibly. New areas of "sensitivity" (and corresponding literary silences) emerged. Libertarians found themselves once again on the back foot.

By the end of the 1970s, after two decades of "permissiveness," claims for new controls (new censorships) were voiced. Feminism, which had broken through into a position of cultural authority (if not quite gender equality) with the formation of the National Organization for Women in 1966, was in the forefront of demands for new "enlightened" control. The movement's most eloquent polemicist, Andrea Dworkin, put the case forcefully: "The old [pre-1960] pornography industry was a right-wing industry; secret money, secret sex, secret promiscuity, secret buying and selling of women, secret profit, secret pleasure … the new pornography is a left-wing industry:

timeline

1711–12
Joseph Addison and Richard Steele launch *The Spectator*, intended to raise the tone of British society

1857
Britain's first obsenity legislatic The Lord Campbell Act

promoted by the boys of the sixties as simple pleasure, lusty fun, public fun." "New pornography" demanded new forms of censorship. QED.

At this point, in the 1980s, a moth-eaten term resurfaced from the lexicon of 1960s Maoist politics, "political correctness." The Great Helmsman had used the term unironically – as something to be aspired to by all good Chinese Communists. In Orwell's Newspeak it would have been a "doubleplusgood word." In its resurfaced form, PC was a pejorative, often applied with satirical contempt by the wilfully incorrect.

The new restrictiveness Whether called "PC" or "sensitivity," there was, demonstrably, a powerful new corrective force in play. The prehistory of Bret Easton Ellis's *American Psycho* illustrated its power. Ellis, one of the new "brat" generation of writers of the early 1990s, secured an advance of $300,000 from Simon and Schuster for the rights to the novel. A whistle-blower editor at the firm, appalled at the novel's misogyny (as she saw it), leaked the proofs to fellow feminists. In the face of concerted protest, Simon and Schuster revoked the contract (sacrificing an undisclosed portion of the massive advance). The novel went to Random House, under whose imprint it came out – reportedly in toned-down form.

Gender politics was one prime area in which new PC orthodoxies made themselves felt. Race was the other.

Philip Larkin had always been rather surprised that his poetry should be installed as a "set book" in the educational syllabuses of Britain. Of his poem "This Be the Verse," with its opening line, "They fuck you up, your mum and dad," he wryly wrote, "I fully expect to hear it recited by a thousand Girl Guides before I die." There was, as the century drew to a close, no problem with the four-letter word that had, before 1960, got so many writers into trouble.

> **"Women have burned their bras and put men in a literary straitjacket."**
> Anonymous (male) complaint about the suppression of *American Psycho*

1959–60	1981	1991	2000
Legislation in the US and the UK legitimizes literary expression previously deemed offensive	Andrea Dworkin publishes *Pornography: Men Possessing Women*	Johnson Bret Easton Ellis publishes *American Psycho*	Philip Roth publishes *The Human Stain*, an all-out attack on political correctness

No-no words

The increasing pressure of political correctness on published writing inspired a number of lexicons, or guidebooks to usage, many satirical. Joel Bleifuss's 2007 list (aided by Lott Hill) is typical. Some examples:

African-American: rather than "Black" (or, worse still, "black") or Negro. Jesse Jackson ordained the AA-word in 1988. Every American newspaper took note.

Boi: "used by young queer people to refer to either young gay males or young females who are presenting as males."

GLBTQ2IA: "the acronym for Gay, Lesbian, Bi, Transgendered, Queer, Questioning, Intersex, Allies of the foregoing."

Hir (*hirs*): "gender neutral for him and her."

Ze: "gender neutral for he or she."

School performances of "Romeo and Julian" (i.e., Juliet, corrected) during Lesbian Gay Bisexual Transgender History month in February 2009 were a sign of the times that caused dangerous rises in blood pressure in conservative quarters.

Larkin's views on race – which became public after his death in 1985 – were something else. His letters and private conversations, it emerged, were peppered with remarks such as that he and his consort Monica Jones, "don't go to [cricket] Test matches now, too many fucking niggers about."

The censorship of enlightenment Lisa Jardine, head of English at the University of London's Queen Mary College, announced in the *Guardian* that henceforth Larkin's poems "would be removed from the core curriculum." They did not sit easily "within our revised curriculum, which seeks to give all of our students, regardless of background, race or creed, a voice within British culture." It may have been obnoxious – but was Larkin's not also a voice?

The curriculum was being revised all over. In the decade following the civil rights legislation of 1964, Joseph Conrad's novella, *Heart of Darkness*, was installed as a central text on every literature course in the US. The West, however, had not read the work carefully enough.

> **❝I believe that political correctness can be a form of linguistic fascism, and it sends shivers down the spine of my generation who went to war against fascism.❞**
>
> **P. D. James**

Following Chinua Achebes" years-long campaign against Conrad as a hater and disparager of Africans the novel was viewed in a new light. The effect was explosive. Students marched on campuses carrying placards such as "Get your racist education at Stanford!" Conrad, like Larkin, was suddenly poison. Being African, Achebe could use the N-word with impunity, as could rap singers. White authors, however, could only handle it with the longest of tongs. Joining Conrad on the not-to-be prescribed list was Mark Twain's *Huckleberry Finn*, for its promiscuous use of the N-word.

There was, as the poet Tom Paulin vividly put it, a sewer running under the whited sepulchres of Anglo-American literature. Anthony Julius's 1995 polemic, *T. S. Eliot and Anti-Semitism*, traced the course of that cloacal tunnel to the most influential poet of the twentieth century. Would his works, too, be purged from the revised curriculum?

There was an inevitable impact on what authors felt free to write and publishers proper to publish in these newly enlightened times. Not all submitted. Philip Roth deplored the PC muzzle put, as he saw it, on their creative freedom. It was the writer's duty to work with the "human stain" – and if that meant misogyny, homophobia, neo-fascism, racism, so be it. The writer's motto should be *nihil humanum mihi alienum est*. Or, as Roth put it, "human beings live here."

the condensed idea
Watch your mouth

46 Literary Lies

Literature routinely sidesteps allegations of mendacity ("it's all lies") with the Sir Philip Sidney defense: "Now for the poet, he nothing affirmeth, and therefore never lieth." Lies and literature – a category error. There are, however, situations in which literature can be culpably caught out in what Huck Finn, self-servingly, calls "stretchers." Closely examined, they tell us something about how literature works.

Varieties One can list the varieties of literary lie on a spectrum of purest white to the deepest black:

1. Least culpable is authorial *gilding of the lily*. Wilkie Collins's novel, *The Woman in White*, was first serialized in Charles Dickens's journal, *All the Year Round*. According to Collins, "quite one third of *The Woman in White* was written before a title could be found for it." Dickens was desperate to begin serialization, but what could they call it? Collins was holed up, writing for his life, at Broadstairs, and after his day's labor, he went for a long walk along the cliffs. "As the sun went down," he recalled in later life, "I threw myself on the grass, contemplating the North Foreland lighthouse ... biting the end of my last cigar I apostrophised the building standing coldly and stiffly in the evening light, "You are ugly and stiff and awkward; you know you are: as stiff and as weird as my white woman." White woman! – woman in white! The title by Jove!" Correspondence shows that Collins actually sent in the title before a word was put to paper.

2. Closely connected to the lily-gilding lie is the *heroic lie*, in which an author exaggerates to make himself/herself grander in the reader's

timeline

1595	1859–60
Sir Philip Sidney asserts in his *Apology* that poetry "never lieth"	Wilkie Collins serializes *The Woman in White*, and perpetrates a white lie about the title

eyes. In his memoir, *A Million Little Pieces* – his chronicle of recovery from the depths of addiction – James Frey, in tough-guy mode, recalls drunken car crashes, being imprisoned for months on end, and the ingestion of enough booze and drugs to kill a woolly mammoth. Cybersleuthing among police reports by the Smoking Gun website gave the lie to much of what Frey wrote. No tough guy, but a wimp.

3. *Suppressio veri.* Jack London published what has traditionally been regarded as a ground-breakingly candid "alcoholic memoir," *John Barleycorn,* in 1913. He bares his soul to the reader. But in the chapters dealing with his early life, he does not disclose something that plausibly accelerated his mid-life descent into dipsomania. While a student at Berkeley, Jack discovered that his father was not the Civil War veteran John London, whose name he bore, but a "footloose astrologer" and rogue, William H. Chaney. London's suppression of the fact was both to save his blushes (bastardy was a painful stigma in 1913) and to protect his living relatives. An understandable lie – the author is not on oath to "tell the whole truth."

4. *The compositional lie.* Even people who have not read Anthony Burgess's fiction know that, on being diagnosed with terminal brain cancer in 1959, he dashed off five novels (to provide for his widow) in a year. They included his masterwork, *A Clockwork Orange.* Biographer Roger Lewis plausibly casts doubt on whether Burgess was actually at death's door. It makes a good story about a good story.

5. *Forgery.* There is a library of noble forgery in literature. One thinks of eighteenth-century writers like Thomas Chatterton, "the marvellous boy," who forged pseudo-medieval poems and when exposed, poisoned himself – ensuring that he and his forgeries

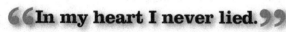

In my heart I never lied.

Blanche Dubois, in *A Streetcar Named Desire*

1960	2006	2008
Anthony Burgess claims to have written *A Clockwork Orange* under sentence of death from brain tumor	James Frey apologizes for the mis-statements in his alcoholic memoir, *A Million Little Pieces*	Herman Rosenblat enjoys huge commercial success with *Angel at the Fence,* later discovered to be fiction

The MacLeod case

Literary forgery is always interesting, because such clever and inventive people commit the crime. William Sharp, a rather dull Victorian of impeccable morality, invented the best-selling novelist (his cousin, he alleged) Fiona MacLeod – a wild child of the Scottish heather. He even invented a *Who's Who* entry for her, and arranged press conferences that – at the last moment – the authoress would regretfully have to cancel (a storm in the mountains or something). Fiona clearly released a pent-up part of Sharp himself. The forgery was creative. It took in everyone for years. Who, though, was the liar? Stuffy old Sharp or bonny Miss MacLeod?

became immortal. Or James McPherson, who forged Scottish "Ossian" epics, dug up – he claimed – from his country's heroic-Gaelic prehistory. Both these forgers can be argued to have produced works of genuine, if perverse, literary merit. Less meritorious is Jerzy Kosinski. A Polish Holocaust survivor, Kosinski – aided by fake documentation – came to the US in his early twenties. Ten years later, he was a best-selling and prize-winning novelist. His early fiction has plausibly been shown to be ghost-written by other hands and plagiaristic. More recently, J. T. LeRoy, a young HIV-positive former drug addict, was caught out writing best-selling fiction under the false identity of "Laura Albert" (including the meaningfully entitled *The Heart Is Deceitful Above All Things*). LeRoy had got by for years hustling in the streets of New York and this was just another profitable scam. What is fascinating about the LeRoy case is that it lays bare the motive behind much literary lying – the need to prove that one is smarter than those suckers, the reading public.

6. *Lies that really hurt.* After the 9/11 atrocity across the river in Manhattan, the then laureate of New Jersey Imamu Amiri Baraka penned a poem called "Somebody Blew Up America." It contained the verse:

> *Who know why five Israelis was filming the explosion*
> *And cracking they sides at the notion?*
> *Who knew the World Trade Center was gonna get bombed*

> **There isn't a great deal of difference between fact and fiction. It's just how you choose to tell a story.**
>
> James Frey, after his "fact" was revealed as "fiction"

Who told 4,000 Israeli workers at the Twin Towers
To stay home that day
Why did Sharon stay away?

Things were not helped by Baraka explaining on his website, "I was not saying Israel was *responsible* for the attack, but that they 'knew' and that our own counterfeit president did too."

The very worst literary lying Fabricated Holocaust memoirs are similarly obnoxious. In 2008, Herman Rosenblat had a huge commercial success with his concentration camp romance, *Angel at the Fence*. While incarcerated at Buchenwald, Rosenblat recalled, he had met at the wire a young girl, who gave him an apple every day. Twelve years later, a survivor, he met "Roma" on a blind date. Miraculously, she was the apple-a-day girl. They married and lived happily ever after. It was proved false. The book was subsequently repackaged as a "novel," *Apple*, in which, as Sidney would say, nothing was "affirmed."

Rosenblat (now rich) offered the lame excuse: "Why did I do that and write the story with the girl and the apple? Because I wanted to bring happiness to people." The unhappy effect of his fibs was to undermine the veracity of genuine Holocaust memoirs. A wholly black literary lie.

the condensed idea
Sometimes literature is just so much fiction

47 Ghost-Writers

If plagiarism and forgery are capital crimes that can be condemned as treachery against literature, "ghost-writing" counts as a mere misdemeanor. Something equivalent to a moving traffic violation: wrong but not criminal. It's a paradox that the more important the politician, the less we expect him or her to write their own speeches. Yet, paradoxically, it's different with literature. We can get very annoyed when we discover that some wizard of Oz, out of sight behind the scenes, has been pulling the authorial strings.

Team writing Ghost-writing can be found as far back as we can track literature itself. The oldest major work in the English canon, *Beowulf*, is anonymous. But a tenth-century monk took it on himself to transcribe the oral (pagan) work, dutifully Christianizing as he went. He's the first ghost we know about – and, like all of his spectral kind, is invisible to the human eye. Whoever he was, Anglo-Saxonists bless him.

Most admirable among the species is the "helping hand" ghost. When Sir Walter Scott suffered a calamitous stroke, his son-in-law (and fellow novelist) J. G. Lockhart took over and completed the work in progress (*Count Robert of Paris*), taking no public credit for his filial act. On his deathbed, Wilkie Collins entrusted the completion of his novel in progress (*Blind Love*) to his friend Walter Besant. One would like to think that Wilkie's actual ghost looked benignly on when the work was published.

Alexandre Dumas, for a wager of 100 louis (a goodly sum in those days), wrote a novel (*Le Chevalier de Maison Rouge*) in three days flat. More economically, he elsewhere used scores of *assistantes*. One of

timeline

c.900	1621	1832
Beowulf, the work of many unidentified minds and hands, is consigned to vellum	Thomas Middleton's adaptation of *Measure for Measure* is printed as Shakespeare's work	*Count Robert of Paris*, written by his son-in-l published under the d Walter Scott's name

them, Auguste Maquet, sued on the grounds that his ghostly (and wholly unacknowledged) hand was largely responsible for *The Three Musketeers* and *The Count of Monte Cristo* (the spat was made into a 2010 film, *L'Autre Dumas*).

The professionalization of the "ghost" "Assisting" is a rather colorless description. The term "ghost-writing," and a profitable commercial line of business based on it, was invented by the literary entrepreneur Christy Walsh in the 1920s. His main interest was "sports celebrity" memoirs by the likes of Babe Ruth.

The 1920s was also the period when the "creative editor" came to the fore. Foremost among these was Maxwell Perkins. Perkins, a former newspaperman, joined Scribner's in 1910 and took over a senior editorial role four years later. Scott Fitzgerald was his first significant "discovery."

American literature has always valued intrusive editors more than its British counterpart. Perkins was among the most brilliantly intrusive. More importantly, as a commissioning editor, he cultivated new voices in American fiction (sometimes against the prejudices of the crusty patriarch of the house, Charles Scribner). Fitzgerald brought his friends Ernest Hemingway and Ring Lardner to Scribner's and Perkins's nurturing care. In 1928, Perkins took on his greatest editorial challenge with the hugely voluminous work of Thomas Wolfe. He was instrumental in hacking works such as *Look Homeward Angel* into shape. "In all my life, until I met you, I never had a friend," Wolfe wrote. Scott Fitzgerald, in a letter to Wolfe, called Perkins our common parent. Could one also call him their "ghost?"

> **I hear it's a terrific book! One of these days I'm going to read it myself.**
> **Ronald Reagan, on his autobiography**

1844	1929	1986	2007
Auguste Maquet claims to have been a principal author of Dumas's *The Three Musketeers*	Thomas Wolfe's *Look Homeward Angel* published, after drastic editing by Maxwell Perkins	V. C. Andrews dies, but writes more novels as a dead author than she did when alive	Robert Harris's *The Ghost* (first novel with a ghost-writer hero) is published to best-selling success

ghost riders on the page

Graham Lord's flagrantly "unauthorized" biography of Dick Francis, published in 1999, alleged outright that the author's university-educated wife Mary ghosted every one of the best-selling novels of the turf. According to Lord, she confirmed his thesis, telling him that her authorship was suppressed in order to preserve the "taut ... masculine" feel of the works. Two pieces of evidence support Lord. First is the fact that the Francises did not sue him. Secondly, on Mary's death in 2000, Francis "retired" from writing. He came back, eight years later, in "collaboration" with his son, Felix. But what does it matter? Horses don't win races by themselves: jockeys don't win races by themselves – they win them in partnership. Why shouldn't it be the same with novels? He was the horse, she was the jockey.

Modern times   The "invisible hand" of literature has become ever busier in the last 50 years. Two varieties of ghosting predominate, "Exploiting the Brand" and "Celebrity Books."

As regards the first, ghosting is the rational commercial response to two shortcomings in traditional authorship. One is that the most valuable authors can't produce enough, fast enough, to satisfy the market. The other is that (damn them) they die. Tom Clancy (still living) pastes his name happily on works by a platoon of writers as invisible to the reader's eye as his Ghost Recon force is to the enemy they invariably defeat. As Clancy's publisher unblushingly puts it: "Tom Clancy creates the ideas for these series, and the writers execute Clancy's ideas. All these titles are subject to Clancy's overall editorial supervision." The output of the Clancy factory is only equaled, in its selling clout, by the output of the James Patterson factory.

Publishers are unwilling to let a best-selling author go quietly to the grave. They are made to ride out, corpses in the saddle, like Charlton Heston at the end of the movie *El Cid*. The website AllBookstores.com lists some 200 authors who have "written" posthumously. Currently there is a bit of a fuss about Robert Ludlum, whose after-death output looks likely to exceed what he produced while still a warm body.

> **❝I don't believe that the readers who enjoy these stories care who actually does the typing, any more than they care whether Mr Kipling actually bakes his own cakes.❞**
>
> Andrew Crofts, ghost writer

But the outright winner in the literary El Cid stakes must be V. C. Andrews. Andrews only got into print in 1979 with a paperback original, *Flowers in the Attic*, published (after much carving on the editorial block) by Pocket Books. She was 56 years old. It was a runaway super-seller and founded a new line of Gothic fiction – the "children in jeopardy" genre. Seven years after *Flowers in the Attic*, Andrews died of cancer, aged 62. Novels, none the less, kept on pulsing out after her death under the auspices of the estate. The ghost in the Andrews machine was, after some years, discovered to be Andrew Neiderman. His name does not appear on the Andrews copyright pages. Louis L'Amour books similarly continued to gallop into the bestseller lists long after he had gone to his rest. Ghost-writers in the sky were suspected.

Celebrity "franchise" books are typically justified by the fact that celebs are too busy to write and can't write anyway. No one expects Katie Price (Jordan) to write her own novels any more than they expect her to sew the clothes she models. As for living, said Marie Antoinette, we have our servants for that. Jordan has the estimable ghost-writer Rebecca Farnworth.

the condensed idea
The thing about ghosts is that you can't see them

48 Fanfic

What, precisely, is fanfic ("fanfiction," "FF")? According to the most authoritative book on the subject, Sheenagh Pugh's *The Democratic Genre*, it's writing by fans who either want more of their favorite works; or who want more *from* their favorite works.

In the past, new literary forms were as rare as new vices (the emperor Heliogabulus offered a prize for any Roman citizen who could come up with one – it was, one is told, never claimed). No more. In the unregulated hothouse that is the Internet, new literary life forms appear and change faster than fruit flies mutate. Fanfic is one of literature's Web-engendered mutations. It looks like a species that will survive and grow. What will that mean for traditional literary life forms?

Fanfic's habitat The environment in which fanfic thrives is the web's "Wild West" freedom from the copyright ownership that shackles the store-bought codex book. The historian Michel de Certeau has neatly called it "textual poaching." It's an error, however, to think of it as narrative anarchy. Fanfic has elaborate rules about such things as "going AU" (i.e., "alternative universe"), "respect for canon," and "character rape" (gross disrespect). It attaches most powerfully to fantasy and science fiction writing. There are also vigorous growth areas around classic fiction. "The Republic of Pemberley," for example (www.pemberley.co.uk), dedicated to "obsessive" lovers of Jane Austen, has a "Bits of Ivory" annexe in which fans devise sequels to the six novels.

Slashfic

One of the interesting variants of fanfic is slash(fic). The term "slash" signals unconventional (i.e., homosexual) relationships, as opposed to the soothingly conventional (heterosexual) ampersand of, say, "Fun with Dick & Jane." A different kind of fun, that is. Slash fiction originated in the dark ages (computerwise) with *Star Trek*. A "Trekkie" cult developed around the TV series. Fans *lived* the series. *Star Trek* fanfic was a by-product that made a pretty penny for its paperback publishers. And some Trekkies boldly went further – they fantasized gay shenanigans between, for example, Kirk and Spock and wrote up their fantasies as stories in hand-circulated underground fanzines. Slash fiction was born. It has since tended to gravitate toward pop-music celebrities.

Jane Austen won't complain. But living authors have a range of views on this "most sincere" form of literary flattery. Lois McMaster Bujold declares on the website dedicated to her fanfic, "I am a fanfic friendly author," adding, "I myself wrote fanfic in my teens." But she won't read it nowadays lest she is sued for stealing from fellow authors.

The current queen of vampire fiction, Anne Rice, thinks differently. She says, "I do not allow fan fiction. My characters are copyrighted. It upsets me terribly to even think about fan fiction." J. K. Rowling (whose fandomain is now cosmically large), however, is tolerant – although not of the raunchier imaginings that Harry Potter has inspired, or of anything with a tincture of paedophilia to it.

Fanfic is, as Pugh's title indicates, democratic. It's like the medieval ballad, and largely anonymous or pseudonymous. But not, perhaps, for much longer. In addition to service-provider controls and infuriated authors, another threat is emerging from within the genre – namely the Big Name Fan (BNF).

2000
Anne Rice posts a warning, "I do not allow fan fiction." Violators are harassed

2001
Cassandra Claire begins posting on her website *The Very Secret Diaries*, based on Tolkien's *Lord of the Rings*

2005
Sheenagh Pugh's *The Democratic Genre* published, defining the nature and rules of fanfic

"Fanon."

Fanspeak for the fanfic canon

The Biggest Name Fan currently writing is Cassandra ("Cassie") Claire. It's a nom-de-web – in real life, Claire is a published nonfiction writer. So far she has produced two epic works of fanfic. *The Very Secret Diaries of Middle Earth* was launched on her website in late 2001. It features the ruminations of a Tolkienian outrider, Aragorn (half-Hamlet, half-Adrian Mole). The *VSD* series has established itself as a cult classic, spawning, inevitably, its own fandom. She has also web-penned a "Draco" trilogy, based on Draco Malfoy. This Rowlingiad, which would, in printed form, run to 1,000 pages, has been, like the *VSD*, phenomenally successful and much translated.

It is important to distinguish fanfic from traditional and conventional varieties of narrative. Fiction typically conforms to commercial circuits of origination (a work is "commissioned" or "accepted" by a paymaster of some kind), production (a work is commercially printed), and distribution, through bookshops, libraries or (more recently) web-based retailers such as Amazon.

Fanfic is, by contrast, coterie-generated and coterie-circulated material. It is not commissioned, nor is it paid for, nor is it reviewed, nor is it bought. It is not, as the term is usually applied, published. It is fiction written principally for the delectation of a readership of those who also, most of them, write such fiction. Its status, in literary terms, is akin to the manuscripts exchanged, for mutual criticism, in a creative writing class. The "shared" aspect of fanfic is a primary feature. It is not a commodity. It is neither commercial nor professional. It is never traded in any kind of market. In many ways it is closer to literary conversation than to the printed word.

The historical origins of fanfic are, broadly speaking, twofold. The more venerable is the fanzine. These were coterie-generated magazines by fans – typically of science fiction. They existed outside the normal circuits of literary production and consumption. They were typically run off on Gestetner copiers, or by carbon paper. They were not sold – although, occasionally, monetary subscription (i.e., membership fees) might be involved to cover costs. Fanzines can be traced back to the 1930s. They often contained *hommage* fiction, as a tribute to particularly admired classic texts.

Fanfic and the computerization of literary culture The second more recent generator and distributor of fanfic is the computer chatroom. These came on the scene in the 1980s, when costless access to the web via the home computer became widespread. The chatroom

❝Unleash Your Imagination!❞

Slogan of the largest fanfic archive, www.fanfiction.net

(later blog and website) has effectively replaced the fanzine. It has also explosively expanded the activity into many thousands of "fandoms."

Fanfic is "affiliation group writing." It involves interactivities, and collectivities (and, often, jealously preserved privacies), which set it apart from what one normally associates with the term "fiction." If the printed novel is in the public domain, fanfic rarely, if ever, emerges from its member-restricted clubs. Finding it is often difficult, requiring registration and password-activated entry.

The standard histories of fanfic usually see it as originating as fan exchanges around cult TV series such as *Star Trek*, or *Buffy the Vampire Slayer*; and cult book-based series, such as "Harry Potter," *Lord of the Rings*, "Discworld," and "Twilight." Although the participatory community was, initially, largely male and juvenile, in recent years the gender and age mix has balanced out.

The essence of fanfic is that it's free. It has the same relationship to the printed novel that a jazz solo does to sheet music (think John Coltrane versus Julie Andrews on "My Favorite Things"). Fanfic can only work on the Web because it's outlaw territory. Does fanfic have its Coltranes? Not yet. Is it the "reader-driven" future of fiction? Perhaps.

the condensed idea
You can publish on the web what you can't print on the page

49 The e-Book

If a poll had been taken in the mid-1960s as to who, currently, was the purveyor of the biggest ideas around, the winner, in all probability, would have been Marshall McLuhan. In the *Gutenberg Galaxy* (his groundbreaking monograph), McLuhan argued that the Western world, after five centuries, was exiting from print culture into something entirely new. What that "new" might be he did not precisely define. Instead he focused on the means by which new culture would be delivered. We are living in an era when those systems are changing faster, and more radically, than ever before.

McLuhan's vision realized? A lover of epigram, McLuhan's biggest idea was expressed as the paradox "the medium is the message." It was punningly glossed as the title of a later, best-selling book, *The Medium is the Massage* (i.e., "mass-age," as well as "manipulator"). For McLuhan, electronic media were, effectively, new "senses." The reader of the future would be "bionic."

McLuhan's work generated a mass cult following. It had the effect of switching attention from "what" to "how" in the discipline that later formed as "media studies" (less sexily, "communication studies"). The new media- connected world would, McLuhan prophesied, coalesce into one "global village." He made this prediction three decades before the Internet became a universal facility. Within the McLuhanite village, communication would be intimately close, planetary in reach. The trend was, in the 1960s, already evident in the worldwide market for popular music. In 1967, the year of love, the Inuit in his igloo and the Muscovite in her dacha probably concurred with Allen Ginsberg that Liverpool, home of the Beatles, was the center of the universe.

timeline

1450s
Johannes Gutenberg prints bibles in Mainz, Germany

1962
Marshall McLuhan publish *The Gutenberg Galaxy: Th Making of Typographic M*

McLuhan's impact on the thinking of his time was explosive, but short-lived. The technological determinism was utopian, and neglected content in favor of the systems by which it was delivered. Ideology and a host of immaterial factors were blanked out by McLuhan's fascinations. He made people think, and look at, mankind's new toys – then mankind moved on and left McLuhanism behind.

Hot or cold? Some of McLuhan's ideas remain thought-provoking. One particularly, where the e-book is concerned. Among various kinds of media and communications, he drew a distinction between what he called "hot" and "cool." It was analogous, he admitted, to the way jazz was currently categorized.

In the 1960s, it was cool to be "cool." It was the cool media (as he saw them) that particularly interested McLuhan. This was how he divided and partnered the two kinds:

HOT	COOL
radio	telephone
printed word	spoken word
photographs	comics and cartoons
movies	TV
lectures	seminars

The difference, he explained, inheres in two things: the "thickness" of the message transmitted and, most importantly, the degree of active participation the medium demanded. As he put it, *hot* media were packed to overflowing with data, or message content. *Cool* data, by contrast, were those which required the audience / reader / spectator to fill in the gaps. Their participation quotient was higher.

As McLuhan modeled it, you cannot stop or start or shape a radio transmission, or a cinema-shown film. A photograph is hot – its message is unambiguous. The reader, however, has to do the work to make a comic or a cartoon meaningful.

2006	**2007**	**2009**
Sony Reader (e-book) launched in the US	Amazon launch the Kindle e-reader in the US	Schwarzenegger announces that e-books will replace printed textbooks in California's schools

The reader as cyborg

Arnold Schwarzenegger may, in future histories of the book, find himself alongside Gutenberg. It was the Governor of California who decreed that henceforth textbooks in schools should be replaced by e-books, on which material could be downloaded. It was economically rational. But increasingly psychologists were speculating that these new access systems were not merely changing the ways in which young brains received information; they might be changing those young brains physiologically. In the British House of Lords, in February 2009, Lady Greenfield, professor of synaptic pharmacology at Lincoln College, Oxford, warned that web-based networking was creating a culture "devoid of cohesive narrative and long-term significance. As a consequence, the mid-21st-century mind might almost be infantilized, characterized by short attention spans, sensationalism, inability to empathise and a shaky sense of identity."

Three decades later – what with iPod, Skype, cell phones, Tivo, iTunes. Photoshop and iPhones – the media are evolved well beyond what was seen as excitingly new (color TV! Wow!) in 1968. Above all, the interactivity that McLuhan perceived as the distinguishing mark of the cool is now much more available.

Without getting into the theologies of McLuhanism (and, for all the epigrams he threw at it, he never succeeded in making the hot/cool thing entirely clear), he was surely right in suggesting that media are not neutral conduits. Which brings one to something that McLuhan (who died in 1980) never lived to see. Namely the e-book. Are the Kindle and the Sony e-reader hot or cool?

Before answering the question, it's worth invoking another McLuhanism – what he niftily called "rear-mirrorism." What he meant by this is that we always see the new in terms of the old. When, for example, it appeared in the late fifteenth century, the printed book was seen as a new form of manuscript codex (to the untrained eye, it is almost impossible to distinguish Gutenberg's print from the script it was in the process of exterminating). Once established, the printed codex book proved astonishingly durable. There are few other items of medieval technology which have lasted as unchangingly. If Gutenberg could be teleported into a current Barnes & Noble, or Waterstone's, he would be gratified by the monuments to his ingenuity which he saw on the shelves.

In fact the e-book is much more than a book. Among other things, it's an archive. Not a library book, but a book library. Secondly, it is a device for receiving and transmitting texts, not merely delivering them. Thirdly, it is a formatting device. Buy a book from a bookshop and you are lumbered with the typography and font size. More novels are read by old eyes than by young. Large print is e-book available.

The future of the e-book That's what it can do now. The e-book has daunting potential. In the very near future it will, for example, allow sound tracks – as in movies. Or voice-over (what does Ian McEwan's voice sound like, reading his own work?). Illustration can be added. Fan fiction liberties can be taken. Above all, annotation can be appended or inserted. If (as in William Gibson's 2008 novel *Spook Country*) the action opens in the Mondrian Hotel, on Los Angeles" Sunset Strip, that fine establishment can be flicked in, visually. This kind of annotation is already being done, on the web, to Gibson's fiction by fans. In the future it will be packed alongside the text itself.

The e-book of the near future, it is safe to say, will need as much instruction and tuition in using it as driving an automobile. And, like the automobile, it will revolutionize.

the condensed idea
Media maketh literature

50 Literary Inundation

One of the great scientific breakthroughs of the last 30 years has been the invention and manufacture of ever more powerful telescopes. The new VLA (very large array) apparatuses, and telescopes like the Hubble in space, have led to extraordinary advances in knowledge about the heavens. But along with the excitement, every time a new telescope has its "first light," the astronomer suppresses a small shudder. The amount of information these technological marvels send back, as their range stretches to the rim of the universe, is crushing: it's like doing marine studies in a tsunami. Literature, in the age of the World Wide Web, the digitized archive and the e-book faces something similar. Inundation.

Can we survive it? "Tsunami" is not hyperbole. There is, in the first decades of the twenty-first century, more new fiction, poetry and literary criticism coming out in a week than even the most culturally athletic reader could cover in a year. In Shakespeare's time there were, it is estimated, some 2,000 volumes in print. He, and other "well-read" men of his time (few women, alas), probably knew pretty well all there was worth knowing – particularly if, like Shakespeare, you had Latin and French.

What does it mean to be "well read" today? The Google Library Project makes available some 15 million books, all just a couple of clicks away, many of them cost-free. There are three times as many

timeline

1757
George II gives the British Museum the privilege of "copyright receipt"

1974
Ray Kurzweil markets Optic Character Recognition syst making Internet publicatio efficient

> ## ❝We are drowning in information but starved for knowledge.❞
> ### John Naisbitt

new books published every year as were published as recently as the 1980s. We are faced with the paradox that our ignorance (with the mass of books necessarily unread by us) is growing faster than our knowledge. It is the sorcerer's apprentice deluge. This is not a new problem, but the scale of it is terrifyingly new.

Ways forward. Perhaps   There are three plausible solutions.

1. *Find your comfort zone and camp out there.* The first, and least adventurous, response to the impossible surplus is simply to fall into one's comfortable genre groove. Read, that is, nothing except science fiction, or murder mysteries, or Mills and Boon romance, or "classic fiction," or poetry. Many who take this option are fearsomely well read within the tight frame of the relatively small territory they have selected. As a strategy, however, it's goldfish bowls and oceans.

2. *Discriminate!* In the middle years of the twentieth century, as the surplus first became worrisome, a different winnowing strategy was fashionable. It promulgated the virtue of "discrimination." Only the best was good enough to invest one's precious time in. This was the era of "must-read" lists, whose main function was to create "don't waste your time on this" lists. The problem with this strategy was that it depended on authority. It was only those who had taken on the heroic task of plunging, discriminatingly, into the mass who could pass on the fruits of their efforts to lesser beings. The 1930s and 1940s was the heyday of the dictatorial literary critic. The necessity of reader obedience to such "leaders" was demanded, without mincing of words, by F. R. Leavis (arguably a critic as dictatorial as Stalin):

   > "In any period it is upon a very small minority that the discerning appreciation of art and literature depends: it is (apart from cases of the simple and familiar) only a few who

1989	1996	2001	2006
Tim Berners Lee writes the proposal for what, five years later, will become the World Wide Web	Google Books Library Project launched; by 2010 it will offer an estimated 15m volumes	First Wikipedia article posted online	Chris Anderson, editor of Wired magazine, publishes *The Long Tail*

are capable of unprompted, first-hand judgement.... Upon this minority depends our power of profiting by the finest human experience of the past; they keep alive the subtlest and most perishable parts of the tradition. Upon them depend the implicit standards that order the finer living of an age, the sense that this is worth more than that, this rather than that is the direction in which to go."

3. *The long tail.* Dictatorship – in literary matters – is nowadays much out of fashion. What is currently fashionable is the so-called long tail strategy, advocated by Chris Anderson. Anderson first outlined his creative solution to the surplus in an article in the magazine *Wired*, and later in a best-selling book.

Anderson's starting point was the unprecedentedly convenient electronic cataloguing and archival systems, which made possible adventurous map-making. The "long tail" approach did not mean keeping within frontiers (like the narcotic genre-followers) but

The end of literature?

In 1992, the historian Francis Fukuyama caused a great stir with his thesis that history had come to an end with the fall of Communism. As he put it: "What we may be witnessing is not just the end of the Cold War, or the passing of a particular period of postwar history, but the end of history as such: that is, the end point of mankind's ideological evolution and the universalization of Western liberal democracy as the final form of human government."

There were predictable squeals of denial. But could one make a similar case that the core beliefs that created literature – made it something special – were also "ending" with the imminent death of the book? Could some Heinrich Heine of the future proclaim, grandly, "where digital files are erased, men are erased?" It would not have the ring of "where books are burned, men are burned." Will the "information age" swallow up the great half-millennium of literature, dependent as it has been on the codex book?

"Life is a series of collisions with the future."
Jose Ortega y Gasset

mapping out whole new, but not dauntingly large, territories, as a kind of mosaic of freshly discovered discriminations. The new taxonomies and stores of cultural wares represented, Anderson hypothesized an entirely new cultural playground—a gigantic smorgasbord in which the onus was on the skill, and idiosyncrasy, of the consumer, no two of whom would pile their plates identically. There is, of course, a significant difference. Few of us need instruction as to how to load our plate at the help-yourself-buffet. Negotiating the huge unstandardized sources of learning, information, scholarship and entertainment now on offer is something very different.

The future is here Will we drown in the deluge of readable matter about to descend on us, or will we – as Anderson optimistically prophesies – learn to surf on it? One thing is clear: the literary environment of the future will be different. And, like the current global warming, the change is happening much faster than in the past. More books are available than ever before, but bookshops and libraries are closing faster than at any time since the printed book appeared on the scene 500 years ago. Delivery systems are changing. With them, history suggests, what is delivered and how it is consumed must change as well. The main problem for the readers of the future was articulated by Arthur Schopenhauer 150 years ago. "Buying books would be a good thing if one could also buy the time to read them in!"

the condensed idea
What you are reading may not be a book, but a coffin.

Glossary

Alliteration: a device used principally in poetry, in which repetition of consonants at the beginning of words is employed for linkage. *Assonance* refers to repetition, or near repetition, of syllables, usually within a series of words. *Onomatopoeia* refers to words echoing actual sounds. All three devices are manifest in the following verse from Tennyson's poem, "Come Down, O Maid:"

> Sweeter thy voice, but
>   every sound is sweet
> Myriads of rivulets,
>   hurrying through the
>   lawn,
> The moan of doves in
>   immemorial elms,
> And murmuring of
>   innumerable bees.

Antagonist: the character who opposes the *protagonist* in the action of a play, or narrative (from the Greek *agon*, meaning "contest").

Anticlimax: not, as commonly misused, that which comes *before* a climax ("ante-climax"), but that which deflates or diminishes a climax. Typically a fault in literary art (e.g., if the villain in a "whodunnit" is disclosed prematurely to the reader).

Aphorism: a compressed thought – similar to the *epigram* or *maxim*; e.g., Shakespeare's "All the World's a Stage."

Ballad: originally music and song that was danced to (as in "ballet"). Now more loosely applied to lyrics, whether or not set to music.

Bathos: a deliberate, or accidental, lowering of the literary tone – common in burlesque and mock epic (for example, the "heroic" urination contest in Pope's *The Dunciad*).

Belles-lettres: literally "fine writing," or "stylishness." Sometimes used to describe a corpus, or body of literature (the first English department, at Edinburgh University in the eighteenth century, was designated a "Department of Rhetoric and Belles Lettres").

Bildungsroman: novels that depict the growth of a character from childhood to maturity. *David Copperfield* is a notable example.

Blank verse: the favorite metrical form in English poetry – a ten-syllable (*decasyllabic*) line, with alternating weak and strong (*iambic*) stress. It is unrhymed, unlike the *couplet*. "To be or not to be, that is the question" is blank verse.

Deus ex machina: a term used by Aristotle (scornfully) to describe an artificial, or factitious, solution to some complex narrative or dramatic situation. For example, "with one bound Jim was free." It literally means the gods descending, in a basket, to rescue the imperiled hero.

Doggerel: "low" or degraded verse.

Dystopia: The opposite of "utopia" – an ideal state. Classic dystopia fictions are George Orwell's *Nineteen Eighty-Four*, and Aldous Huxley's *Brave New World*. The root term, utopia (it means "nowhere"), was invented by Sir Thomas More in his pioneering work in the genre, in 1516.

Elegy: literature, typically in verse, of grief and bereavement. A famous example is Milton's poem on his dead fellow-poet, Edward King, *Lycidas*.

Epigraph: a "paratextual" short passage, at the head of a work, often allusive to other literary works, set typically on its own page, summing up the contents that follow. For example the epigraph to Mary Shelley's *Frankenstein* (from Milton's *Paradise Lost*):

> Did I request thee, Maker, from my clay
> To mould me man, Did I
>   solicit thee
> From darkness to promote
>   me?

Epistle: Literally (from the Latin) "letter" – as in correspondence. The Horatian Epistle was a favorite form of poetry in the eighteenth century (particularly with Alexander Pope), as was the epistolary novel – or narrative in letters – which, notably, Samuel Richardson specialized in.

Euphuism: a style pioneered by the writer John Lyly's *Euphues* in the seventeenth century, marked by circumlocution, elaboration, and an unwillingness to say anything directly. Shakespeare parodies it in the person of the fop Osric, in *Hamlet*. Euphemism is close in meaning to *periphrasis* – roundabout expression (e.g., "finny tribe" for "fish").

Exposition: that section (usually the opening section) of a drama or narrative that lays out the antecedent facts that the audience, or reader, must know?

Haiku: a Japanese poetic form of great attraction to imagist schools of poetry. It is, as practiced in English, nonideographic, one to three short lines. Extreme, poignant compression is its characteristic.

Hubris: a term used by Aristotle to describe, in tragedy, that pride that goes before the inevitable fall, or reversal of fortune (*peripeteia*). It relates to what Aristotle calls *hamartia* – loosely translated as the hero's "tragic flaw," or shortcoming.

Indeterminacy: a term applied principally to contemporary literature that avoids easy conclusions, summary or closures. The French *nouveau roman* ("new novel") is a prime example of indeterminacy, or "openness."

In medias res: literally "in the middle of things." Aristotle notes that epic typically opens in the middle. In modern literature, the "flashback" often accompanies literature that opens *in media res*.

Juxtaposition: the placement of two things, not obviously connected, close together. In Pope's *The Rape of the Lock*, for example, the description of the objects on the beauty, Belinda's dressing table:

Here Files of Pins extend
　their shining Rows,
Puffs, Powders, Patches,
　Bibles, Billet-doux

Laureate: derived from the laurels placed on the brow of the winner in ancient Greek literary tournaments, it is now principally applied to the winners of major prizes, such as the Nobel, or writers with official appointments, such as the English monarch's poet laureate.

Litotes: literally "understatement" (from the Greek meaning "plain," or "simple") – a powerful ironic device; as in, for example, "Houston, we have a problem."

Magic realism: a term current in Germany in the 1920s, which has been applied to a major genre of late-twentieth-century fiction, of whom the most famous exponent is Salman Rushdie.

Metonymy: the substitution of one thing to describe another – as, for example, "the press" for the newspaper industry. It is close in application to *synechdoche*, in which the part stands for the whole – as in "all hands on deck."

Mise en scène: from the French, literally scene-setting: bringing the reader, or audience, up to speed.

Novella: a work of fiction longer than a short story, but shorter than a novel. Conrad's *Heart of Darkness* is an example. Not to be confused with *novelette*, which is pejorative and dismissive.

Ode: a term that in ancient literature involved a precise architecture but in modern verse suggests spontaneity and unmeditated response, as in Shelley's *Ode to the West Wind*.

Parable: a tale, or anecdote, with a central moral or religious meaning. Bunyan's *The Pilgrim's Progress* can be read as an extended parable on the human condition.

Paratactic: from the Greek, it describes poetry, or prose, that lacks logical *syntactic* or grammatical joins.

Personification: the device by which things are described as if they were people.

Realism: one of the most contentious terms in literature – and one that is used by both creative writers and critics. As a literary ideal, and topic of contention, realism became central in the nineteenth century, with the aim of depicting the actual world as it really was: antiromantically. But realism operates within, typically, a fictional framework. The result was what the poet Marianne Moore wittily called "imaginary gardens with real toads in them."

Rhetoric: language used principally to persuade, rather than to prove a point.

Roman-à-clef: from the French, literally "novel with a key" – that is to say, a novel in which "originals" (characters or situations) are transparently recognizable to the knowing reader. *Primary Colors* (see p. 84) is a good example.

Simile: a device in which two things, not naturally conjoined, are compared, as in "my love is like a red, red rose."

Syntax: in grammar, the connectivity of parts of speech. It is also extended to mean the ways in which scenes, or larger units of narrative, cohere.

Thesis/antithesis: literally "argument," or a "proposition" for which an argument is made. The "thesis" of *Uncle Tom's Cabin*, for example, is that slavery is bad and should be abolished. Antithesis is more loosely used as meaning "opposite."

Unities: ideally, Aristotle decreed, drama should observe the three unities of time (the action should be contained in a single day), of place (one location only) and of action (no subplots). Perhaps as a challenge, Shakespeare's play *The Tempest* is the only one of his works that conforms to the unities.

Unreliable narrator: a term that became current in the 1960s and after, referring to the fact that omniscient, or autobiographical, narrators in fiction are not always to be trusted (for example, should we take everything that Nellie Dean tells Lockwood in *Wuthering Heights* at face value?).

Verisimilitude: a term used in judgment of the closeness of a literary effect, or situation, to real life.

Index

A

Achebe, Chinua 101–2, 148–50, 183
affective qualities 5–6, 24–7
alienation 105–7
allegory 88–91, 92
allusion 100–3
ambiguity 8–11
American Psycho (Ellis) 181
Amis, Martin 175
Anderson, Chris 202–3
Andrews, Dame Lucilla 166
Andrews, V.C. 191
anthropology 108–9
antiquity 17
apocrypha 61
Aristotle 4–7, 24
Arnold, Matthew 48–9
Arnott, Jake 173
Austen, Jane 20–1, 117–18
Auster, Paul 67
authenticity 150
author intent 20–3
authority, critical 80–3
authorship 76–8, 131, 188–91
see also ownership
Axolotl Roadkill (Hegemann) 167

B

Bakhtin, Mikhail 140–3
Baldwin, James 49–50
Baraka, Imamu Amiri 186–7
Bartheleme, Donald 114
Barthes, Roland 14–15, 78, 82, 122–4, 131, 157–8
base/superstructure model 56–9
Bateson, Gregory 134
Beckett, Samuel 137, 139
beginnings 69
belletrism 130–1
Bellow, Simon 173–4
Benjamin, Walter 30–1, 44
Beowulf 32, 34, 47, 188
best-seller lists 158
Bible 46, 89–90
Big Name Fans (BNFs) 193–4
"big story" endings 69–71
binarisms 152–4
blasphemy 176–9
Bleak House (Dickens) 28, 98
Bloom, Harold 135
Bloomsbury Group 53–4
BNFs (Big Name Fans) 193–4
book commerce 64–5, 157–8, 203
Booker Prize 80–1
see also Man-Booker prize
Booth, Wayne C. 94, 95
Breath (Beckett) 137
Brecht, Bertolt 7, 56–7, 105–7, 141
bricolage 108–11
British Empire 148–9
Brontë, Charlotte 70, 161, 163

Brontë, Emily 43
Brown, Dan 71, 99, 166

C

canons 51, 60–3, 150–1
see also classics
carnivalesque 141
The Castle of Otranto (Walpole) 41
Catch-22 (Heller) 134–5
The Catcher in the Rye (Salinger) 31, 45–6, 79, 100–1
catharsis theory 5–6, 24
celebrity writers 191
censorship 60, 146, 171, 180–3
Chandler, Raymond 86
Chaucer, Geoffrey 103
cinema epics 34
City of Glass (Auster) 67
civilization 16–17, 48–50, 180
Clancy, Tom 190
class factors 48–51, 57, 82–3, 141–3
classics 16–19
see also canons
Cleland, John 169–70
closure 68–71, 202
Coleridge, Samuel Taylor 104–5
Collins, Wilkie 184
colonialism 148–51
comedians 175
commerce 64–5, 157–8, 203
Commonwealth 148–9
compositional lies 185
computer chatrooms 194–5
The Confessions of Nat Turner (Styron) 150
Conrad, Joseph 150, 182–3
"consciousness" 59
"contemporary" literature 137–8
contextuality 129
"cool" media 197–9
copyright 77, 78–9, 164–7
coterie 53–5, 194
counter-culture 51
Crichton, Michael 110–11
criticism see literary criticism
Culler, Jonathan 122
culture 48–51, 57, 194–5

D

The Da Vinci Code (Brown) 71, 99, 166
de Certeau, Michel 192
de Graef, Ortwin 127
de Man, Paul 125–7
death scenes 26–7
deconstruction 121, 124–7
defamiliarization 104–7
Defoe, Daniel 20–1, 57–8, 116
Derrida, Jacques 67, 124, 126
detail 116–19
Detective Writers Club 65–6
Dickens, Charles 26–8, 58, 70–1, 98–101, 109, 128, 141, 184
dilemmas 132, 133
discriminating reading 201–3
Dostoevsky, Fyodor 141

double bind situations 132–5
Doyle, Arthur Conan 110–11
Dumas, Alexandre 188–9

E

e-books 196–9
Eco, Umberto 71, 155
education 62–3, 150
Eliot, George 58, 69
Eliot, T.S. 3, 8–9, 16–18, 48, 50, 103, 140–1
elitism 50, 51
Elizabethan age 145–6
see also Shakespeare, William
Ellis, Bret Easton 181
emblem books 98
emotion 5–6, 24–5, 107
empire see imperialism
Empson, William 10, 11
endings 68–71, 202
English language 37–8, 46–7
Enlightenment thought 139
epics 32–5, 112
equivalency 44
eroticism 169–70
essentialism 44
European Union 18
exile 4, 7
explanatory images 98–9

F

fallacies 22, 24–7
fanfiction (FF) 192–5
Fanny Hill 169–70
fanzines 194
Federman, Raymond 113
feelings 24–5
feminism 160–3, 180–1
FF (fanfiction) 192–5
fiction 64, 66–7, 69–70, 112–15, 192–5
see also individual works
FIS (free indirect style) 86–7
Fish, Stanley 21, 22–3, 159
Fitzgerald, Scott 52–4, 189
Foden, Giles 174
forgery 185–6
Forster, E.M. 25
Foster, Professor Don 85, 86
Foucault, Michel 82, 131
Francis, Dick and Mary 190
free indirect style (FIS) 86–7
French language 9, 110
Freud, Sigmund 10, 41, 99
Fukuyama, Francis 202

G

Geertz, Clifford 147
gender see sexual politics
genre 21, 64–7, 86, 110–11, 192–5, 201
ghost-writers 188–91
Gilbert, Sandra 163
"gilded-lily" lies 184
Golding, William 149
Gore, Al 174
Gothic literature 40–3
Great Expectations (Dickens) 70–1, 101, 109
The Great Gatsby (Fitzgerald) 52–4

Greenblatt, Stephen 146–7
Greene, Graham 94–5
Greer, Germaine 162
Gubar, Susan 163
Gulliver's Travels (Swift) 95

H

Haley, Alex 165–6
Hamlet (Shakespeare) 6, 8–11, 13–14, 97, 118, 141–2
Hardy, Thomas 93
Hassan, Ihab 138–9
The Heart of the Matter (Greene) 94–5
"Heathcliff" character 43
Hegemann, Helene 167
Heller, Joseph 134–5
Hemingway, Ernest 52–3
hermeneutics 12–15, 96
heroic epics 32–4
heroic lies 184–5
heteroglossia 140–3
historical novels 118
history/historicism 74, 144–5, 147, 157–8
see also new historicism
Holocaust memoirs 187
homage fiction 112, 194
Hopkins, Gerard Manley 10–11, 37–8
"hot" media 197–9

I

idiolect 85, 86
imagery 96–9
imitative authors 65–6
see also mimesis
immateriality of words 78, 123
imperialism 17–19, 148–51
intentionalism 20–3
Internet 167, 192–5, 198, 200–3
interpretive communities 23, 159
intertextuality 100, 129
irony 92–5
Iser, Wolfgang 156–7
Islam 179

J

Jacobs, W.W. 94
James, Henry 29–30, 116–18, 157
Jane Eyre (Brontë) 70, 161, 163
Jewish writers 55, 127
Johnny Come Home (Arnott) 173
Johnson, Dr 143
Johnson, Samuel 61
Joyce, James 154
Jurassic Park (Crichton) 110–11

K

Keneally, Thomas 166
Kermode, Frank 17–19, 28, 30, 68–70
King Lear (Shakespeare) 19
King, Stephen 65, 66–7
Klein, Joe 85

L

labels 26
Lacan, Jacques 124
Lady Chatterley's Lover (Lawrence) 168, 170–1

langue 85
Larkin, Philip 181–2
law 78–9, 164–8, 170–9
Lawrence, D.H. 50, 168, 170–1
LeRoy, J.T. 186
Lévi-Strauss, Claude 108–9
libel 172–9
lies in literature 184–7
lines in literature 120–1
linguistics and style 85–6
literary canons see canons
literary criticism 3, 11, 22, 74
  authority of 80–3
  deconstruction 124
  discrimination 201–2
  sexual politics 162
  textuality 129, 130–1
literary epics see epics
literary inundation 200–3
literary lies 184–7
literary ownership see ownership
literary texts see textuality
literary translation 44–7
"Little Nell" character 26–7
Lodge, David 21, 124–5
"long tail" strategy 202–3
Lord of the Flies (Golding) 149
Lord, Graham 190
The Lost World (Doyle) 110–11
lyric poetry 33, 36–9

M
McCarthy, Cormac 102–3
McEwan, Ian 80–3, 166
McLuhan, Marshall 196–8
Man-Booker prize 80–1, 149
Marxism 56–9, 146–7
mass civilization 48–9
meaning 12–15, 159
media, e-books 196–9
metafiction 112–15
A Midsummer Night's Dream (Shakespeare) 6, 162
milieux 52–5
Millett, Kate 160–2
mimesis 4–7, 24
  see also imitative authors
minority cultures 48–9
modern epics 33–5
modern poetry 36–9
modernism 136–9
The Monkey's Paw (Jacobs) 94
monsters 42, 161, 163
Mother Courage (Brecht) 106
"motivated" narrative 117–19
Mrs. Dalloway (Woolf) 87
multiple ownership 76–7
music and poetry 38–9
myth 108

N
Nabokov, Vladimir 47, 130
The Name of the Rose (Eco) 71, 155
narrative 28–31, 68–71, 116–19
narratology 30
nations/nationalism 35, 86
Naylor, James 176
neo-Marxism 147

neo-Victorianism 114–15
new criticism 11, 22
new historicism 3, 144–7
Nineteen Eighty-Four (Orwell) 92, 118–19, 134
No Country for Old Men (McCarthy) 102–3
novels 21, 28–9, 31, 57–8, 112–15, 118
  see also individual novels
Noyes, Alfred 74–5

O
obscenity 168–71
Oedipus complex 135
Old Curiosity Shop (Dickens) 26–7
originality 114–15
Orwell, George 7, 56–7, 92, 118–19, 134
Othello (Shakespeare) 94
ownership 30–1, 76–9

P
panegyric 32
pantextuality 130
paradigm shifts 72–5
paradoxes 6, 13–15, 44–7
paranoia 71
paraphrase 79
paratextuality 129
parody 112
parole 85, 86
patriarchy 161–2
PC (political correctness) 181–3
Perkins, Maxwell 189
permissiveness 180–3
philosophy and allegory 90–1
plagiarism 164–7
Plato 4–7, 88–9
Poe, Edgar Allan 33, 36, 89
poetry 32–4, 36–9, 104, 204–5
political correctness (PC) 181–3
politics 160–3, 180–3
polyphony 140–2
polyvalence 8–9
pornography 168
postcolonialism 148–51
postmodernism 136–9
poststructuralism 120, 121
poststructuralism 11, 22
Primary Colors 84–5
printing technology 83, 198–9
prizes for literature 80–1, 149
prose, poetry and 38–9
prosody 36–9
psychoanalytic ambiguities 10–11

Q
Queen Mab (Shelley) 177–8

R
race 52, 55, 182–3
rationalism 138–9
reader response theory 156–9
reader's role 23–7, 96, 121–2, 156–9, 200–3
real living people (RLPs) 172–5
realism 6, 89, 98, 116–18, 205
reception theory 156–9
reductionism 58, 62, 145

referencing 100–3
The Republic (Plato) 4, 7, 88–9
revolutionary work 73–4, 142–3
rhythm in poetry 38–9
RLPs (real living people) 172–5
The Road to Wigan Pier (Orwell) 56, 58
Robinson Crusoe (Defoe) 20–1, 57–8, 116
roman-à-clef 172–3, 205
romantic fiction genre 66–7
Romanticism 42
Romola (Eliot) 58
Roots (Haley) 165–6
Rosenblat, Herman 187
Roth, Philip 183
Rushdie, Salman 151, 179

S
Said, Edward 151
Salinger, J.D. 31, 45–6, 79, 100–1
The Satanic Verses (Rushdie) 179
Satires of Circumstance (Hardy) 93
Saussure, Ferdinand de 85, 152–3, 155
Schopenhauer, Arthur 90–1
science 72–5, 108–9
science fiction 66, 110–11
Scott, Walter 118
Segal, Erich 174
semiology 152–5
sexual content 168–71
sexual politics 160–3, 180–3
Shakespeare, William 3, 17–19, 60
  ambiguity 8–9, 10–11
  copyright 78
  defamiliarization 106–7
  hermeneutics 13–14
  heteroglossia 141–3
  imagery 97–8
  irony 94
  milieu 54–5
  mimesis 6
  new historicism 145–7
  plagiarism 165
  realism 118
  sexual politics 162
  translation problems 46–7
Sharp, William 186
Shelley, Mary 42
Shelley, Percy Bysshe 177–8
Shklovsky, Viktor 104–5
Showalter, Elaine 162, 163
signification 152–5
slander 172
slash fiction 193
social heteroglossia 141–2
  see also class factors
solidity of specification 116–19
songs 39
Sontag, Susan 14
specification solidity 116–19
Spender, Stephen 137–8
Stanislavski, Constantin 107
state education 62–3
Sterne, Laurence 113
story/story-telling 28–31, 68–71

see also narrative
stress-structured verse 37–8
structuralism 3, 120–3
style 84–7
Styron, William 150
subjectivity 156–7, 159
subtextuality 129
subversion 146–7
superstructure/base model 56–9
suppressio veri lies 185
surfiction 113
Swift, Jonathan 95
symbolic code 15

T
Taine, Hippolyte 52, 54
team writing 188–9
"telling" detail 118–19
The Tempest (Shakespeare) 147
textuality 128–31, 157
theater pits 146
theories 3
Things Fall Apart (Achebe) 101–2, 149
time factors 13, 47, 75, 98
The Time Machine (Wells) 59
Tompkins, Jane 159
totalitarianism 22
translation paradox 44–7
Tristram Shandy (Sterne) 113
Trollope, Anthony 117
truth 4–5, 12, 90–2
The Turn of the Screw (James) 29–30

U
Ulysses (Joyce) 154

V
verbal ambiguity 9–10
Victorian fiction 70, 114–15
  see also individual works
Virgil 16
visual images 97
  see also imagery

W
Walpole, Horace 41
The War of the Worlds (Wells) 91, 111
The Waste Land (Eliot) 140–1
Wells, H.G. 59, 91, 111
Whitehouse, Mary 177–8
Whitman, Walt 36–7
The Windhover (Hopkins) 10
women and politics 160–3
Woolf, Virginia 87, 138, 162
working-class culture 50–1
"works" versus "texts" 128
Wuthering Heights (Brontë) 43

Y
Yeats, W.B. 38–9, 101–2, 126

Z
"Zapp" character 21, 124–5

Answers to Quizzes

Test your CL (see p. 49)

1. London Review of Books, New York Review of Books. The American journal came first.
2. Benjamin Disraeli's *Sybil*, 1845.
3. Lisbon. His last literary work is a memoir of his voyage there.
4. James Joyce's *Finnegans Wake*.
5. Percy Bysshe Shelley.
6. Salman Rushdie's *Midnight's Children* – the second two victories were in "best of the best" Booker competitions.
7. Twenty-five; Hyperion.
8. It's never quite clear, but probably a bull male sperm whale.
9. The heroine's murdered daughter.
10. A line of verse with 12, not 10, syllables. It is more popular in French than in English poetry.

How well read are you? (see p. 102)

1. James Joyce's *Portrait of the Artist as a Young Man*, itself an allusion to Rembrandt's picture of himself.
2. A line in Shakespeare's Sonnet 30, itself a reference to the phrase in the Bible.
3. A sermon of the divine and poet John Donne.
4. The music hall song that begins "Oh lucky Jim, How I envy him."
5. A line in Thomas Gray's "Elegy Written in a Country Church-yard."
6. A line in Keats's "Ode to a Nightingale."
7. A line in Spinoza's Ethics.
8. The Bible, Book of Revelation, Chapter 14.
9. A poem by Walt Whitman of the same name.
10. Philip Sidney's pastoral fable, of the same name.

Quercus Publishing Plc
21 Bloomsbury Square
London WC1A 2NS

First published in 2010

A catalogue record of this book is available from the British Library

UK and associated territories:
ISBN 978 1 84866 060 1

Printed and bound in China

10 9 8 7 6 5 4 3 2 1

Prepared by Starfish Design, Editorial and Project Management Ltd.